LEONOR **CORRADI**

#HASHTAG ENGLISH 3
PRE-INTERMEDIATE

STUDENT'S BOOK
and e-book

with **Online Practice**

Pearson

Catalogue Publication Data

Hashtag English 3 Pre-intermediate Student's Book and e-book with Online Practice

Authors: Leonor Corradi

Pearson Educación de México, S.A. de C.V., 2023

ISBN: 978-607-32-5686-5

Area: Schools

Format: 20,5 × 24,7 cm   Page count: 168

Product Vice President: Marianne Lewis ■ **ELT Director:** Marjorie Robles ■ **Product Managers:** Anita Heald, Priscila Marconi ■ **Product Developers:** Renata S. C. Victor, Carolina Andrade ■ **Editor:** Elaine Mendonça ■ **Art and Design Coordinator:** Anderson Ferreira ■ **Art and Design Editors:** Andréia A. Santa Rosa, Patricia Santos, Luiz Rubio ■ **Layout:** Casa de Ideias ■ **Cover & Interior Design:** Apis Design ■ **Cover Photo:** Shutterstock ■ **Digital Development Supervisor:** Isabel Silva ■ **Digital Content and Development Editors:** Rafaela de Mendonça, Fernanda Patucci, Lara Tasso, Mirella Armentano ■ **Digital Content Authors:** 2014 Solucões Editoriais, Ohana Editorial, Bella Szyszkowska ■ **Audiovisual Coordinator:** Lucas Domingues ■ **Audiovisual Editor:** Lucas Motta ■ **R&P Coordinator:** Maiti Salla ■ **R&P team:** Maricy Queiroz, Cristiane Gameiro ■ **Content Support:** 2014 Soluções Editoriais (Editors: Carla Maurício Coelho da Silva Vianna, Joyce Rocha Gomes, Marcos Carvalho Mendonça, Rebeca Pasqua de Andrade. Assistants: Cristine Zanela Monte, Elani Souza Gomes, Juliana Aga, Pedro Zanela) ■ **Proofreading:** 2014 Soluções Editoriais, Silva Serviços de Educação ■ **Picture Credits:** Pearson Asset Library, Shutterstock, 123RF, Alamy Stock Photo

Contact: soporte@pearson.com

First published, 2023

ISBN PRINT BOOK: 978-607-32-5686-5

Impreso en México. *Printed in Mexico.*

1 2 3 4 5 6 7 8 9 0 - 25 24 23 22

D.R. © 2023 por Pearson Educación de México, S.A. de C.V.
Avenida Antonio Dovalí Jaime #70
Torre B, Piso 6, Colonia Zedec Ed. Plaza Santa Fe
Delegación Álvaro Obregón, México, Ciudad de México, C. P. 01210

www.PearsonELT.com

Pearson

Pearson Hispanoamérica

Argentina ■ Belice ■ Bolivia ■ Chile ■ Colombia ■ Costa Rica ■ Cuba ■ República Dominicana ■ Ecuador ■ El Salvador ■ Guatemala ■ Honduras ■ México ■ Nicaragua ■ Panamá ■ Paraguay ■ Perú ■ Uruguay ■ Venezuela

STUDENT'S BOOK INDEX

#TABLE OF CONTENTS

SPEAKING	WRITING	PRONUNCIATION	VOCABULARY	USE OF ENGLISH	PROJECT
Talking About an Online Course	Writing a Note to A Classmate	Pronunciation of *–ed* Adjectives	Adjectives with *-ed / -ing*	Saying What I Like About Online Courses	A Poster
Describing What Someone is Wearing	Writing a Social Media Post	Sounds /b/ and /p/	Clothes and Accessories	Describing Clothes for Donation	An Interactive Board Presentation
Interviewing Classmates About Their Eating Habits	Writing a Restaurant Review	Sounds /e/ and /ei/	Fruit and Vegetables Food Containers Adjectives for Describing Food Collocations – *Drink / Eat / Have*	Ordering Food in a Restaurant	A Blog
Talking About the Technology Use in the Past	Writing a Biography	Sounds /n/and /ŋ/	Gadgets and Inventions	Demonstrating Agreement and Disagreement in a Conversation	A Virtual Bulletin Board
Interviewing a Classmate About a New Technological Gadget	Writing an Informal E-mail	Phrasal Verbs Stress	Phrasal Verbs	Discussing Future Plans and Arrangements	An Online Graphic Organizer
Telling Your Classmates About Animal Habitats	Writing a Short Article	Compound Adjectives	Endangered Animals Compound Adjectives	Giving Opinions and Justifying Them	An Online Slideshow
Teaching Your Friend How to Use a Travel App	Writing a Factual Article	Sounds /æ/ and /a:/	Means of Transportation Travel-related Words	Talking About Travel Arrangements	A Travel Newsletter
Talking About Different Media	Writing a Review	Word Stress	Music, Movies, and TV	Talking About How I Feel About Art	A Digital Poster
Taking About Movements in Favor of Women's Protection	Writing an Opinion Essay	Sentence Stress	Crimes and Criminals	Describing Advantages and Disadvantages	An Online Bulletin Board

#BOOK WALKTHROUGH

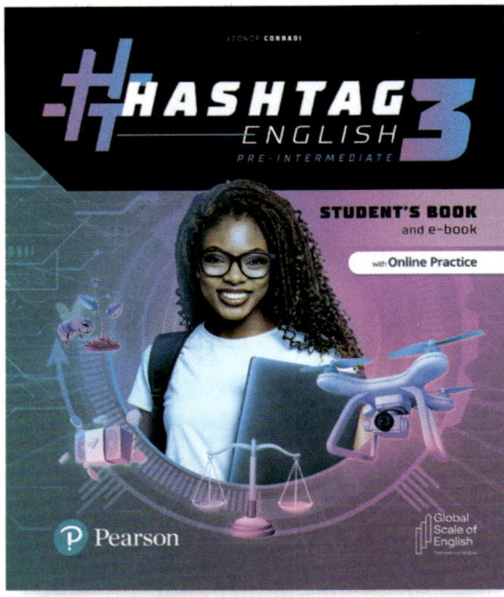

WELCOME TO HASHTAG ENGLISH!

Hashtag English is a six-level course for lower- and upper-secondary students. You are going to interact with technology to learn English through task-based learning activities, working with UNESCO's Sustainable Development Goals, (SDG) Bloom's Taxonomy, and 21st century skills. *Hashtag English* aims at providing thought-provoking content that recognizes your ability to observe and make a difference to the world around you, while still retaining a light-hearted and fun approach that is age appropriate.

OPENER

Each unit starts with a picture to arouse your curiosity about the theme and to introduce the focus on the SDG.

In this unit, you will learn how to:
This shows the learning outcomes of the unit.

Say what you know:
This activates your prior knowledge of the language goals of the unit.

UNESCO'S Sustainable Development Goal

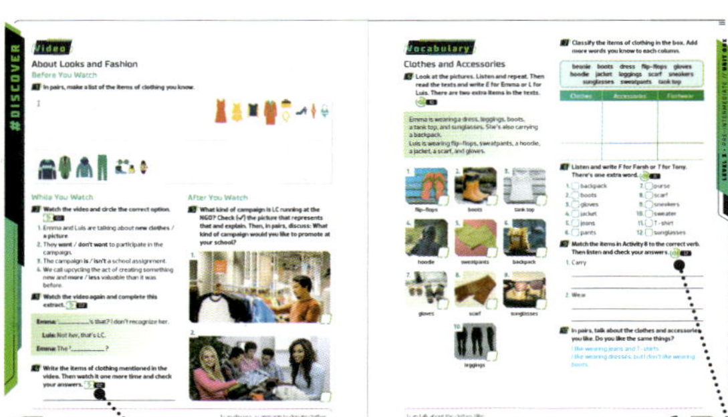

DISCOVER

The first page of this double-page section is based on a video in which two characters discuss the unit topic and the language is introduced in context. The second page introduces the vocabulary of the unit.

VIDEO **AUDIO** **FLASHCARDS**

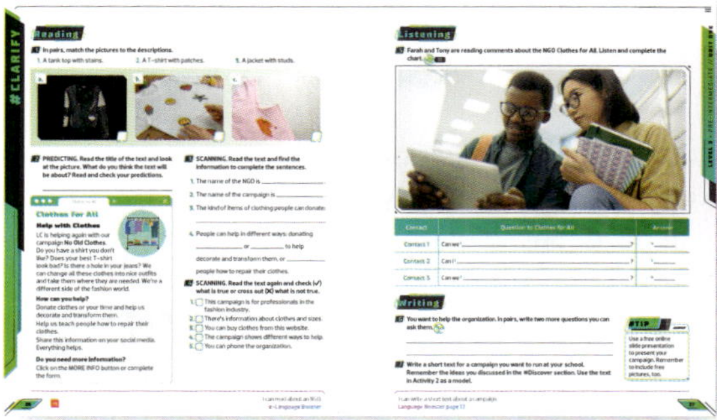

CLARIFY

This double-page section includes one or more texts that develop the SDG and work on a reading skill, a listening text, and a writing task on the topic of the text.

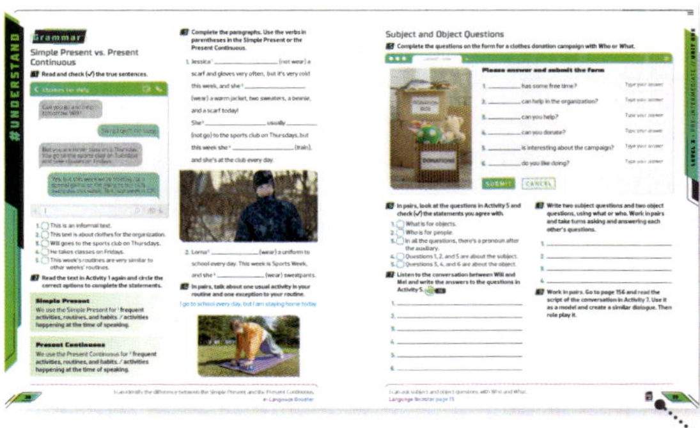

UNDERSTAND

This double-page section develops the grammar focus of the unit in an inductive manner. Grammar is presented in context and you are encouraged to work out the form for yourself.

EXAM PRACTICE

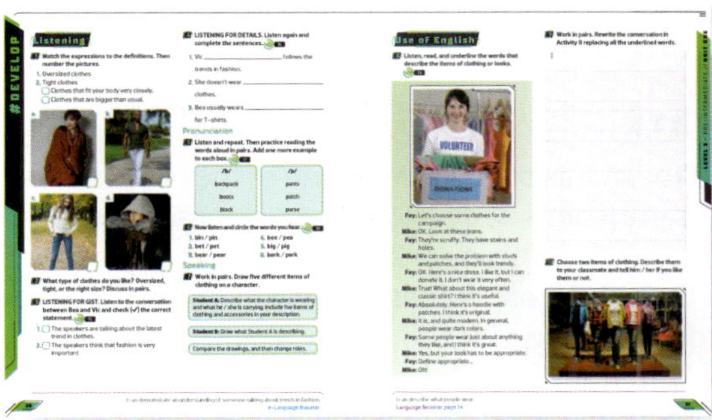

DEVELOP

The first page of this double-page section contains a listening text that develops a listening skill and sometimes a second vocabulary topic. The second page is where you develop speaking skills in natural, communicative contexts that use the grammar focus of the unit.

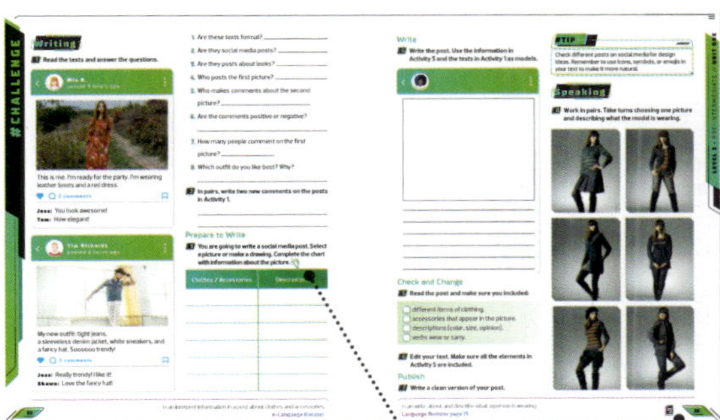

CHALLENGE

This double-page section develops your writing skills through a step-by-step writing task that puts into practice everything you have learned in the unit. The section culminates in a speaking task.

21ST CENTURY SKILL **EXAM PRACTICE**

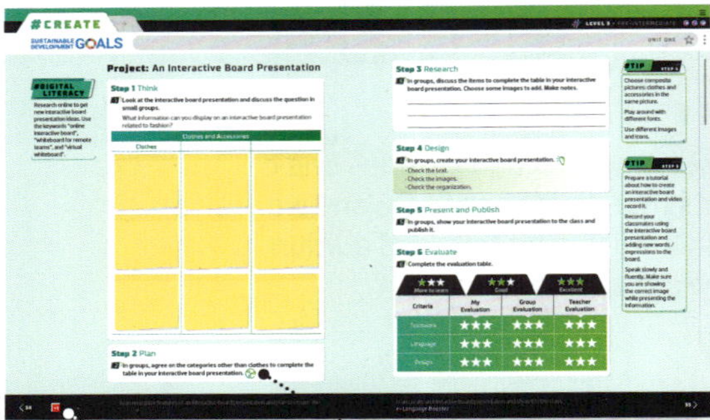

CREATE

In this section, you work collaboratively on a project to identify, critically analyze, and present a problem or potential solution related to the SDG of the unit.

21ST CENTURY SKILL

UNESCO'S SUSTAINABLE DEVELOPMENT GOAL

SELF-ASSESSMENT

This end-of-unit section presents a list of *can-do* statements related to the unit content that help you identify your progress and opportunities for improvement.

UNIT TEST

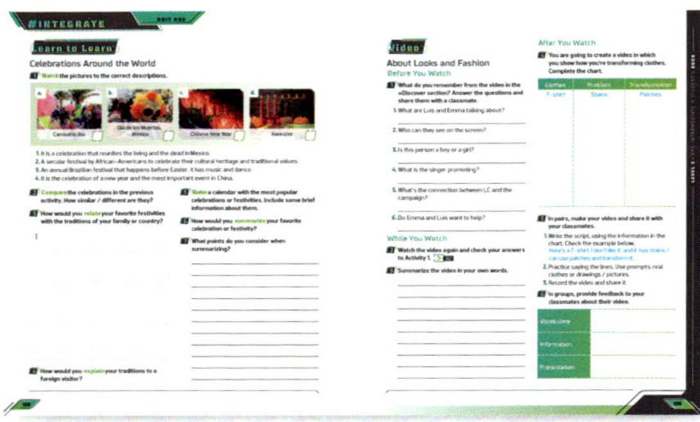

INTEGRATE

The first page of this section at the end of the book is called Learn to Learn. It aims at developing your learning skills using Bloom's Taxonomy. The second page contains new activities based on the video from the Discover section and proposes the recording of a new video to review the unit content.

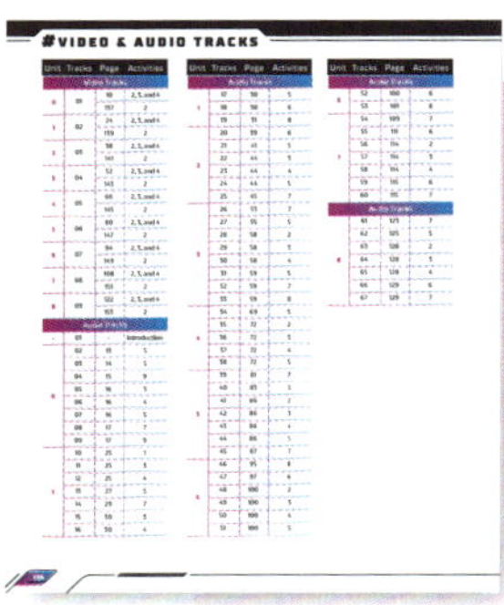

VIDEO & AUDIO TRACKS

This section at the end of the book lists the video and audio tracks from all the units.

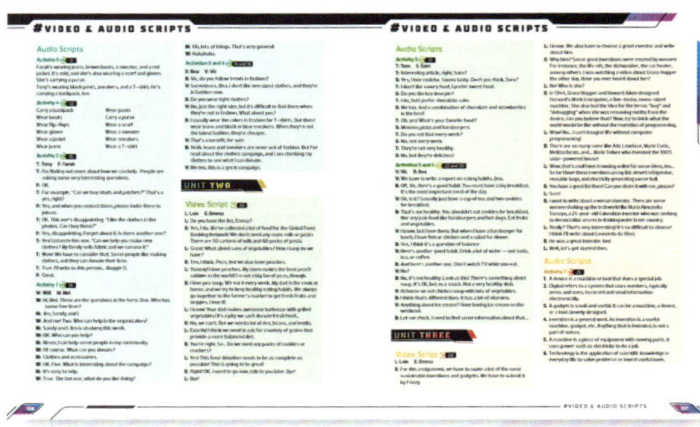

VIDEO & AUDIO SCRIPTS

This section at the end of the book contains the video and audio scripts from all the units.

WE CAN ALL LEARN

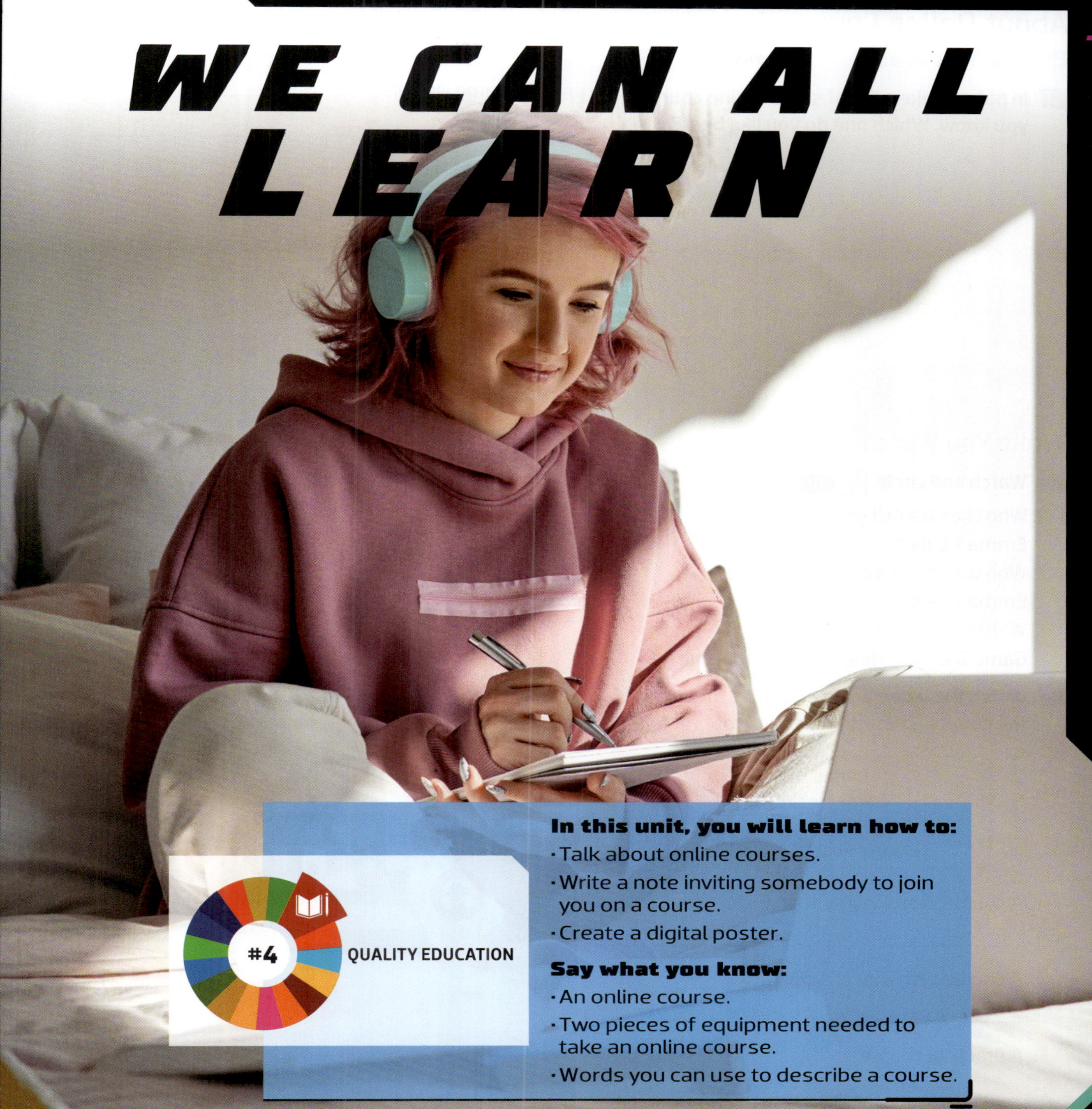

#4 QUALITY EDUCATION

In this unit, you will learn how to:

- Talk about online courses.
- Write a note inviting somebody to join you on a course.
- Create a digital poster.

Say what you know:

- An online course.
- Two pieces of equipment needed to take an online course.
- Words you can use to describe a course.

Video

About Online Courses

Before You Watch

1 **In pairs, make a list of some online courses you know. Which one do you like best?**

While You Watch

2 **Watch and circle.** ▷ 01

1. Who likes Game Design?
   Emma / Luis
2. Who would like a practical course?
   Emma / Luis
3. Which course is practical?
   Game Design / Healthy Food at Home

3 **Watch the video again and write the name of the course. There's an extra name.** ▷ 01

Clothes DIY
Game Design
Great Classics Trap
Healthy Food at Home

1. A course that's longer than the others: ______
2. A course with a lot of activities: ______
3. A practical course: ______

4 **Write the adjectives from the video to describe the courses. Then watch the video one more time and check your answers.** ▷ 01

1. All courses: ______
2. Game Design: ______
3. Great Classics Trap: ______
4. Healthy Food at Home: ______

After You Watch

5 **What do you think of the courses? Write two adjectives for each one.**

1. Game Design: ______
2. Great Classics Trap: ______
3. Healthy Food at Home: ______

6 **What are the advantages and disadvantages of online courses?**

I can talk about online courses.
e-Language Booster

Vocabulary

Adjectives with *-ed / -ing*

7 **Read the excerpts from the video. Then answer the questions.**

I like the courses, they look **amazing**!

I'm **tired** after school.

1. What does Luis call amazing?

____

2. How does Luis feel after school?

____

8 **Label the pictures with an adjective from the box.**

annoyed	confusing	excited	exhausted	fascinating	interesting

1. 

____

2. 

____

3. 

____

4. 

____

5. 

____

6. 

____

9 **Circle the correct option.**

1. The students are **amazing** / **amazed** at the online courses.
2. Luis is **tiring** / **tired** of walking to school every morning.
3. Jessica's project is **fascinating** / **fascinated**.
4. Are you **interesting** / **interested** in that game?
5. Her instructions were really **confusing** / **confused**.
6. He has this **annoying** / **annoyed** habit of interrupting when we are speaking.

10 **In pairs, talk about online courses. Use the adjectives you studied in this lesson.**

I feel excited when I join online classes.

Oh, no. I get annoyed when the connection is lost.

I can describe people and things using adjectives with *-ed* / *-ing*.

Language Booster page 5

Reading

1 **PREDICTING. Read the title of the text and look at the picture. What kind of information do you expect to find in the text?**

Climate Change: Human... +

http://www.greatonlinecourses.com

Climate Change: Human Responsibility

This online course is one of the 30 best online courses.

Learn what climate change is and what it does to our planet.

Climate change is a problem for our world. Do you want to save our home? Then we must understand climate change.

In this course, you will learn details of climate change and how to make Earth a better place.

Duration:
4 weeks

Weekly study: 3 hours
(for videos, articles, and activities)

Extra benefits:
100 % online

2 **SCANNING. Read the text and find the information to complete the sentences.**

1. The address of the website is ________________________.
2. Climate Change is one of the top ____________ courses.
3. In this course, you learn what climate change does to the ____________.
4. The course takes ________ weeks, and you need ________ hours of study time per week.
5. Climate Change is an ________ course.

3 **SKIMMING. Read the text again and mark the sentences T (True) or F (False).**

1. ☐ This online course is for scientists.
2. ☐ This online course is for people who like ecology.
3. ☐ Humans are also responsible for saving the planet.
4. ☐ Some classes are face-to-face.
5. ☐ You will only read articles in this course.

I can read about a course on climate change.

e-Language Booster

Listening

4 **Answer the questions below individually. Then share your answers with a classmate.**

Do you usually read or listen to ads? What information do they include?

____

____

5 **Listen to the ad and complete the information about the courses.** 02

	Great Civilizations	Food Medicine
Topic	1 ____________	5 ____________
Duration	2 ____________	6 ____________
Weekly study	3 ____________	7 ____________
Activities	4 ____________	8 ____________

Writing

6 **Complete the following text with the information from the chart in Activity 5.**

Great Civilizations is an interesting course about 1 ____________. You'll learn about the Egyptians, the Greeks, and the Romans. The course lasts 2 ____________ weeks. You need 3 ____________ hours a week to 4 ____________ 5 ____________, and 6 ____________.

Food Medicine is a practical course about 7 ____________. You don't need any cooking experience to take this course. It lasts 8 ____________ weeks. You need 9 ____________ hours a week to read recipes, 10 ____________ and 11 ____________.

7 **Write about an online course.**

- Use the table in Activity 5 and complete it with information about your course.
- Use the text in Activity 6 as a model and write about your online course.

#TIP

You can use an online shared document to write about your course. If possible, use pictures or icons to illustrate the information.

I can write a description of an online course.

Language Booster page 6

#UNDERSTAND

Grammar

Comparatives and Superlatives

1 **Read and check (✓) the true sentences.**

Online courses

Today

OK, we have to choose one course for us.

Course A is interesting.

Yes, but it's a long course.

I think it's worse than the others.

I guess course A is the worst of all the courses.

And it's the most difficult, too. What about B?

It's the most practical course.

B is shorter than A. What about C?

C is more expensive than A, but it is the shortest course.

Yes, it's the best!

1. ☐ Students are comparing courses.
2. ☐ They choose one course.
3. ☐ One student thinks course A is more difficult than B.
4. ☐ Course A is short.
5. ☐ One student thinks that course C is the best.

2 **What words are used to describe the courses? Circle them in the text.**

3 **Fill in the gaps based on the text in Activity 1.**

Comparatives

Short adjectives: + [1] ________ + than

Long adjectives: [2] ________ + adjective + [3] ________

Irregular adjectives: good → [4] ________ than / bad → [5] ________ than

Superlatives

Short adjectives: the + [6] ________

Long adjectives: the [7] ________ + adjective

Irregular adjectives: good → the [8] ________ / bad → the [9] ________

4 **In small groups, compare three online courses.**

Hate / Like / Love + -ing Forms

5 **Listen to Emma and Luis talking about other courses. Answer the questions.** 03

1. Does Emma like online courses?

____

2. Does Luis like practicing sports?

____

6 **Read and circle the correct option. Use the information in Activity 5.**

Likes and Dislikes: *hate / like / love*

1. Verb + noun: you hate / like / love **a person, place, or object / an action or experience**
2. Verb + *-ing* form: you hate / like / love **a person, place, or object / an action or experience**

I can use comparatives and superlatives with people and things.

7 **Read the sentences and underline the correct option.**

1. I love **study** / **studying** about the Romans. It's a very interesting topic!
2. I hate **watch sports** / **watching sports** on TV. It's boring.
3. I don't like **make** / **making** cakes.

8 **Look at the example. In pairs, find three activities you have in common. Record the conversation.**

I like swimming.

I hate it, but I like riding a bike.

Me too! I also love playing soccer.

Would like for Offers and Requests

9 **Listen to a new conversation between Emma and Luis and write T (True) or F (False).** 04

1. ☐ Luis offers his paper to Emma.
2. ☐ Luis wants to read Emma's paper.

10 **Read Emma's and Luis's sentences and identify them. Write *offer* or *request*.**

1. Would you like some help with your homework, Luis?

____

2. I'd like to read your paper.

____

11 **Based on the pictures, write an offer or a request. Then, in pairs, take turns making offers and requests to each other.**

1. 

____
____
____

2. 

____
____
____

3. 

____
____
____

4. 

____
____
____

12 **Work in pairs. Read the dialogues aloud. Then role play different situations.**

Jake: Do you like singing?
Beth: I love singing.
Jake: Would you like to study music?
Beth: Definitely!

Anne: Do you like dancing?
Joshua: I hate dancing.
Anne: Would you like to play basketball then?
Joshua: That would be great!

I can say what I like and make offers and requests.
Language Booster page 7

#DEVELOP

Listening

1 Match the activities to the pictures.

1. Do / Complete a geography assignment.
2. Submit an assignment.
3. Take online classes.
4. Use different resources.

a. 

b. 

c. 

d. 

2 Look at the pictures again. Do you also do these activities? Talk to a classmate.

3 LISTENING FOR GIST. Listen and check (✓) the correct option. 05

1. ☐ The speakers are teachers.
2. ☐ The testimonials are about courses.

4 LISTENING FOR DETAILS. Listen again and complete the sentences. 06

1. Kelly's [1] ________________ online classes. The classes are [2] ________________. She loves [3] ________________ the assignments.

2. Rajesh's [4] ________________ a course on Space Science. He's satisfied with it. He has to [5] ________________ his first assignment next week, and he's [6] ________________. He likes [7] ________________ online.

Pronunciation

5 Listen to the pronunciation of the *–ed* adjectives. Then say the words and complete the chart. 07

/t/	/d/	/id/
perplexed	bored	excited

Speaking

6 Work in pairs. Talk about an online course. Ask and answer about likes / dislikes and ask each other to do something.

I can identify information in a listening text about online courses.
e-Language Booster

Use of English

7 **Listen, read, and underline the sentences with *like*.** 08

Monica: I'd like to take an online course. What about you two?
Dan: Me too. I like learning online.
Liz: Maybe. I like online activities, but they're tiring. After an hour, I'm exhausted!
Monica: We can do a short course. Would you like to choose one?
Liz: Do you like doing assignments? In some courses, you have to do assignments.
Dan: I'd like to do one assignment only. An exciting one.
Monica: What's an exciting assignment?
Dan: Making a video, writing a poem...
Liz: Not very interesting... I like more practical activities.
Dan: OK. A short course, with only one practical assignment.
Liz: Yes!
Monica: Fine by me!

8 **Write the sentences you underlined in Activity 7 in the correct category.**

1. Like + object

____

____

2. Like + action

____

____

3. Offer

____

____

4. Request

____

____

9 **Listen to the conversation in Activity 7 again. Then role play it in groups of three.** 09

10 **Practice the conversation in Activity 7 again. Now use true information about your likes and dislikes.**

I can say what I like about online courses.

Language Booster page 8

#CHALLENGE

Writing

1 Read the text and answer the questions.

Hi, Ivan!

Have you seen our homework? We have to take an online course and write a report on it. There are some interesting courses on the list; others are boring. I like making things, so I'd like to take the Vegetable Garden course. It's longer than the others, but it's the most practical. I'm excited! Would you like to do it with me? We can start a vegetable garden at home.

See you!

Jess

1. Is this text a note? ______________
2. Is this text formal? ______________
3. Is Ivan the writer of the text? ______________
4. Are Ivan and Jess classmates? ______________

2 Read the text in Activity 1 again. Then check (✓) the true information.

1. ☐ It's a short text.
2. ☐ It's a formal text.
3. ☐ There are lots of ideas and topics.
4. ☐ It contains the writer's name.
5. ☐ It contains the recipient's name.

3 Go back to the note in Activity 1 and complete the template below. Use the words from the box.

Body   Ending   Greeting   Writer's name

1

2

3

4

4 Go back to the note once again and underline the different parts. Use color coding.

Introduce the situation	red
Describe the situation	blue
Invite the person to join you	green
Give a suggestion	pink

5 Copy the sentences from the note with -*ed* and -*ing* adjectives.

____

____

Prepare to Write

6 You are going to write a note to a classmate. Think of these items and complete the chart.

Situation	
Description of the situation	
Invitation	
Positive information	

I can identify some of the characteristics of a note.
e-Language Booster

Write

7 **Write your note. Use the information in Activity 6 and the text in Activity 1 as a model.**

Check and Change

8 **Read your note and make sure you included:**

- ☐ a greeting.
- ☐ the recipient's name.
- ☐ the situation.
- ☐ an invitation.
- ☐ some positive information.
- ☐ a goodbye.
- ☐ your name.

9 **Edit your note. Make sure all the elements in Activity 8 are included.**

Publish

10 **Write a clean version of your note.**

#TIP

Search online for samples of notes.

Speaking

11 **Read your classmate's note and answer the questions.**

1. What is the recipient's name?
2. What adjectives does your classmate use to describe the courses?
3. What course does he / she want to take?
4. How does he / she invite the recipient?

I can write a note about online courses.

Language Booster page 9

#CREATE

SUSTAINABLE DEVELOPMENT GOALS

Project: A Poster

#DIGITAL LITERACY

To search for the ideal courses your school could offer, it is important to follow some guidelines:

1. Spend some time exploring online and use keywords for your search.
2. Make sure you read the course description in detail.
3. Check the website offering the course and see if it has good reviews from users. Reliability is very important.

#TIP STEP 3

Always look for the most popular online courses websites. They usually have courses for a broader audience in many different subjects.

#TIP STEP 4

You can look for graphic organizers to write the key points of the course. They can be found online and for free.

Step 1 Think

1 Discuss in groups.

1. What are the advantages of online courses?
2. Does your school offer online courses? Which ones?
3. What online courses would you like your school to offer?
4. Do you like taking online courses? What kind of online courses do you like?
5. Are different resources important in online courses?

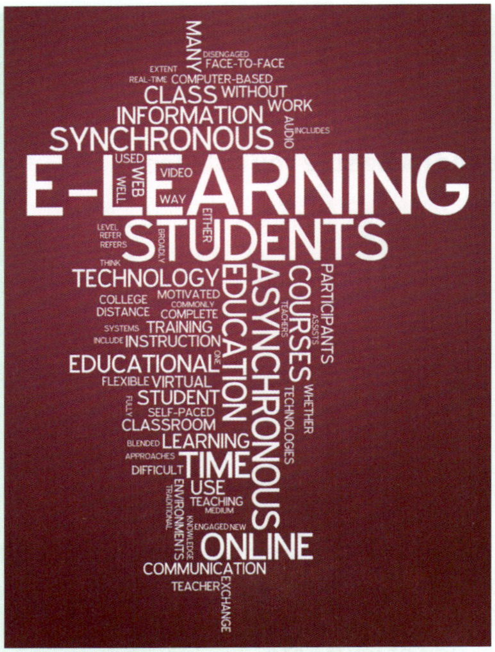

Step 2 Plan

2 In groups, agree on the main points for an online course. List them.

____

____

____

I can discuss the main points of online courses and plan a poster to create one.

Step 3 Research

3 Go online and search for different online courses. Select five courses you think are more appropriate for your school. Complete the chart. In groups, agree on a course to present.

	Course 1	Course 2	Course 3	Course 4	Course 5
Course					
Topic					
Duration					
Activities					

Step 4 Design

4 In groups, create a poster about the course you have chosen. Use a free online platform for design and artwork.

#TIP STEP 4

- Choose a template that you all like.
- Play around with different fonts.
- Use different images and icons.

Step 5 Present and Publish

5 In groups, present your posters to the class. Publish your posters.

#TIP STEP 5

You can practice the presentation and record it on video.

Don't read out the poster. Name the most important points.

Speak slowly and fluently.

Step 6 Evaluate

6 Complete the evaluation table.

★☆☆ More to learn · ★★☆ Good · ★★★ Excellent

Criteria	My Evaluation	Group Evaluation	Teacher Evaluation
Teamwork	☆☆☆	☆☆☆	☆☆☆
Language	☆☆☆	☆☆☆	☆☆☆
Design	☆☆☆	☆☆☆	☆☆☆

I can create a digital poster and present it to class.

#SELF-ASSESSMENT

1 **Mark the learning objectives according to the key.**

★☆☆ I don't understand.	★★☆ I understand, but I need help.	★★★ I can do it!

Learning Objectives	Rating
To talk about online courses.	☆☆☆
To describe people and things using adjectives with *-ed / - ing*.	☆☆☆
To read about a course on climate change.	☆☆☆
To write a short description of an online course.	☆☆☆
To use comparatives and superlatives with people and things.	☆☆☆
To say what I like and make offers and requests.	☆☆☆
To identify information in a listening text about offers and requests.	☆☆☆
To say what I like about online courses.	☆☆☆
To identify some of the characteristics of a note.	☆☆☆
To write a note about online courses.	☆☆☆
To discuss the main points of online courses.	☆☆☆
To create a digital poster and present it to the class.	☆☆☆

2 **Work in pairs. Discuss the questions.**

1. What did I find most interesting to learn? Why?
2. How did I learn it?
3. How can I use it in real life?

UT Language Booster page 10

WHAT'S FASHION TO YOU?

#1 NO POVERTY

In this unit, you will learn how to:

- Talk about trends and fashion.
- Write clothing descriptions.
- Create an interactive digital whiteboard presentation.

Say what you know:

- Clothes, accessories, and shoes.
- A description of a person's clothing.
- A description of what a classmate is wearing.

Video

About Looks and Fashion

Before You Watch

1 **In pairs, make a list of the items of clothing you know.**

While You Watch

2 **Watch the video and circle the correct option.** ▷ 02

1. Emma and Luis are talking about **new clothes** / **a picture**.
2. They **want** / **don't want** to participate in the campaign.
3. The campaign **is** / **isn't** a school assignment.
4. We call upcycling the act of creating something new and **more** / **less** valuable than it was before.

3 **Watch the video again and complete this extract.** ▷ 02

Emma: [1]__________'s that? I don't recognize her.

Luis: Not *her*, that's LC.

Emma: The [2]__________?

4 **Write the items of clothing mentioned in the video. Then watch it one more time and check your answers.** ▷ 02

____

After You Watch

5 **What kind of campaign is LC running at the NGO? Check (✓) the picture that represents that and explain. Then, in pairs, discuss: What kind of campaign would you like to promote at your school?**

1.

2.

I can discuss a campaign to donate clothes.

e-Language Booster

Vocabulary

Clothes and Accessories

6 **Look at the pictures. Listen and repeat. Then read the texts and write E for Emma or L for Luis. There are two extra items in the texts.** 10

Emma is wearing a dress, leggings, boots, a tank top, and sunglasses. She's also carrying a backpack.
Luis is wearing flip-flops, sweatpants, a hoodie, a jacket, a scarf, and gloves.

1. 
flip-flops

2. 
boots

3. 
tank top

4. 
hoodie

5. 
sweatpants

6. 
backpack

7. 
gloves

8. 
scarf

9. 
sunglasses

10. 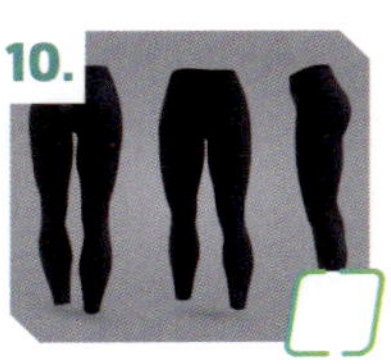
leggings

7 **Classify the items of clothing in the box. Add more words you know to each column.**

beanie boots dress flip-flops gloves hoodie jacket leggings scarf sneakers sunglasses sweatpants tank top

Clothes	Accessories	Footwear

8 **Listen and write F for Farah or T for Tony. There's one extra word.** 11

1. ☐ backpack
2. ☐ boots
3. ☐ gloves
4. ☐ jacket
5. ☐ jeans
6. ☐ pants
7. ☐ purse
8. ☐ scarf
9. ☐ sneakers
10. ☐ sweater
11. ☐ T-shirt
12. ☐ sunglasses

9 **Match the items in Activity 8 to the correct verb. Then listen and check your answers.** 12

1. Carry

____

____

2. Wear

____

____

10 **In pairs, talk about the clothes and accessories you like. Do you like the same things?**

I like wearing jeans and T-shirts.
I like wearing dresses, but I don't like wearing boots.

I can talk about the clothes I like.
Language Booster page 11

Reading

1 In pairs, match the pictures to the descriptions.

1. A tank top with stains.
2. A T-shirt with patches.
3. A jacket with studs.

a. 

b. 

c. 

2 **PREDICTING. Read the title of the text and look at the picture. What do you think the text will be about? Read and check your predictions.**

____

Clothes for All

Clothes for All

Help with Clothes

LC is helping again with our campaign **No Old Clothes**. Do you have a shirt you don't like? Does your best T-shirt look bad? Is there a hole in your jeans? We can change all these clothes into nice outfits and take them where they are needed. We're a different side of the fashion world.

How can you help?

Donate clothes or your time and help us decorate and transform them.

Help us teach people how to repair their clothes.

Share this information on your social media. Everything helps.

Do you need more information?

Click on the MORE INFO button or complete the form.

3 **SCANNING. Read the text and find the information to complete the sentences.**

1. The name of the NGO is ____________________.
2. The name of the campaign is ________________.
3. The kind of items of clothing people can donate: ______________________________.
4. People can help in different ways: donating ______________ or ____________ to help decorate and transform them, or ______________ people how to repair their clothes.

4 **SCANNING. Read the text again and check (✓) what is true or cross out (✗) what is not true.**

1. ☐ This campaign is for professionals in the fashion industry.
2. ☐ There's information about clothes and sizes.
3. ☐ You can buy clothes from this website.
4. ☐ The campaign shows different ways to help.
5. ☐ You can phone the organization.

I can read about an NGO.
e-Language Booster

#CLARIFY

Listening

5 Farah and Tony are reading comments about the NGO *Clothes for All*. Listen and complete the chart. 13

Contact	Question to *Clothes For All*	Answer
Contact 1	Can we [1] ______________________________?	[4] ______
Contact 2	Can I [2] ______________________________?	[5] ______
Contact 3	Can we [3] ______________________________?	[6] ______

Writing

6 You want to help the organization. In pairs, write two more questions you can ask them.

____

____

7 Write a short text for a campaign you want to run at your school. Remember the ideas you discussed in the #Discover section. Use the text in Activity 2 as a model.

#TIP

Use a free online slide presentation to present your campaign. Remember to include free pictures, too.

I can write a short text about a campaign.

Language Booster page 12

#UNDERSTAND

Grammar

Simple Present vs. Present Continuous

1 Read and check (✓) the true sentences.

1. ☐ This is an informal text.
2. ☐ This text is about clothes for the organization.
3. ☐ Will goes to the sports club on Thursdays.
4. ☐ He takes classes on Fridays.
5. ☐ This week's routines are very similar to other weeks' routines.

2 Read the text in Activity 1 again and circle the correct options to complete the statements.

Simple Present

We use the Simple Present for [1] **frequent activities, routines, and habits.** / **activities happening at the time of speaking.**

Present Continuous

We use the Present Continuous for [2] **frequent activities, routines, and habits.** / **activities happening at the time of speaking.**

3 Complete the paragraphs. Use the verbs in parentheses in the Simple Present or the Present Continuous.

1. Jessica [1] ____________ (not wear) a scarf and gloves very often, but it's very cold this week, and she [2] ____________ (wear) a warm jacket, two sweaters, a beanie, and a scarf today!
   She [3] ____________ usually ____________ (not go) to the sports club on Thursdays, but this week she [4] ____________ (train), and she's at the club every day.

2. Lorna [5] ____________ (wear) a uniform to school every day. This week is Sports Week, and she [6] ____________ (wear) sweatpants.

4 In pairs, talk about one usual activity in your routine and one exception to your routine.

I go to school every day, but I am staying home today.

I can identify the difference between the Simple Present and the Present Continuous.

e-Language Booster

Subject and Object Questions

5 **Complete the questions on the form for a clothes donation campaign with *Who* or *What*.**

Clothes Donation

Please answer and submit the form

1. __________ has some free time? Type your answer
2. __________ can help in the organization? Type your answer
3. __________ can you help? Type your answer
4. __________ can you donate? Type your answer
5. __________ is interesting about the campaign? Type your answer
6. __________ do you like doing? Type your answer

SUBMIT CANCEL

6 **In pairs, look at the questions in Activity 5 and check (✓) the statements you agree with.**

1. ☐ *What* is for objects.
2. ☐ *Who* is for people.
3. ☐ In all the questions, there's a pronoun after the auxiliary.
4. ☐ Questions 1, 2, and 5 are about the subject.
5. ☐ Questions 3, 4, and 6 are about the object.

7 **Listen to the conversation between Will and Mel and write the answers to the questions in Activity 5.** 14

1. ______________________________
2. ______________________________
3. ______________________________
4. ______________________________
5. ______________________________
6. ______________________________

8 **Write two subject questions and two object questions, using *what* or *who*. Work in pairs and take turns asking and answering each other's questions.**

1. ______________________________
2. ______________________________
3. ______________________________
4. ______________________________

9 **Work in pairs. Go to page 156 and read the script of the conversation in Activity 7. Use it as a model and create a similar dialogue. Then role play it.**

I can ask subject and object questions with Who and What.

Language Booster page 13

#DEVELOP

Listening

1 **Match the expressions to the definitions. Then number the pictures.**

1. Oversized clothes
2. Tight clothes

☐ Clothes that fit your body very closely.
☐ Clothes that are bigger than usual.

a.

☐

b.

☐

c.

☐

d.

☐

2 **What type of clothes do you like? Oversized, tight, or the right size? Discuss in pairs.**

3 **LISTENING FOR GIST. Listen to the conversation between Bea and Vic and check (✓) the correct statement.** 15

1. ☐ The speakers are talking about the latest trend in clothes.
2. ☐ The speakers think that fashion is very important.

4 **LISTENING FOR DETAILS. Listen again and complete the sentences.** 16

1. Vic ______________________ follows the trends in fashion.
2. She doesn't wear ______________________ clothes.
3. Bea usually wears ______________________ for T-shirts.

Pronunciation

5 **Listen and repeat. Then practice reading the words aloud in pairs. Add one more example to each box.** 17

/b/	/p/
backpack	**p**ants
boots	**p**atch
black	**p**urse

6 **Now listen and circle the words you hear.** 18

1. bin / pin
2. bet / pet
3. bear / pear
4. bee / pea
5. big / pig
6. bark / park

Speaking

7 **Work in pairs. Draw five different items of clothing on a character.**

Student A: Describe what the character is wearing and what he / she is carrying. Include five items of clothing and accessories in your description.

Student B: Draw what Student A is describing.

Compare the drawings, and then change roles.

I can demonstrate an understanding of someone talking about trends in fashion.
e-Language Booster

Use of English

8 **Listen, read, and underline the words that describe the items of clothing or looks.** 19

Fay: Let's choose some clothes for the campaign.
Mike: OK. Look at these jeans.
Fay: They're scruffy. They have stains and holes.
Mike: We can solve the problem with studs and patches, and they'll look trendy.
Fay: OK. Here's a nice dress. I like it, but I can donate it. I don't wear it very often.
Mike: True! What about this elegant and classic shirt? I think it's useful.
Fay: Absolutely. Here's a hoodie with patches. I think it's original.
Mike: It is, and quite modern. In general, people wear dark colors.
Fay: Some people wear just about anything they like, and I think it's great.
Mike: Yes, but your look has to be appropriate.
Fay: Define appropriate...
Mike: Oh!

9 **Work in pairs. Rewrite the conversation in Activity 8 replacing all the underlined words.**

10 **Choose two items of clothing. Describe them to your classmate and tell him / her if you like them or not.**

I can describe what people wear.
Language Booster page 14

#CHALLENGE

Writing

1 **Read the texts and answer the questions.**

Mia B.
posted 3 hours ago

This is me. I'm ready for the party. I'm wearing leather boots and a red dress.

2 comments

Jess: You look awesome!
Tom: How elegant!

Tim Richards
posted 2 hours ago

My new outfit: tight jeans,
a sleeveless denim jacket, white sneakers, and a fancy hat. Soooooo trendy!

2 comments

Jess: Really trendy! I like it!
Shawn: Love the fancy hat!

1. Are these texts formal? __________
2. Are they social media posts? __________
3. Are they posts about looks? __________
4. Who posts the first picture? __________
5. Who makes comments about the second picture? __________
6. Are the comments positive or negative? __________
7. How many people comment on the first picture? __________
8. Which outfit do you like best? Why? __________

2 **In pairs, write two new comments on the posts in Activity 1.**

____

____

Prepare to Write

3 **You are going to write a social media post. Select a picture or make a drawing. Complete the chart with information about the picture.**

Clothes / Accessories	Descriptions

I can interpret information in a post about clothes and accessories.
e-Language Booster

Write

4 **Write the post. Use the information in Activity 3 and the texts in Activity 1 as models.**

____

____

____

____

____

____

Check and Change

5 **Read the post and make sure you included:**

- ☐ different items of clothing.
- ☐ accessories that appear in the picture.
- ☐ descriptions (color, size, opinion).
- ☐ verbs *wear* or *carry*.

6 **Edit your text. Make sure all the elements in Activity 5 are included.**

Publish

7 **Write a clean version of your post.**

#TIP

Check different posts on social media for design ideas. Remember to use icons, symbols, or emojis in your text to make it more natural.

Speaking

8 **Work in pairs. Take turns choosing one picture and describing what the model is wearing.**

I can write about and describe what a person is wearing.

Language Booster page 15

SUSTAINABLE DEVELOPMENT GOALS

Project: An Interactive Board Presentation

#DIGITAL LITERACY

Research online to get new interactive board presentation ideas. Use the keywords *online interactive board, whiteboard for remote teams*, and *virtual whiteboard.*

Step 1 Think

1 Look at the interactive board presentation and discuss the question in small groups.

What information can you display on an interactive board presentation related to fashion?

Clothes and Accessories		
Clothes		

Step 2 Plan

2 In groups, agree on the categories other than clothes to complete the table in your interactive board presentation.

I can recognize features of an interactive board presentation and plan to create one.

Step 3 Research

3 **In groups, discuss the items to complete the table in your interactive board presentation. Choose some images to add. Make notes.**

____

____

____

Step 4 Design

4 **In groups, create your interactive board presentation.**

- Check the text.
- Check the images.
- Check the organization.

Step 5 Present and Publish

5 **In groups, show your interactive board presentation to the class and publish it.**

Step 6 Evaluate

6 **Complete the evaluation table.**

★☆☆ More to learn | ★★☆ Good | ★★★ Excellent

Criteria	My Evaluation	Group Evaluation	Teacher Evaluation
Teamwork	☆☆☆	☆☆☆	☆☆☆
Language	☆☆☆	☆☆☆	☆☆☆
Design	☆☆☆	☆☆☆	☆☆☆

#TIP STEP 4

Choose composite pictures: clothes and accessories in the same picture.

Play around with different fonts.

Use different images and icons.

#TIP STEP 5

Prepare a tutorial about how to create an interactive board presentation and video record it.

Record your classmates using the interactive board presentation and adding new words / expressions to the board.

Speak slowly and fluently. Make sure you are showing the correct image while presenting the information.

I can create an interactive board presentation and show it to the class.

#SELF-ASSESSMENT

1 **Mark the learning objectives according to the key.**

★☆☆ I don't understand.	★★☆ I understand, but I need help.	★★★ I can do it!

Learning Objectives	Rating
To discuss a campaign to donate clothes.	☆☆☆
To talk about the clothes I like.	☆☆☆
To read about an NGO.	☆☆☆
To write a short text about a campaign.	☆☆☆
To identify the difference between the Simple Present and the Present Continuous.	☆☆☆
To ask subject and object questions with *Who* and *What*.	☆☆☆
To demonstrate an understanding of someone talking about trends in fashion.	☆☆☆
To describe what people wear.	☆☆☆
To interpret information in a post about clothes and accessories.	☆☆☆
To write about and describe what a person is wearing.	☆☆☆
To recognize features of an interactive board presentation and plan to create one.	☆☆☆
To create an interactive board presentation and show it to the class.	☆☆☆

2 **Work in pairs. Discuss the questions.**

1. What did I find most interesting to learn? Why?
2. How did I learn it?
3. How can I use it in real life?

FT Language Booster page 16

HEALTHY EATING HABITS

#2 ZERO HUNGER

In this unit, you will learn how to:

- Talk about food and eating habits.
- Write a review.
- Create a blog.

Say what you know:

- Fruit and vegetables.
- Food adjectives and food containers.
- Your favorite food.

Video

About Food

Before You Watch

1 **In pairs, make a list of ten food items. List the items in order of preference. (1 most favorite, ten least favorite)**

01
02
03
04
05
06
07
08
09
10

While You Watch

2 **Watch and check (✓) the food items Luis and Emma talk about.** ▷ 03

1.

2.

3.

4.

5.

6.

3 **Watch again and circle the correct option.** ▷ 03

1. They are **collecting** / **selling** food.
2. Emma **loves** / **hates** pea soup.
3. They need **some** / **a lot of** rice.
4. They have cans of **vegetables** / **beans**.

4 **Watch one more time and write what foods they cannot donate.** ▷ 03

After You Watch

5 **How important is it to help organizations like the Global Food Banking Network? Do you and your family support any such groups? If so, how? If not, why not? Answer in a short paragraph.**

I can demonstrate an understanding of a conversation about food donation.
e-Language Booster

Vocabulary

Fruit and Vegetables

6 **Label the fruit and vegetables with the words from the box. Then listen and check your answers.** 20

corn	eggplant	grapes	peas	pineapple	strawberry

1.  ____________
2.  ____________
3.  ____________
4.  ____________
5.  ____________
6.  ____________

Food Containers

7 **Match the pictures to the words. Then work in pairs. Discuss the foods stored in each container.**

1. 

2. 

3. 

4. 

☐ bag ☐ bottle ☐ carton ☐ pot

Adjectives for Describing Food

8 **Read the sentences and underline the words that describe the food items.**

1. I don't like bitter chocolate. I love sweet chocolate.
2. My sister loves sweets, but I prefer savory food like potato chips.
3. I am a big fan of spicy food. I always put a lot of pepper in my food.
4. I love salty crackers, but my brother only eats cookies. He loves sweet food.
5. I want to go back to that restaurant. The food was so tasty!

Collocations – *Drink / Eat / Have*

9 **Observe the expressions in bold in the sentences. Then answer the questions in pairs.**

1. I usually **have lunch** at noon.
2. I **eat ice cream** in the summer.
3. Sometimes I don't **have dinner** with my family because I work late.
4. My family likes to **have a barbecue** every Sunday.
5. I **drink water** while I exercise.

How often do you have lunch with your family?
Do you like eating ice cream in the summer?
How much water do you drink every day?
What do you enjoy most about having barbecues with your family?

10 **In pairs, discuss which food items are more appropriate for donations to food banks and explain why.**

I can talk about food and how it is stored.

Language Booster page 17

#CLARIFY

Reading

1 USING PRIOR KNOWLEDGE. In pairs, describe the foods in the pictures. Use the adjectives from the box.

savory	spicy	sweet	tasty

1. 
____

2. 
____

3. 
____

4. 
____

2 PREDICTING. Look at the pictures. What is the text about?

Typical Dishes Around...

http://www.worldfood.com

1. 
____

2. 
____

3. 
____

4. 
____

Typical Dishes Around the World

Every place in the world offers a special, typical dish. Here are some choices.

Are you traveling to Peru? Then you should try ceviche. It's pieces of cold fish in lime juice, onions, and tomatoes. It's pretty spicy!

Tourists in Brazil have to try *feijoada*. It's a typical dish with black beans, pork, and beef. To go with *feijoada*, Brazilians often have rice, cassava flour, and slices of orange, among other things. It's very tasty, but not very spicy.

A typical dessert in the United States is the famous key lime pie. Don't confuse it with a lemon pie. It's made with fresh lime juice and condensed milk.

Ropa Vieja. This means "old clothes" and it's the unofficial national dish of Cuba. It's made with pieces of meat and vegetables: pork, chicken, beef, various types of vegetables, and spices like oregano, pepper, etc.

What's the typical dish in your country? Write and tell us!

I can read about typical dishes around the world.

e-Language Booster

3 **SCANNING. Read the text quickly. How many countries can you find?**

____

4 **SKIMMING. Read the text again and check (✓) the correct statements or cross out (✗) the incorrect statements. Then go back to the text in Activity 2 and label the dishes.**

1. ☐ There's information about the ingredients in the typical dishes.
2. ☐ There are recipes and instructions to make the typical dishes.
3. ☐ The United States and England have the same typical dish.
4. ☐ The author invites the readers to write about typical dishes in their country.
5. ☐ There's information about restaurants where you can eat the typical dishes.

Listening

5 **Listen and write T for Tom, S for Sam, or B for both.** 21

1. ☐ I love ceviche.
2. ☐ I prefer sweet food.
3. ☐ I prefer chocolate cake.
4. ☐ I love chocolate and strawberries.
5. ☐ My favorite food is pizza and hamburgers.

6 **In pairs, ask questions about your classmate's taste in food. Use the conversation in Activity 5 as a model.**

Writing

7 **Work in groups. Write to the author of the text in Activity 2 and tell him / her about a typical dish in your country.**

#TIP

You can look for a picture of your dish online to add it to your text. Check some free picture websites.

I can write about typical dishes.

Language Booster page 18

#UNDERSTAND

Grammar

Countable and Uncountable Nouns

1 Write the words from the box in the correct column. Then add three more words to each column.

apple egg hamburger milk
peas pizza soda tea water yogurt

Drinks	Foods

2 Answer the questions. Then circle the correct words to complete the statements.

1. Can you count water? ______________

2. Can you count apples? ______________

3. Which words in Activity 1 have a plural form?

____

4. Which words don't have a plural form?

____

- We [1] **can** / **can't** count countable words.
- We [2] **can** / **can't** count uncountable words.
- [3] **Countable** / **Uncountable** words are singular or plural.
- [4] **Countable** / **Uncountable** words are always singular.

Plural Nouns, Quantifiers, *How many*, *How much*

3 Read the conversation. Then write the shopping list.

A: There are **some** strawberries in the refrigerator, Mom. Can I make a cake?
B: Yes. **How many** are there?
A: There aren't **many**, only five or six. And I need **some** milk.
B: OK. I'll go to the supermarket. **How much** milk?
A: One bottle.
B: Are there **any** eggs? And yogurt? Is there **any** yogurt?
A: There are **a lot of** eggs- 18, but there isn't **any** yogurt.
B: OK. **How much** yogurt do you need?
A: Not **much**, a small pot of vanilla yogurt. And a bag of chocolate cookies!
B: For the cake?
A: No, I'm hungry!

Shopping List

1 ______________________________

2 ______________________________

3 ______________________________

4 Read the conversation again and check (✓) the correct statements. In pairs, discuss how to correct the incorrect statements.

1. ☐ We use *how much* and *how many* to ask about quantity.
2. ☐ We use *a lot*, *much*, and *many* to describe small quantities.
3. ☐ We use *some* and *any* to describe undefined quantities.
4. ☐ We use *some* and *any* with countable and uncountable nouns.
5. ☐ We use (*not*) *many* with uncountable nouns.
6. ☐ We use *any* in negative statements and in questions.

I can identify and use countable and uncountable nouns and quantifiers.

e-Language Booster

5 **Complete the dialogue. Use *any*, *some*, *much*, *many*, *how much*, or *how many*.**

A: Is there [1]__________ water in the refrigerator?

B: Yes, there's [2]__________. But we need to buy two or three more bottles!

A: Is there [3]__________ milk?

B: Yes, there is.

A: [4]__________ milk is there?

B: Not [5]__________ – a carton.

A: Do you need [6]__________ oranges?

B: Yes, I do.

A: [7]__________ oranges do you need?

B: Not [8]__________ – two or three.

6 **In pairs, role play the conversation in Activity 5. Replace the underlined words.**

Indirect Questions

7 **Read the examples and answer the questions.**

Is this Dr. Mendez's room?
Can you tell me if this is Dr. Mendez's room?
What's this?
Can you tell me what this is?

1. Do the questions have the same meaning?
____
2. Which question is more formal?
____
3. Which one is a direct question?
____
4. Which one is an indirect question?
____
5. What happens to the structure of the question in indirect questions?
____
____
____
6. When do we use indirect questions?
____

8 **Match the questions to the pictures.**

1. Can you tell me if the supermarket closes at 5?
2. Do you know where the restaurant is?
3. Would you mind telling me what this is?

a. 

b. 

c. 

9 **In pairs, practice turning direct questions into indirect questions. Use some of the questions in this unit.**

A: *How often do you meet them?*
B: *Can you tell me how often you meet them?*

I can use indirect questions.
Language Booster page 19

#DEVELOP

Listening

1 Label the pictures.

eat ice cream	eat soup
go grocery shopping	have breakfast

1.

____

2.

____

3.

____

4.

____

2 Work in small groups. Read the example below and talk about your routine and your family's. Use the pictures in Activity 1.

My mom goes grocery shopping on Tuesdays.

3 LISTENING FOR GIST. Listen and check (✓) the correct sentence. 22

1. ☐ The speakers talk about good and bad eating habits.
2. ☐ The speakers have good eating habits.

4 LISTENING FOR DETAILS. Listen again and circle the correct options to complete the sentences. 23

1. Vic has a / an **healthy** / **unhealthy** breakfast.
2. Vic **likes** / **doesn't like** hamburgers.
3. According to Bea, we should eat **some** / **a lot of** fruits and vegetables.
4. Vic eats chicken soup with lots of **vegetables** / **cheese**.
5. Vic **likes** / **doesn't like** to have ice cream on the weekend.

Pronunciation

5 Listen and write the words in the correct column. Look back through the unit and find more words with these vowel sounds. 24

eggplant	grapefruit
taste	lettuce

/e/	/ei/

Speaking

6 Interview three classmates. Ask about their eating habits and complete the chart. Then tell them if they have a healthy diet.

	Classmate 1	Classmate 2	Classmate 3
Breakfast			
Junk Food			
Weekends			

I can talk about healthy and unhealthy food.

e-Language Booster

Use of English

7 Complete the conversation with the sentences from the box. Then listen and check. 25

Any drinks?	Can I take your order?	I'd like to have some fruit.	No dessert, then.

At the Restaurant

Ed: Good morning! [1] ______________________
Fay: Yes. I'd like a veggie burger and a salad.

Ed: [2] ______________________
Fay: Yes! A lemonade.
Ed: Any sweet treats for dessert?

Fay: [3] ______________________ Do you have any?
Ed: Sorry, no. Only ice cream.

Fay: [4] ______________________
Ed: OK, that's $12.80. For here or to go?
Fay: Here.
Ed: Is it cash or credit card?
Fay: Credit card.
Ed: OK. Be right back.
Fay: Thank you.

8 Circle the correct alternatives to complete the sentences.

1. **A:** Is there **any** / **some** juice left in the carton?
   B: Yes, there is **any** / **some**.
2. I need to go to the supermarket. There isn't **any** / **some** food for lunch today.
3. **Any** / **Some** restaurants downtown don't serve typical food.
4. Poor, Leon! He doesn't have **any** / **some** healthy eating habits.

9 Complete the sentences with *many*, *much*, *how much*, or *how many*.

1. **A:** ______________ sugar do you need to make the pie?
   B: Not ______________.
2. **A:** ______________ glasses of water a day does the doctor recommend?
   B: It depends on your weight.
3. ______________ tourists try *feijoada* when they are in Brazil.
4. I don't know ______________ cream you like in your coffee.

10 Work in pairs. Role play the conversation in Activity 7. Replace the foods and drinks according to your likes and dislikes.

I can order food in a restaurant.
Language Booster page 20

#CHALLENGE

Writing

1 Read and check (✓) what you think you will find in the restaurant review in Activity 2.

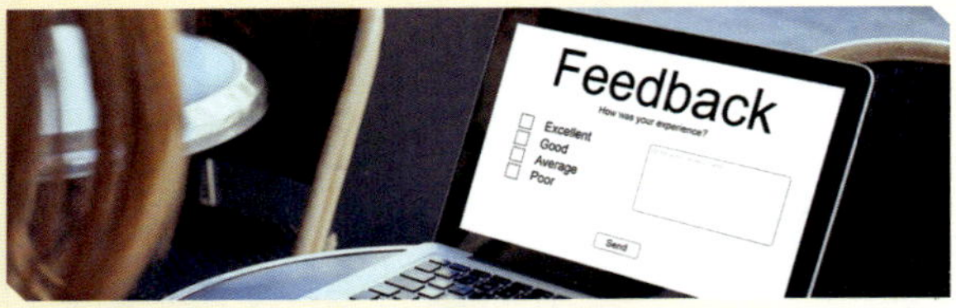

I think I'll find information about

1. ☐ orders.
2. ☐ operating hours.
3. ☐ the menu.
4. ☐ prices.
5. ☐ reservations.
6. ☐ the service.

2 Read the review and check your answers in Activity 1. Then answer the questions.

Best Places +

www.bestplaces.com

The Club Restaurant

The Club Restaurant is a new restaurant near the Galana Shopping Mall. It's the favorite place for families, couples, and small groups of friends.

There's a bar at the entrance. You can have a drink or just sit on the comfortable couches and armchairs before your table is ready. Tip: make a reservation, it's usually full.

The menu shows a variety of dishes for vegans, people with allergies, for those who like fast food, and for those who prefer a homemade dish. The dessert list is quite short, but the options are amazing. The Club Restaurant is not a cheap place, but it's definitely cheaper than most famous restaurants in the area.

The service is OK. You do not get much information about the dishes from the waiters.

We considered the place, the quality of the food, the service, and the prices, and we give it...

★★★★

Ben Hutchins
The Global Tribune

1. Where's the restaurant?
____
2. Does Ben recommend making a reservation?
____
3. Are there options for gluten intolerant people?
____
4. Are there negative comments in the review?
____
5. Who is the author of the review?
____
6. Where does the author of the review work?
____

3 Read the review again and complete the chart.

Sections of the review	Key information
Description of the place	*New, bar at the entrance, couches and armchairs.*
Information about the menu	1
Name, location, and who it is for	2
Recommendation	3
Service	4
Score	5

I can read a restaurant review.
e-Language Booster

Prepare to Write

4 You are going to write a review of a restaurant. The restaurant can be fictitious or real. Complete the chart with information for your review. Select a picture or make a drawing.

Sections of the review	Key information
Description of the place	
Information about the menu	
Name, location, and who it is for	
Recommendation	
Service	
Score	

Write

5 Write the review. Use the information in Activity 4 and the text in Activity 2 as a model.

#TIP

Check different restaurant reviews for design ideas.

Check and Change

6 Read the review and make sure you included:

- ☐ a description of the place.
- ☐ information about the menu.
- ☐ name, location, and who it is for.
- ☐ recommendation.
- ☐ service.
- ☐ score.

7 Edit your text. Make sure all the elements in Activity 6 are included.

Publish

8 Write a clean version of your review.

Speaking

9 In pairs, talk about a restaurant you have been to. Comment on the service, the menu, and special features.

I can write a restaurant review.

Language Booster page 21

Project: A Blog

#DIGITAL LITERACY

Blogs may reflect only the personal opinion of the blogger. Make sure you check if information is real before reusing it or sharing it on social media.

Step 1 Think

1 Work in groups.

1. Discuss: What's in a blog? What different types of blogs can you think of?
2. Read the blog page below.

Food Blogger

https://www.foodblogger.com

Help with Food

July 10th

We did it!

At school, we always help an NGO. This year we're collecting food for an organization called Food Sharing. There are a lot of donations from all our classmates' families and friends: bottles of milk, bags of pasta, cans of fruit and vegetables... Lots and lots of food! We're very happy.

June 28th

We can all help

Food Sharing is an amazing organization that helps people who need food. They collect food from restaurants and send it to communities in need. They also help local organizations start their food banks. It's not difficult, and you get a lot of help and ideas from the NGO.

We can help end hunger. How? With food banks. Click here and find out more.

Step 2 Plan

2 You are going to create a food blog and write a post for it. Decide what information you want to include. Use the mind map to help organize your ideas.

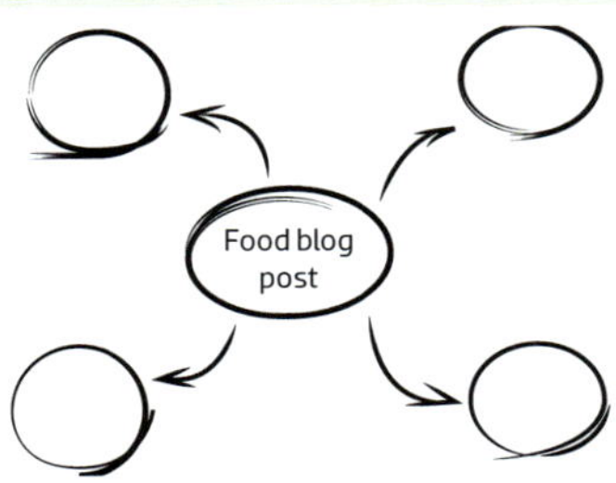

Step 3 Research

3 **Research food blogs and try to find the information you included in Step 2. Make notes.**

____

____

____

____

____

#TIP STEP 3

You can use a free online website to look for different types of design for blogs, according to the one you intend to create.

Step 4 Design

4 **In groups, create your food blog and write your post. Use the information from the previous activities.**

- Check the text.
- Check the images.
- Check the organization.

#TIP STEP 4

1. You can practice the presentation and video record it.
2. Describe what the blog is about.
3. Don't read out the text.
4. Speak slowly and fluently.

Step 5 Present and Publish

5 **In groups, present your blog to the class and read your post.**

Step 6 Evaluate

6 **Complete the evaluation table.**

★☆☆ More to learn | ★★☆ Good | ★★★ Excellent

Criteria	My Evaluation	Group Evaluation	Teacher Evaluation
Teamwork	☆☆☆	☆☆☆	☆☆☆
Language	☆☆☆	☆☆☆	☆☆☆
Design	☆☆☆	☆☆☆	☆☆☆

I can create a food blog, write a post for it, and present it to the class.

#SELF-ASSESSMENT

1 Mark the learning objectives according to the key.

★☆☆ I don't understand.	★★☆ I understand, but I need help.	★★★ I can do it!

Learning Objectives	Rating
To demonstrate an understanding of a conversation about food donation.	☆☆☆
To talk about food and how it is stored.	☆☆☆
To read about typical dishes around the world.	☆☆☆
To write about typical dishes.	☆☆☆
To identify and use countable and uncountable nouns and quantifiers.	☆☆☆
To use indirect questions.	☆☆☆
To talk about healthy and unhealthy food.	☆☆☆
To order food in a restaurant.	☆☆☆
To read a restaurant review and prepare to write one.	☆☆☆
To write a restaurant review.	☆☆☆
To recognize features of a blog and plan to create one.	☆☆☆
To create a food blog, write a post for it, and present it to the class.	☆☆☆

2 Work in pairs. Discuss the questions.

1. What did I find most interesting to learn? Why?
2. How did I learn it?
3. How can I use it in real life?

UT Language Booster page 22

GREAT INVENTIONS

#11 SUSTAINABLE CITIES AND COMMUNITIES

In this unit, you will learn how to:

- Talk about great inventions and inventors.
- Write a biography.
- Create a virtual bulletin board.

Say what you know:

- Useful gadgets.
- Inventions that changed the world.
- Sustainable inventions.

#DISCOVER

Video

Past Inventions

Before You Watch

1 **In pairs, talk about the gadgets and inventions that contribute to a better, more sustainable world. What do you know about them? What would you like to know? Make a list.**

While You Watch

2 **Watch and check (✓) the inventors you see in the video.** ▷ 04

1. ☐ Grace Hopper
2. ☐ Ada Lovelace
3. ☐ Ellen Eglin
4. ☐ Marry Kenner
5. ☐ Maria Telkes
6. ☐ Melitta Bentz

3 **Watch again and mark the sentences T (True) or F (False).** ▷ 04

1. ☐ Emma and Luis are talking about technology.
2. ☐ Women haven't created any inventions.
3. ☐ Emma was watching a video about a woman inventor.
4. ☐ Emma mentions a young Colombian inventor.
5. ☐ Luis will write about a woman inventor.
6. ☐ Emma thinks Da Vinci was a great inventor.
7. ☐ Luis has some inventions on his list already.

4 **Check (✓) the information Emma and Luis discuss. Then watch again and check your answers.** ▷ 04

1. ☐ Details of the content of the assignment.
2. ☐ Date of submission of the assignment.
3. ☐ Number of words for the assignment.
4. ☐ Website with information about Da Vinci.
5. ☐ Some women inventors.

After You Watch

5 **Make a list of the gadgets and inventions Emma and Luis talk about and answer the questions.**

1. Do these inventions /gadgets contribute to sustainability? How?

____

____

____

2. Is this invention / gadget used in your city / neighborhood?

____

____

____

6 **In small groups, discuss these questions.**

1. How many electronic devices do you have at home?
2. Which ones do you use? How often do you use them?

I can name some gadgets and inventions.

e-Language Booster

Vocabulary

Gadgets and Inventions

7 **Match the words to their definitions. Then listen and check.** 26

1. device
2. digital
3. gadget
4. invention
5. machine
6. technology

- [ ] New machines, equipment, and ways of doing things that are based on modern knowledge about science and computers.
- [ ] A machine or tool that does a special job.
- [ ] A piece of equipment with moving parts that uses power (for example, electricity) to do a particular job.
- [ ] Using a system in which information is recorded or sent out electronically in the form of numbers, usually ones and zeros.
- [ ] A small, useful, and cleverly designed machine or tool.
- [ ] A useful machine, device, etc. that has been invented.

8 **In pairs, use the words in Activity 7 to refer to the items below. More than one word is possible.**

1. 

____
____

2. 

____
____

3. 

____
____

4. 

____
____

9 **Look at these devices. Match them to their descriptions.**

- [ ] A massage chair
- [ ] A smart fridge
- [ ] A touch screen monitor
- [ ] An electric car
- [ ] VR headset

1. A refrigerator with Internet connectivity and the ability to detect and handle objects placed in it.
2. An eye-covering device worn on the head that provides a fully immersive 3D experience.
3. Motors inside this gadget generate vibrations that massage your muscles as it spins.
4. Rechargeable batteries act as a fuel source in this device, providing energy to the engine to power the vehicle.
5. It's a type of display that lets you interact with a computer using your finger or a pen.

10 **In pairs, choose a gadget or device from Activity 8. Describe it to the whole class. Who can guess what it is?**

I can talk about gadgets and inventions.

Language Booster page 23

#CLARIFY

Reading

1 Read and match the pictures to the descriptions. There is an extra picture.

a. 

b. 

c. 

d. 

1. This machine scans a document and transfers the data to another machine of the same type. This other machine decodes the data and prints out the document. They use special paper and a telephone line.
2. This invention started in the United States in the 1920s. Individual firms, such as oil companies and hotels started issuing them to customers. At present, there are millions. People use them all over the world instead of paper money.
3. This is a very old invention. The first ones go back 6,000 years. They were made of wood. At present, there are metal ones and magnetic ones, too. The purpose is the same: protection.

2 MAKING AND CONFIRMING PREDICTIONS. Read the title of the text and look at the pictures. What do you think the text will be about? Read and check your predictions. Then label the pictures.

Technology Can Help +

http://www.greatinventionsandgadgets.com

Technology Can Help

The desert refrigerator is a container within another container. Between the two containers is wet sand. As the water evaporates, the sand becomes cooler. This way, people in areas without electricity can keep food in good condition for weeks.

Would you like to play soccer and generate electricity? Now there is a soccer ball that generates energy when you play soccer with it. After 30 minutes of play, you can keep a LED lamp going for three hours.

A straw that can turn dirty water into drinking water. No chemicals, just a special membrane. It reduces bacteria and parasites in the water. A great invention for places where there is no access to good drinking water.

The fog catcher is an amazing invention for desert areas. It has nets with very small openings. These openings catch the tiny water droplets of the fog. The droplets collect in the net and flow into a channel. From there, the water is directed to containers at the base of the mountains and is ready for immediate use.

The light emitting diode (LED) is currently the most energy efficient lighting technology. LED lights are more expensive than regular light bulbs, but they last much longer and do not use much energy.

1. 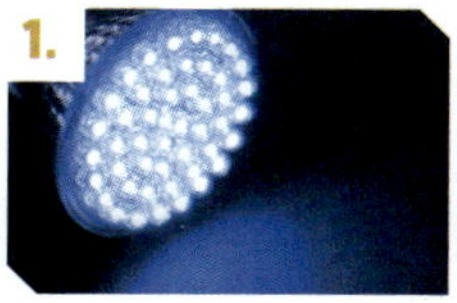
______

2. 
______

3. 
______

4. 
______

5. 
______

I can give examples of sustainable inventions.

3 SCANNING. Read the text again and complete.

1. Inventions which are sustainable: ______
2. An invention that reduces the use of energy: ______
3. Inventions related to water: ______
4. Inventions related to eating and drinking: ______

4 SKIMMING. Read the sentences and check (✓) what is true according to the text.

1. ☐ In this website, there's information about the cost of the inventions.
2. ☐ The desert refrigerator uses digital technology.
3. ☐ The soccer ball is for amateur players.
4. ☐ The membrane in the straw is very effective.
5. ☐ You can use the fog catcher to generate energy.
6. ☐ LED lights are more ecological than regular light bulbs.

Listening

5 Listen and mark the sentences T (True) or F (False). 27

1. ☐ There are better inventions than the smartphone.
2. ☐ The boy listens to music on his smartphone.
3. ☐ He uses pen and paper to take notes.
4. ☐ He drives.
5. ☐ The boy rides a bike.
6. ☐ He likes talking on the phone.

Writing

6 In pairs, research about a useful invention. Make notes of the main points.

______

______

7 Write a short text about the invention. Use the text in Activity 2 a model.

______

______

______

I can write a short text about an invention.

Language Booster page 24

#UNDERSTAND

Grammar

Past Continuous

1 **Read and circle the parts that show an ongoing action in the past. Then answer the questions.**

Vic: I called you an hour ago, and you didn't answer.
Kay: Oh, I was playing with my new gadget, and my mom and dad were testing their new invention. I didn't hear the phone.
Vic: Ah, a family of inventors...
Kay: Haha. Why did you call me?
Vic: I was writing the geography report and I needed help.
Kay: Sorry! I can help you now.
Vic: It's almost 5:00, and I have my Italian class. Don't worry.

1. What was Kay doing when the phone rang?
____
____
2. What were her parents doing when the phone rang?
____
____
3. What was Vic doing when she called Kay?
____
____

2 **Read an extract from the dialogue. Check (✓) the correct statements. Then underline the correct options to complete the sentences.**

Kay: I was playing with my new gadget, and my mom and dad were testing their new invention.

1. ☐ These are past actions.
2. ☐ Kay started playing an hour ago.
3. ☐ Kay's parents started testing their invention before 4:00.
4. ☐ At 4:00, the activities were in progress.

- We use the Past Continuous to talk about [1] **present events / activities in progress in the past**.
- The Past Continuous is formed by [2] ***was*** **or** ***were*** **/** ***did*** + [3] **to verb / verb** ***ing***.

3 **Work in pairs. Answer the questions.**

What were you doing...

1. last night at 10 p.m.? _______________
2. two days ago in the morning? _______________
3. at noon last Saturday? _______________
4. at 4 p.m. last Sunday? _______________

4 **In pairs, take turns talking about your answers in Activity 3.**

A: *What were you doing last night at 10p.m.?*
B: *I was watching a movie on TV.*

I can express ongoing actions in the past.
e-Language Booster

Simple Past and Past Continuous

5 **Read the post and vote.**

Amy R.
posted 3 hours ago

Yesterday was a holiday, and I wanted to enjoy my day. I was making breakfast when Grandma called. She wanted to talk. My breakfast was ruined. 🙁 OK, cookies. Later, while I was watching the last episode of my favorite series, the lights went out. 😤 OK, be positive. I decided to ride my bike. A cat ran in front of me while I was riding, and I fell off my bike. 😭 What do you think?
Vote! Did I have a good day? YES! 👍 NO! 👎

5 comments

6 **Read the post in Activity 5 and choose the correct option.**

1. The post is about **the past** / **the present**.
2. We use the Simple Past for **completed actions** / **actions in progress** in the past.
3. We use the Past Continuous for **completed actions** / **actions in progress** in the past.
4. We use *when* to introduce the **completed action** / **action in progress**.
5. We use *while* to introduce the **completed action** / **action in progress**.

7 **Look at the pictures and write sentences in the Past Continuous and the Simple Past.**

1.

____

____

2.

____

____

____

3.

____

____

____

4.

____

____

8 **In pairs, write a social media post. Use the post in Activity 5 as a model.**

Amy R.
posted 3 hours ago

____

____

____

____

____

____

____

____

I can demonstrate actions in the past using the Simple Past and the Past Continuous.

Language Booster page 25

Listening

1 **Read the captions and match them to the pictures.**

1. Generation Y
2. Generation X
3. Generation Z
4. Generation Alpha

2 **LISTENING FOR GIST. Listen to the podcast and check (✓) the correct statement.** 28

1. ☐ The podcast is about technology in different generations.
2. ☐ The podcast shows which generation is the best.

3 **LISTENING FOR DETAILS. Listen again and circle the correct options to complete the sentences.** 29

1. Generation X is the **phone** / **smartphone** generation.
2. Generation X had **basic** / **modern** computers at home.
3. Generation Y is also known as **Centennials** / **Milennials**.
4. There was technology for Generation Y **when** / **after** they were born.
5. The Z generation is the **Millennial** / **Centennial** generation.
6. They **are** / **aren't** the smartphone generation.
7. The Alpha Generation **uses** / **doesn't use** smartphones.
8. They're **always** / **sometimes** connected to the Internet.
9. Their social life will be mostly **online** / **face to face**.
10. We **know** / **don't know** the name of the next generation.

Pronunciation

4 **Listen to the words and write them in the correct column. Can you think of other words with these sounds? Practice saying them.** 30

calling phone thanking young

/n/	
/ŋ/	

5 **Now listen and circle the words you hear.** 31

1. **thin** / **thing**
2. **sin** / **sing**
3. **win** / **wing**
4. **sun** / **sung**
5. **hang** / **hanging**

Speaking

6 **Work in pairs. Talk about the use of technology in the past. What do you think people were doing 20 years ago?**

Talk about these areas:

1. The use of smartphones.
2. The use of landlines.
3. Technology, devices, and gadgets.
4. The use of the Internet.

I can identify different generations and how they use technology.

Use of English

7 **Listen and read. Then underline the phrases that show agreement and disagreement.** 32

June: Hey! Cheer up! What's wrong with you?
Ivan: I listened to the podcast. I don't think it's quite right.
June: I see your point, but don't forget that these are general characteristics and tendencies.
Ivan: I don't think so. The speaker was absolutely sure about what the generations have done in the past.
June: I think we need to read more.
Ivan: Me too. I don't like just repeating what people say.
June: Me neither!
Ivan: Let's look online. That's where we get the best information.
June: Sorry, I'm afraid I have to disagree with you on that. We also have to check the information, too. Sometimes it isn't correct.
Ivan: I agree. Let's check the Internet and check with some teachers at school.
June: Great! By the way, I think you belong to Generation Alpha...

8 **Listen again and role play the conversation in pairs.** 33

9 **Complete the chart with the expressions from the conversation.**

Agreement	
Disagreement	

10 **Work in pairs. Write a conversation. Use the conversation in Activity 7 as a model. Then role play it.**

1. Give your opinion about one of the generations.
2. Show agreement or disagreement.
3. Agree or disagree with your classmate's comment.

____
____
____
____
____
____

I can demonstrate agreement and disagreement in a conversation.
Language Booster page 26

#CHALLENGE

Writing

1 **Check (✓) the information you can find in a biography.**

1. ☐ Place and date of birth
2. ☐ Family
3. ☐ Education
4. ☐ Important facts about the person's life
5. ☐ Opinion about the person
6. ☐ Place and date of death

2 **Read the text and check your answers in Activity 1.**

All About Leonardo Da Vinci

☐ Leonardo Da Vinci was an artist, scientist, inventor, engineer, and architect.

☐ He was born in Vinci, Italy, in 1452. When Leonardo was 14 years old, he studied with Verrocchio in the city of Florence. He learned art, drawing, painting, and sculpting.

☐ In 1482, he moved to Milan and lived there for 17 years. During this time he painted one of his most famous works: The Last Supper.

☐ After some stays in Venice and other cities, he returned to Florence. It was a time of intense scientific study, but he also painted his other most famous work: The Mona Lisa.

☐ Leonardo was interested in science. In his diary he wrote down his observations about the world on more than 13,000 pages. He made drawings of helicopters, a flying machine, tanks, musical instruments, and many other useful machines that we use today.

☐ He had a deep knowledge of the human body. He made detailed drawings of muscles, tendons, the human skeleton, the heart, and other organs. His Vitruvian Man is very close to a scientific sketch. He also had an interest in animals.

☐ Leonardo never registered any of his inventions. He kept a personal diary in which he recorded them. The diary was discovered only after his death.

☐ He died in 1519 in Amboise, France.

3 **Circle the correct option.**

1. Verrocchio was **his father** / **an artist**.
2. He was in **Florence** / **Milan** when he painted The Last Supper.
3. He painted The Mona Lisa while he was in **Venice** / **Florence**.
4. He died in **France** / **Italy**.
5. He **built** / **drew** machines we use today.
6. His Vitruvian Man is **a scientific** / **a non-scientific** sketch.

4 **Read the text again and number the sections in Activity 2 according to the headings below.**

1. Job / profession
2. Place and date of birth and early years
3. His career
4. Place and date of death

I can identify the features of a biography.

Prepare to Write

5 You are going to write a biography. Choose one inventor, complete the chart, and select a picture of the person.

Sections	Information
1. Job / profession	
2. Place and date of birth and early years	
3. Career	
4. Place and date of death	

Write

6 Write the biography of an inventor. Use the information in Activity 5 and the text in Activity 2 as a model.

____

____

____

____

____

Check and Change

7 Read the biography and make sure you included:

- ☐ job / profession.
- ☐ place and date of birth and early years.
- ☐ career.
- ☐ place and date of death.

8 Edit your text. Make sure all the elements in Activity 7 are included.

Publish

9 Write a clean version of the biography.

Speaking

10 Work in pairs. Take turns talking about the person in the biography you wrote. Ask and answer questions.

#TIP

You can use a timeline maker to illustrate your biography.

I can write a biography.

Language Booster page 27

Project: A Virtual Bulletin Board

#DIGITAL LITERACY

Virtual boards can be used for collaborative work. They can be used to brainstorm, to make notes, and to keep track of projects.

Step 1 Think

1 **Discuss in groups. What's in a virtual bulletin board?**

Best and Most Useful Gadgets and Inventions

This is the best invention ever! It's an example of artificial intelligence. It talks to you, gives you information about the weather, about your calendar... By using only your voice, this gadget can answer questions, set alarms, create to-do lists, and read the news. It's amazing!!!

Milton C.

I love this device. I use it every day. My food and my tea is never cold, and it takes two minutes! A microwave oven (also known as a microwave) is an electric oven that warms and cooks food by exposing it to microwave-frequency electromagnetic radiation. Fantastic!

Carla D.

Step 2 Plan

2 **In groups, agree on the information you want to include in your virtual board.**

____

____

____

____

____

I can recognize features of a virtual bulletin board and plan to create one.

Step 3 Research

3 In pairs, research some virtual bulletin boards. Choose some pictures to add. Make notes.

____

____

____

Step 4 Design

4 In groups, create your virtual bulletin board.

- Check the text.
- Check the pictures.
- Check the organization.

Step 5 Present and Publish

5 In groups, show your virtual bulletin board to the class.

Step 6 Evaluate

6 Complete the evaluation table.

★☆☆ More to learn · ★★☆ Good · ★★★ Excellent

Criteria	My Evaluation	Group Evaluation	Teacher Evaluation
Teamwork	☆☆☆	☆☆☆	☆☆☆
Language	☆☆☆	☆☆☆	☆☆☆
Design	☆☆☆	☆☆☆	☆☆☆

#TIP STEP 4

You can use different online virtual boards and explore the different functionalities among them.

#TIP STEP 5

1. Prepare a tutorial about how to create a virtual bulletin board and video record it.
2. Record your classmates using the virtual bulletin board and adding new words / expressions to the board.
3. Speak slowly and fluently. Make sure you are showing the correct picture while presenting the information.

I can create a virtual post bulletin and show it to the class.

#SELF-ASSESSMENT

1 Mark the learning objectives according to the key.

★☆☆ I don't understand.	★★☆ I understand, but I need help.	★★★ I can do it!

Learning Objectives	Rating
To name some gadgets and inventions.	☆☆☆
To talk about gadgets and inventions.	☆☆☆
To give examples of sustainable inventions.	☆☆☆
To write a short text about an invention.	☆☆☆
To express ongoing actions in the past.	☆☆☆
To demonstrate actions in the past using the Simple Past and the Past Continuous.	☆☆☆
To identify different generations and how they use technology.	☆☆☆
To demonstrate agreement and disagreement in a conversation.	☆☆☆
To identify features of a biography.	☆☆☆
To write a biography.	☆☆☆
To recognize features of a virtual bulletin board and plan to create one.	☆☆☆
To create a virtual bulletin board and show it to the class.	☆☆☆

2 **Work in pairs. Discuss the questions.**

1. What did I find most interesting to learn?
2. How did I learn it?
3. How can I use it in real life?

UT Language Booster page 28

TECHNOLOGY AND THE FUTURE

#9 INDUSTRY, INNOVATION AND INFRASTRUCTURE

In this unit, you will learn how to:

- Talk about future technology.
- Write an informal e-mail.
- Create an online graphic organizer.

Say what you know:

- Phrasal verbs.
- Technological innovations.
- The future of cars, schools, and computers.

#DISCOVER

Video

Jobs of the Future

Before You Watch

1 **In pairs, read the definition and discuss the questions.**

to automate: to start using computers and machines to do a job, rather than people

1. What services are automated in stores or other places in your town?

___

___

2. What services do you think will be automated in the future?

___

___

While You Watch

2 **Watch the video. What automated process do Emma and Luis talk about?** 05

___

3 **Watch again and mark the sentences T (True) or F (False).** 05

1. ☐ Jaime is going to an interview for a training program.
2. ☐ His old boss sent him on a training program.
3. ☐ Jaime is going to learn to be a robotics engineer.
4. ☐ Jaime is going to study every day for three years.
5. ☐ His salary will be higher than before.

After You Watch

4 **Work in pairs. Make a list of school services and activities that could be automated in the future.**

___

___

5 **Choose one of the options from your list. Write a short presentation for the school principal. Then record yourself giving the presentation.**

We believe that grading tests can be automated. This can save time for the teacher, and the grades would be more accurate.

___

___

I can interpret a conversation about technology and innovation.

e-Language Booster

Vocabulary

Phrasal Verbs

6 **Read the sentences and match them to the pictures.**

1. I have to **put away** all these toys. My room is a mess.
2. Joe is **looking for** his glasses, but he can't find them.
3. Kate is **looking forward to** her trip to Canada.
4. Let's **hang out** again tomorrow.
5. My mom **works out** at the gym every afternoon. She loves physical exercise.
6. He was very tired, but he didn't **give up**.
7. He **turned off** the machine before leaving.
8. He needs to **set up** the printer.

a. 

b. 

c. 

d. 

e. 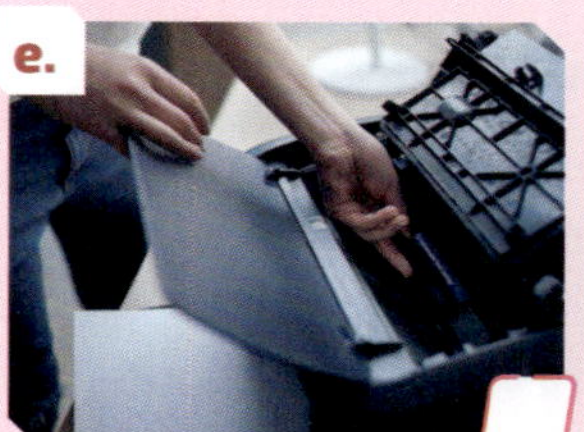

f. 

g. 

h. 

7 **Pay attention to the verbs in bold in the sentences in Activity 6. In pairs, answer the questions.**

1. How many parts do most of the verbs have, one or two? ____________________
2. If we read the two parts separately, do the verbs have the same meaning? ____________________
3. Can phrasal verbs have more than two parts? ____________________
4. Can you give an example of a three-part verb in Activity 6? ____________________

8 **Look up other phrasal verbs in a dictionary. Make a list of at least three new phrasal verbs. Compare your list to a classmate's.**

____

____

9 **In small groups, use the phrasal verbs in Activity 6 and on your list to talk about yourself.**

I can use phrasal verbs to talk about myself.

Language Booster page 29

Reading

1 USING PRIOR KNOWLEDGE. Look at the pictures and answer the questions.

1. Do you think these are examples of technology? Why? Why not?

____

2. How can you make a connection between technology in the future and these items?

____

____

2 MAKING PREDICTIONS. In pairs, read the title of the text. How does it relate to the pictures in Activity 1? Read the text and confirm your guesses.

The Future of Technology +

http://www. techtechnologyforthefuture.com

The Future of Technology

How will technology change the world in the next ten years?

1 ______________________________

The world is changing. The population is growing, and there's not enough food for everyone. Climate change is getting worse, pollution is everywhere... Everything points to a very negative future. The good news is that the future can be brighter.

2 ______________________________

Over the next decade, we'll see profound changes in the way technology can help make our planet a better place. A group of students from 100 high schools on five continents have shared their ideas. Four of them are presented below.

3 ______________________________

Technological milk. Scientists will produce milk, cheese, and other dairy products in laboratories. The system won't be expensive. Even better, the dairy industry isn't environmentally friendly and this will change it forever.

Wearable technology isn't new, but how about clothing that "scans" your body, tracks your health, and sends reports to your primary care physician? People will be healthier and live better.

Homes that are smarter than ever before. Special bricks will collect energy from the sun for all your appliances. And it's clean energy. A central computer will help you conserve water, reduce or avoid carbon emissions, recycle materials, and many other benefits.

Smart planters. Do you live in a house without a garden? You can grow your own fruit and vegetables in these smart planters. No energy, no chemicals, the planters use your trash and garbage and turn it into fertilizer.

What will you do to help?

3 **SCANNING. Read the article and find examples of the following.**

1. A current problem in the world:

____

____

2. Eco-friendly technology:

____

____

3. Technology related to food:

____

4. Technology related to health:

____

4 **SKIMMING. Read the text again and write the heading of each section. Use the headings from the box. There is an extra one.**

A worrying situation Ideas to change the world Natural disasters Technology in the future

Listening

5 **Listen and complete the sentences.** 34

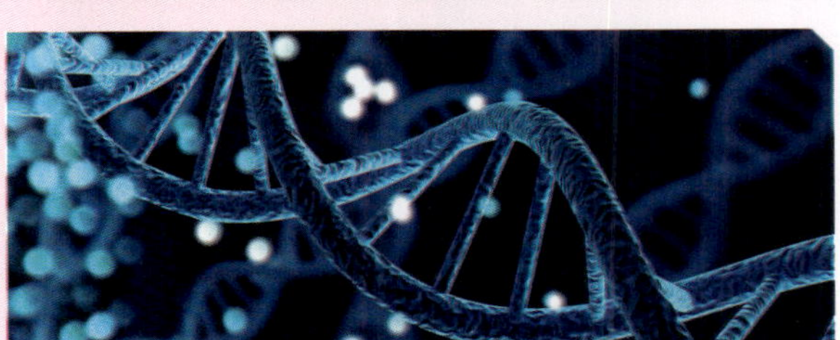

1. Teo's idea is about a ______________________.
2. The car will use a ______________________.
3. Chiara's idea can be useful at ______________________.
4. Her idea is about a chip that can ______________________.
5. Her idea can help save ______________________.

Writing

6 **In pairs, think about a technological invention that could help students.**

1. Describe what it does.

____

2. Say how it can help.

____

7 **Write a short text about your technological invention. Use the texts on the previous pages and the information in Activity 6 to help you.**

I can write about future technology.

Language Booster page 30

#UNDERSTAND

Grammar

Talking About the Future

1 **Read the conversation and answer the questions.**

Don: "Hi, I'm Don, and here's my idea: delivery drones. People will no longer drive to work, they'll work at home, but they'll need deliveries. To reduce carbon emissions, drones will deliver goods and products. They'll be powered by solar batteries, making them environmentally friendly. I'm going to work on that." Is that OK?

Luce: Yes, I like that, but I think it needs some more information. I'm going to help you out.

Don: Good. Can you tell me what changes you want me to make?

Luce: Not right now, sorry. My bus leaves at 3:00, that's in 30 minutes. And at 5:00, I'm meeting my friends to study. I'll send you a message when I'm done.

Don: Thanks a lot!

1. Is the conversation informal? ______
2. Is Luce going to help Don? ______
3. Is Luce helping Don now? ______

2 **Check (✓) the correct explanation according to the extracts from the conversation. Then complete the table with future with *be going to*, future with *will*, Present Continuous, or Simple Present.**

1. **Don:** "People won't travel to work. They'll need deliveries. Drones will use solar batteries."
   - **a.** ☐ They're Don's intentions.
   - **b.** ☐ They're definite plans for the future.
   - **c.** ☐ They're predictions about the future.
2. **Don:** "I'm going to work on that."
   - **a.** ☐ It's Don's intention.
   - **b.** ☐ It's a definite plan for the future.
   - **c.** ☐ It's a prediction about the future.
3. **Luce:** "My bus leaves at 3:00."
   - **a.** ☐ It's Luce's intention.
   - **b.** ☐ It's a planned schedule for the future.
   - **c.** ☐ It's a personal plan for the future.
   - **d.** ☐ It's a prediction about the future.
4. **Luce:** "I'm meeting my friends to study."
   - **a.** ☐ It's Luce's intention.
   - **b.** ☐ It's a planned schedule for the future.
   - **c.** ☐ It's a personal arrangement for the future.
   - **d.** ☐ It's a prediction about the future.

Predictions	Plans / Intentions
1 ______	3 ______
Schedules	**Arrangements**
2 ______	4 ______

I can use different ways of talking about the future.
e-Language Booster

3 **Work in groups. Talk about your plans / intentions and arrangements for next week. What do you have in common with your classmates?**

____

____

4 **In pairs, tell each other about your other classmates. What are their plans / intentions and arrangements for next week?**

A: *Luis is traveling to the United States next week.*
B: *Sandra is going to study for the English test on Wednesday afternoon.*

5 **Work in pairs. Make predictions for life in ten years' time.**

Too and *Enough*

6 **Read the sentences and answer the questions.**

The air is **too polluted** here!
There's **too much** traffic in big cities.
There are **too many** people living in cities.
The sea here isn't **clean enough** for people to swim.
The Earth's climate is **hot enough** to melt glaciers.
A lot of people don't have **enough money** to pay their bills.
He might not have **enough time** to stop global warming.

1. Look at the phrases with *too* and *enough*. Do they refer to the amount of something? ______
2. Is the amount exact? ______
3. Does *too* go before or after adjectives, *much*, and *many*? ______
4. Does *enough* go before or after an adjective? ______
5. Does *enough* go before or after a noun? ______

7 **Read the text and complete the paragraph with *too* and *enough*.**

Situation: a conference about the future of the world
Number of participants: 50 people
Size of room: 3m x 6m
Chairs: 45
Tables for six people: 20
Drinks: six bottles of water (1.5 liter)
Food: 300 sandwiches, 400 chocolate cookies, and candy bars.

The room is [1] ______________ (small). There aren't [2] ______________ (chairs), but there are [3] ______________ (many) tables. There isn't [4] ______________ (water), and there is [5] ______________ (much) food. I think the organizers are not [6] ______________ (good).

8 **In pairs, discuss whether you agree or disagree with the statements below.**

1. There are too many people living in this city.
2. There is enough public transportation for everybody where I live.
3. The universe is too big.
4. Robots are good enough to do people's jobs.

9 **Write a short paragraph about one of the problems you discussed in Activity 8. Use *too* and *enough*.**

____

____

____

I can use *too* and *enough* in my conversations.
Language Booster page 31

Listening

1 **Read the captions and match them to the pictures.**

1. Learning in the future **2.** Life in the future **3.** Love in the future **4.** Traveling in the future

a.

b.

c.

d.

2 **LISTENING FOR GIST. Listen to some students make predictions about the future. Which topic in Activity 1 is not mentioned?** 35

____

3 **LISTENING FOR DETAILS. Listen again and mark the sentences T (True) or F (False).** 36

In the future:

1. ☐ Computers and technology will change human relations.
2. ☐ People will do the housework.
3. ☐ People will need their bikes.
4. ☐ Planes won't be necessary.
5. ☐ Technology will have a negative impact on people.
6. ☐ Teletransportation will be possible.
7. ☐ There will be too many people.

4 **Listen again and write down the phrasal verbs used by each speaker.** 37

1. Speaker 1: ______________________

2. Speaker 2: ______________________

3. Speaker 3: ______________________

Pronunciation

5 **Listen to the phrasal verbs in context and complete the table. Which word is stressed?** 38

Stress on the first word	Stress on the second word / particle
1	4
2	5
3	6

Speaking

6 **Make a list with four questions about a new technological gadget to ask a classmate. Use phrasal verbs. Then interview your classmate.**

____

____

____

____

I can understand a conversation about the future and discuss it.

e-Language Booster

Use of English

7 Read the conversation. Underline the sentences that express future plans and arrangements.

Mitch: I'm going to Mike's birthday party tomorrow. Do you want to come?
Mora: I'd love to, but I'm going to travel to my grandma's in the country.
Mitch: Oh, I love the country! What are you going to do there?
Mora: I'm going to visit my grandma and get some fresh air!
Mitch: My parents are moving to the country next month. They're sick of the big city.
Mora: Good for them! Are you going to move, too?
Mitch: No way! And be far away from you? Never!
Mora: Haha! Well, I have to go now! I'm taking my little sister to her friend's house.
Mitch: See you around, Mora! Nice chatting with you!
Mora: Bye!

8 In pairs, role play the conversation in Activity 7. Add your own ideas to change the sentences expressing future plans and arrangements.

9 Now change the conversation one more time using *too* and *enough*. Make sure the conversation makes sense.

Mitch: *I'm going to Mike's birthday party tomorrow. Do you want to come?*
Mora: *I'd love to, but I am too busy tomorrow.*

10 Work in groups. Write your own conversation and role play it. Include ways of talking about the future and *too* and *enough*.

I can discuss future plans and arrangements.
Language Booster page 32

#CHALLENGE

Writing

1 **Read and write *I* if the writing format should be informal and F if it should be formal. Write *B* if it can be both.**

You write to:

1. ☐ the head of your school.
2. ☐ an influencer.
3. ☐ the manager of a store.
4. ☐ a member of your family.
5. ☐ a YouTuber.
6. ☐ a friend.

2 **Read the e-mail. Then circle the correct options to complete the sentences.**

CANCEL SEND

TO nick.kent@hashtagmail.com

SUBJECT The holidays!!!

☐ Hi, Ann, how are you? How is Uncle John?

☐ I'm doing fine at school. We're studying about jobs and careers, and next week we're celebrating Career Day. On that day, different people come to school and tell us about their jobs. Do you feel like joining us? We can arrange a virtual meeting. I think my classmates will love you and Uncle John. You're scientists and inventors, and your gadgets are amazing! Your latest invention, the helping hand, is just awesome! I use it all the time.

☐ Are you doing anything next weekend? We can come to your house and spend the weekend there. I promise to help you and Uncle John in your workshop. I want to be an inventor, too.

☐ Please write back.
Love, Olivia

1. This e-mail is **formal** / **informal**.
2. **Olivia** / **Ann** writes the mail.
3. Ann is Olivia's **mom** / **aunt**.
4. **Olivia** / **John** is an inventor.
5. **Olivia** / **John and Ann** invented the helping hand.
6. Olivia wants to spend next weekend at **home** / **Ann's house**.

3 **Read the e-mail in Activity 2 again and write the number of each section according to the list below.**

1. Body
2. Closing
3. Greeting
4. Request

Prepare to Write

4 **You are going to write an informal e-mail asking your friend to help you with a school project on technological innovations and new gadgets. Complete the chart with the information you want to include in each section.**

Section	Information
1. Greeting	
2. Body	
3. Request	
4. Closing	

I can identify the parts of an informal e-mail.
e-Language Booster

Write

5 **Write your e-mail. Use the information in Activity 4 and the text in Activity 2 as a model.**

CANCEL SEND

TO

SUBJECT

Check and Change

6 **Read the e-mail and make sure you included:**

- ☐ a greeting.
- ☐ a body (small talk and relevant information).
- ☐ a request.
- ☐ a closing.
- ☐ different ways of talking about the future.

#TIP

Since you are writing to a friend, your language can be casual and friendly. So use contracted forms, common phrasal verbs, and colloquial expressions.

7 **Edit your e-mail. Make sure all the elements in Activity 6 are included.**

Publish

8 **Write a clean version of your e-mail.**

Speaking

9 **In pairs, write a conversation. Then role play it.**

Situation: You're Ann, and you received Olivia's e-mail today. You're talking to Uncle John.

1. Inform Uncle John about the e-mail.
2. Ask for information about Career Day.
3. Answer the questions in the e-mail. Talk about your plans for next weekend.

I can write an informal e-mail.

Language Booster page 33

Project: An Online Graphic Organizer

#DIGITAL LITERACY

Graphic organizers, also called mind maps, are used to connect ideas visually. They can be very useful when studying for a test, for example.

Step 1 Think

1 In pairs, look at the graphic organizers and answer the questions.

1. How is the information organized?
2. What is the purpose of a graphic organizer?
3. When are graphic organizers useful?
4. Which graphic organizer do you use the most often? Why?

Venn Diagram

Purpose:
to compare and contrast two items.

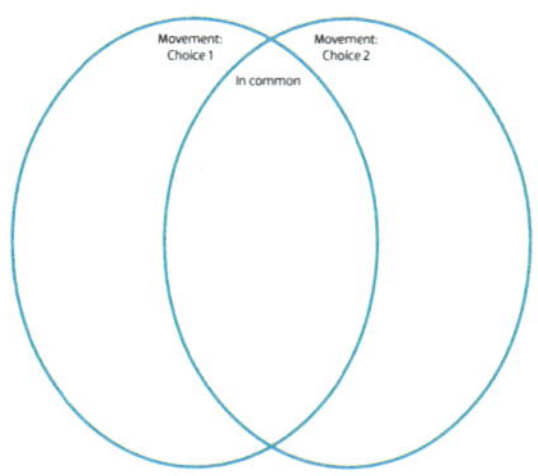

Bubble Map

Purpose:
to describe a person, thing, place, or event.

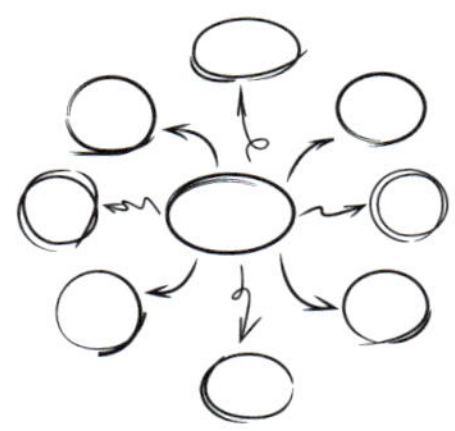

Important Contributions

Purpose:
to record ideas or contributions in relation to a topic.

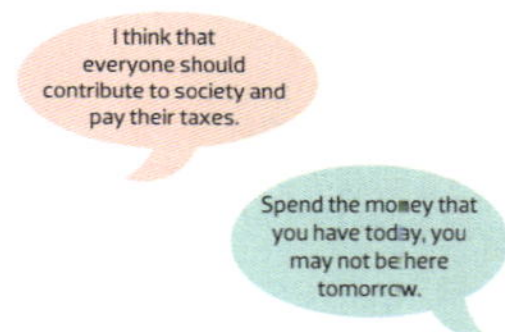

Step 2 Plan

2 You are going to make an online graphic organizer with predictions for the future. In groups, check (✓) the topics you want to include in your graphic organizer. Then decide which graphic organizer is the most appropriate.

- ☐ Learning
- ☐ Love
- ☐ Lifestyle
- ☐ Work
- ☐ Homes
- ☐ Vacations

I can identify different kinds of graphic organizers and plan to create one.

Step 3 Research

3 In groups, do some research into the topics you chose in Activity 2 and complete the table below.

Topic	
Current research in this area	
Future possibilities	

Step 4 Design

4 In groups, create your graphic organizer. Use the information from your research.

- Check the text.
- Check the purpose.
- Check the organization.

Step 5 Present and Publish

5 In groups, show your graphic organizer to the class.

Step 6 Evaluate

6 Complete the evaluation table.

★☆☆ More to learn | ★★☆ Good | ★★★ Excellent

Criteria	My Evaluation	Group Evaluation	Teacher Evaluation
Teamwork	☆☆☆	☆☆☆	☆☆☆
Language	☆☆☆	☆☆☆	☆☆☆
Design	☆☆☆	☆☆☆	☆☆☆

#TIP STEP 4

1. Play around with different kinds of organizers.
2. Use different pictures and icons.
3. Change the organizeraccordingto the purpose.

#TIP STEP 5

1. You can practice the presentation and video record it.
2. Talk about the topic using the information in the graphic organizer.
3. Speak slowly and fluently.

I can create a graphic organizer and present it to the class.

#SELF-ASSESSMENT

1 **Mark the learning objectives according to the key.**

★★★ I don't understand.	★★★ I understand, but I need help.	★★★ I can do it!

Learning Objectives	Rating
To interpret a conversation about technology and innovation.	★★★
To use phrasal verbs to talk about myself.	★★★
To interpret a text about technology in the future.	★★★
To write about future technology.	★★★
To use different ways of talking about the future.	★★★
To use *too* and *enough* in my conversations.	★★★
To understand a conversation about the future and discuss it.	★★★
To discuss future plans and arrangements.	★★★
To identify the parts of an informal e-mail.	★★★
To write an informal e-mail.	★★★
To identify different kinds of graphic organizers and plan to create one.	★★★
To create a graphic organizer and present it to the class.	★★★

2 **Work in pairs. Discuss the questions.**

1. What did I find most interesting to learn? Why?
2. How did I learn it?
3. How can I use it in real life?

MT UT Language Booster page 34

THE ENVIRONMENT AND US

#15 LIFE ON LAND

In this unit, you will learn how to:

- Talk about life experiences.
- Write a short article about animals and us.
- Create an online slideshow.

Say what you know:

- Endangered animals.
- Animal habitats.
- Environmental problems.

Video

Endangered Animals

Before You Watch

1 **In pairs, make a list of the wild animals you know. Which ones can be found in your country?**

2 **What do you know about endangered species? Discuss with a classmate.**

While You Watch

3 **Watch the video and check (✓). What is the main purpose of their conversation?** ▷ 06

1. ☐ Plans and intentions
2. ☐ Exchange of information
3. ☐ A request to do something

4 **Watch the video again and complete the sentences.** ▷ 06

1. They have a ______________ assignment to do.
2. Luis watched a documentary about ______________ .
3. The animal they talk about is the ______________ .
4. There are only 2,500 pandas left in ______________ .
5. One of the reasons why pandas are endangered is ______________ of habitat.
6. Luis and Emma are going to meet to do the ______________ together.

5 **Watch the video again and underline the information Emma and Luis talk about.** ▷ 06

1. The science assignment.
2. A documentary on endangered animals.
3. Watching the documentary together.
4. Meeting to do the assignment together.

After You Watch

6 **Go back to your notes in Activity 1. Which species are endangered?**

I can demonstrate an understanding of a conversation about endangered animals.
e-Language Booster

Vocabulary

Endangered Animals

7 **Read the names of the animals and match them to the pictures. Then listen, check, and repeat.** 39

- ☐ Asian elephant
- ☐ Giant panda
- ☐ Victoria crowned pigeon
- ☐ Snow leopard
- ☐ Tasmanian devil
- ☐ Sea otter

8 **Label the definitions with the animals in Activity 7.**

1. This **large-eared** animal is the second largest land animal.

   ____

2. This black and white, **world-famous** animal is in danger of extinction.

   ____

3. This is the largest pigeon in the world. It is **blue-feathered** and has beautiful feathers on its head.

   ____

4. This **black-spotted** animal is also threatened with extinction.

   ____

5. This **four-legged** mammal is threatened with extinction.

   ____

6. The problem of these small, **pink-eared**, and **black-haired** animals is not man, but cancer.

   ____

Compound Adjectives

9 **In pairs, look at the phrases with a hyphen (-) in Activity 8 and answer the questions. Then complete the explanations.**

Why are those words called compound adjectives? Are they one-word or two-word adjectives?

____

____

1. A **black-striped** animal: its stripes are ____________.
2. A **large-eared** animal: its ears are ____________.
3. A **world-famous** animal: it's ____________ all over the ____________.
4. A **black-spotted** animal: it has ____________.

10 **Work in pairs. Describe the nouns using compound adjectives.**

1. a run that takes ten minutes
   a ten-minute run
2. a girl who is seven years old

   ____

3. kids who behave well

   ____

4. an animal with red eyes

   ____

I can describe animals, people, and things using compound adjectives.

Language Booster page 35

Reading

1 USING PRIOR KNOWLEDGE. Look at the pictures and answer the questions.

1. Are these real or imaginary animals?

____

2. Are they ordinary animals?

____

2 PREDICTING. Read the title of the article. What type of animals do you expect to read about? Mention three animals you expect to find in the article. Then read the text and check your answers.

____

Extraordinary Animals +

Extraordinary Animals

Animals are great, but some of them are extraordinary. Animals, in terms of living things, are almost equal to humans, and their use in studies is extremely important. Rats, for example, share more than 98% of DNA with humans. Animals have helped scientists discover the causes and treatments of various diseases.

The axolotl is a special kind of salamander. Its nickname is *walking fish* because it is four-legged but does not live on land. It has no hair or beard. The six parts on its head are the external gills. Axolotls and fish do not have lungs. They breathe through their gills.

There is nothing unusual or strange about goats, but the Markhor is a fancy wild goat. Like other goats, the markhor has horns. Why fancy? Because the Markhor's horns are very long and shaped like a corkscrew. It also has a very long beard, much longer than other goats.

The red-lipped batfish is a truly amazing creature from the Galapagos Islands. What makes it special is its red lips. Its scientific name, *Ogcocephalus darwini*, is a reference to Darwin.

Some people think the narwhal is an imaginary animal, the aquatic version of a unicorn. But this is not so. The narwhal is a real whale. The most important visual feature is its tusk. Sometimes it is longer than 2.5 meters. Another strange feature is that it only has two teeth.

3 SCANNING. Read the article again and write one characteristic for each animal.

1. Axolotl: _______________
2. Markhor: _______________
3. Red-lipped bat fish: _______________
4. Narwhal: _______________

4 MONITORING COMPREHENSION. Read the article again and answer the questions.

1. How do animals help scientists?

____

2. Why is the axolotl known as the walking fish?

____

3. How can you describe the markhor's horns?

____

4. Where is the red-lipped batfish from?

____

5. How long is the narwhal's tusk?

____

Listening

5 **Listen and mark the sentences Y (Yes) or N (No).** 40

1. ☐ The lady has visited Indonesia.
2. ☐ Dragons are real.
3. ☐ The Komodo dragon is a lizard.
4. ☐ Some lizards are bigger than the Komodo dragon.
5. ☐ It eats only small animals.
6. ☐ There are only female dragons.
7. ☐ The male dragon is necessary in the reproduction process.
8. ☐ Asexual reproduction is possible.

Writing

6 **Look up information online about an unusual animal. Complete the table below.**

Animal name	Animal description	Why it's unusual

7 **Write a podcast script about the unusual animal in Activity 6. Use the script on page 159 as a model. Audio record your script.**

#TIP

To stay on track, follow your script or notes. If you catch yourself going down the wrong path, steer the conversation back to your plan. If you have interesting ideas while recording, you can incorporate them, but be careful not to go off track.

I can write about an unusual animal.

Language Booster page 36

#UNDERSTAND

Grammar

Present Perfect with *Ever* and *Never*

1 **Read the sentences from the box and check (✓) the correct statements.**

Has she ever been to a nature reserve?
Have you ever seen an unusual animal?
I have never traveled to the rainforest.
He has never watched a documentary about nature.

1. ☐ All the sentences refer to life experiences.
2. ☐ The word *ever* means *at no time*.
3. ☐ The word *ever* means *at any time*.
4. ☐ The word *never* means *at no time*.
5. ☐ The word *never* means *at any time*.
6. ☐ The word *ever* is used in questions.
7. ☐ For affirmative sentences, we use *subject* + *has / have* + *never* + *verb* in the past participle.
8. ☐ For questions, we use *have / has* + *subject* + *ever* + verb in the simple past.

2 **Complete the sentences with the past participle form of the verbs in parentheses.**

1. I have never ______________ (see) a lizard.
2. Have you ever ______________ (be) to a campground?
3. She has never ______________ (travel) to a nature reserve.
4. Has he ever ______________ (walk) in a park?
5. We have never ______________ (miss) a science class.
6. I have never ______________ (have) a pet.
7. Has she ever ______________ (visit) China?

3 **Work in groups. Interview your classmates. Then complete the chart. Use the Present Perfect with ever and never.**

A: Have you **ever** traveled abroad?
B: Yes, I have.
C: No, I haven't. I have **never** traveled abroad.

Experiences	Verb phrase
All the people in this group have...	
Nobody in this group has...	
Most people in this group have...	
Only one person in this group has...	

4 **In pairs, write a dialogue asking each other about life experiences. Use the Present Perfect with *ever* and *never*. Then role play the dialogue.**

I can use the Present Perfect with ever and never.
e-Language Booster

Present Perfect with *for* and *since*

5 **Read the dialogue and pay attention to the parts in bold. Then complete the statements.**

Mia: I have had my pet **since 2016**; she's a dog, Rosie. Do you have a pet, too?
Val: Yes, I have a parrot. We've had him **for two years** now. His name's Pepo.
Mia: I love his name!

1. We use the ________ Perfect for something that started in the past and continues in the present.
2. We can use ________ and a date, day, time, or event.
3. We can use ________ and a period of time.

6 **Write the time expressions from the box in the correct line.**

2014 7 o'clock five years four months Jim's birthday Monday 3rd ten days the beginning of the year this morning three hours

for	
since	

7 **Complete the sentences about yourself.**

1. I have lived in the same city for ________________.
2. I have studied English since ________________.
3. I have been here today for ________________.
4. I have known my best friend since ________________.

8 **Write five questions about duration of time with the Present Perfect. Then work in pairs. Interview your classmate. Change roles and answer his / her questions using for and *since*.**

A: How long *have we studied together?*
B: *We have studied together* **for** *two years.*

1. ________________
2. ________________
3. ________________
4. ________________
5. ________________

I can use the Present Perfect with *for* and since.
Language Booster page 37

#DEVELOP

Listening

1 **Read the captions and match them to the pictures.**

1. A desert 2. Grasslands 3. A polar habitat 4. A rainforest 5. A snowy forest

a.  ☐

b.  ☐

c.  ☐

d.  ☐

e.  ☐

2 **LISTENING FOR GIST. Listen and check (✓) the topic of the podcast.** 41

1. ☐ Endangered animals.
2. ☐ Habitats.
3. ☐ The Solar System.

3 **LISTENING FOR DETAILS. Listen again and mark the sentences T (True) or F (False).** 42

1. ☐ It doesn't rain in the grasslands.
2. ☐ Grasslands cover a very small part of the earth's land surface.
3. ☐ There are two seasons at the poles.
4. ☐ You can see the sun in the winter at the poles.
5. ☐ You can't see any plants or animals in the desert.
6. ☐ There are a lot of trees in forests because of the weather conditions.
7. ☐ Trees in rainforests are very tall.
8. ☐ Animals do not live in the canopies.

4 **Listen again and write the compound adjectives.** 43

1. ____________________.
2. ____________________.
3. ____________________.
4. ____________________.

Pronunciation

5 **Listen and practice saying these words. Then go over the unit, find other compound adjectives, and say them.** 44

1. Four-**legged**
2. Two-**legged**
3. Ice-**cold**
4. Green-**leaved**

Speaking

6 **Work in groups. Go online and find more information about the habitats in Activity 1. What animals live there? Tell your classmates.**

I can demonstrate an understanding of a podcast about animal habitats.

e-Language Booster

Use of English

7 **Listen, read, and underline the phrases used to justify an opinion. Then role play the conversation with a classmate.** 45

Eve: Have you ever been to the poles?
Ron: No, I haven't. I don't think they're nice places. The reason is that the temperatures are extreme.
Eve: Oh. I'd like to go there sometime. There are indications that tourists like them. They say that they're different from anything they have seen.
Ron: Maybe. I prefer other places. From my point of view, there are more tourists in every other place than at the poles.
Eve: Well, yes. But they're protected areas. That's why there are more tourists in other parts.
Ron: In my opinion, we all have our reasons.
Eve: Sure!

8 **Read the dialogue again and find one affirmative sentence and one question in the Present Perfect.**

______

______

______

9 **Read the statements. Then agree or disagree with them and justify your opinion. Use the phrases you underlined in Activity 1.**

1. I like spending my vacation at the beach.

______

2. I would never travel to the poles because it is too cold.

______

3. I think everybody should protect the environment.

______

4. The Amazon Forest is important because of its biodiversity.

______

10 **Work in pairs. Write a conversation, and then role play it. Follow these steps.**

1. Choose an endangered species. Check this unit.
2. Give your opinion on why they're endangered. Justify your opinion.
3. Agree or disagree with your classmate's opinion. Give yours and explain why.
4. Use the Present Perfect with *ever*, *never*, *for*, or *since*.

______

______

______

______

______

______

______

______

______

______

______

I can give opinions and justify them.
Language Booster page 38

#CHALLENGE

Writing

1 **Read the statements about articles. Circle YES or NO.**

1. Articles are always long texts.	YES	NO
2. Articles are informative texts.	YES	NO
3. Articles can include pictures.	YES	NO
4. Articles have a headline.	YES	NO
5. Some articles are divided into paragraphs.	YES	NO
6. You can find articles in comic books.	YES	NO
7. You can find articles in magazines and newspapers.	YES	NO
8. All articles are anonymous.	YES	NO

2 **Read the article and check your answers in Activity 1. Then complete the sentences with the phrases from the box.**

describes different causes for extinction | **introduces the topic** | **describes the current situation** | **short**

Endangered Species and Our Responsibility

Animals are called endangered when they are threatened with extinction. This is because there are very few of them on our planet. Since the Earth was formed 4.5 billion years ago, the situation has changed drastically.

Since the beginning of Earth's history, there have been five major extinction events. They were triggered by dramatic events, including meteorite impacts, climate changes, and major volcanic activity. Currently, our planet is experiencing its sixth major extinction event. It is the result of human activity. Scientists estimate that between 100 and 10,000 species become extinct each year. Humans hunt animals and fish with little control and destroy their habitats. They are also polluting the environment and introducing new species into areas.

Our planet is in danger. Humans have done too much damage to it in the last few decades and need to stop damaging the planet. Education is one of the most important ways to help people become aware of this.

By **Emma C.**

1. This article is ____________________.

2. The first paragraph ____________________.

3. The second paragraph ____________________.

4. The third paragraph ____________________.

I can identify parts of an article and prepare to write one.

Prepare to Write

3 You are going to write a short article about animals and us. Complete the chart with key information you want to include in your text.

Paragraph	Key information
1	
2	
3	

#TIP

Use an online search engine to look for information about the topic.

Write

4 Write a short article. Use the information in Activities 1 and 3 to help you and the text in Activity 2 as a model. Include the Present Perfect and at least two compound adjectives in your article.

Check and Change

5 Read your article and make sure you included:

- ☐ the Present Perfect tense.
- ☐ compound adjectives.
- ☐ a headline.
- ☐ an introductory paragraph.
- ☐ a description of the topic.
- ☐ the current situation.

6 Edit your text. Make sure all the elements in Activity 5 are included.

Publish

7 Write a clean version of your article.

Speaking

8 Work in groups. Share your article with your group. Then write two sentences, one true and one false, about your article. Read the sentences to your group. Can they guess which is true and which is false based on your article? Justify your opinion.

1. ____________________

2. ____________________

I can write a short article.

Language Booster page 39

Project: An Online Slideshow

#DIGITAL LITERACY

You can use the picture tab of different search engines online to find pictures. Some pictures have a watermark because they are not free for use. Improve your search by using more specific key words.

Step 1 Think

1 Discuss in groups. Go online and check your answers.

1. What is a slideshow?
2. When are presentations useful?
3. Are pictures helpful?
4. Should we write long sentences or key phrases?
5. Do we use bullet points?
6. Should the font be big enough for everybody to see?

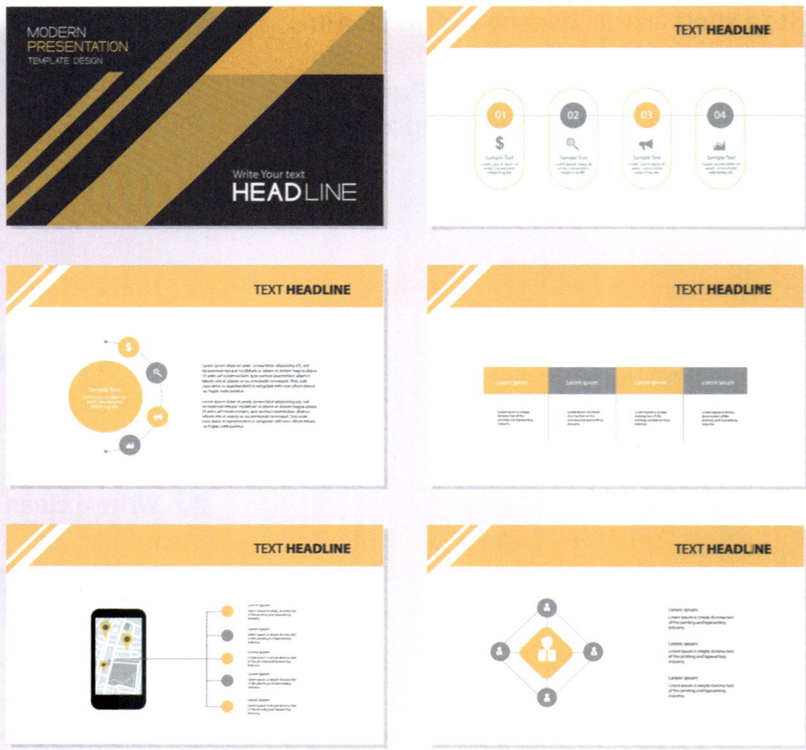

Step 2 Plan

2 You are going to create an online slideshow about the article you have written. Make a list of the key points of each slide and the pictures you would like to use. Use your notebook.

Step 3 Research

3 **Go online and search for the pictures you would like to include in each slide to illustrate your points. Save those pictures to be included in your slideshow.**

Step 4 Design

4 **Create your online slideshow. Use the information from the previous activities.**

- Check the text.
- Check the pictures.
- Check the organization.

Step 5 Present and Publish

5 **Work in groups. Show your slideshow to your group.**

Step 6 Evaluate

6 **Complete the evaluation table.**

★☆☆ More to learn | ★★☆ Good | ★★★ Excellent

Criteria	My Evaluation	Group Evaluation	Teacher Evaluation
Teamwork	☆☆☆	☆☆☆	☆☆☆
Language	☆☆☆	☆☆☆	☆☆☆
Design	☆☆☆	☆☆☆	☆☆☆

#TIP STEP 4

1. Work on your slides carefully and make sure all the key points are there.
2. Choose pictures that will help people understand your key points.
3. Keep your slides clean and clear. Do not use many words.

#TIP STEP 5

1. You can practice the presentation and video record it.
2. Don't read out the slides as if they were scripts.
3. Speak slowly and fluently.

I can create an online slideshow and present it to the class.

e-Language Booster page

SELF-ASSESSMENT

1 **Mark the learning objectives according to the key.**

★☆☆ I don't understand.	★★☆ I understand, but I need help.	★★★ I can do it!

Learning Objectives	Rating
To demonstrate an understanding of a conversation about endangered animals.	☆☆☆
To describe animals, people, and things using compound adjectives.	☆☆☆
To understand an article about unusual animals.	☆☆☆
To write about an unusual animal.	☆☆☆
To use the Present Perfect with *ever* and *never*.	☆☆☆
To use the Present Perfect with *for* and *since*.	☆☆☆
To demonstrate an understanding of a podcast about animal habitats.	☆☆☆
To give opinions and justify them.	☆☆☆
To identify parts of an article and prepare to write one.	☆☆☆
To write a short article.	☆☆☆
To plan to create an online slideshow.	☆☆☆
To create an online slideshow and present it to the class.	☆☆☆

2 **Work in pairs. Discuss the questions.**

1. What did I find most interesting to learn? Why?
2. How did I learn it?
3. How can I use it in real life?

UT Language Booster page 40

TRAVELING AROUND

#10 REDUCED INEQUALITIES

In this unit, you will learn how to:

- Talk about traveling.
- Write a factual article.
- Create a travel newsletter.

Say what you know:

- Famous vacation destinations.
- Different kinds of transportation.
- Inclusive tourism.

#DISCOVER

Video

Traveling Together

Before You Watch

1 **In pairs, make a list of the means of transportation you know. Which one is used most in your region?**

____

____

While You Watch

2 **Watch and check (✓) the main purpose of the conversation.** ▷ 07

1. ☐ To talk about a trip to a specific place.
2. ☐ To compare means of transportation.
3. ☐ To describe towns or cities.

3 **Watch again and answer the questions.** ▷ 07

1. Who's Emma having a video call with?
____
2. Where does her grandma live?
____
3. How does Emma describe Natureville?
____
4. What activities does Emma do in Natureville?
____
5. Does Emma like the educational trips?
____
6. Has Emma invited Luis?
____
7. Is Natureville in another country?
____
8. Where are Emma and Luis going?
____

4 **Watch again and check (✓) the topics Emma and Luis talk about.** ▷ 07

1. ☐ Transportation to Natureville.
2. ☐ Activities on educational trips.
3. ☐ Activities Emma's parents don't allow her to do.
4. ☐ Price of educational trips.
5. ☐ Time to get to Natureville.
6. ☐ Ecotourism and inclusive tourism in Natureville.

After You Watch

5 **Work in pairs. Go back to your list in Activity 1 and do some research. Are those means of transportation eco-friendly? Complete the table.**

Means of transportation	Is it eco-friendly?	Why?

I can interpret a conversation about traveling.
e-Language Booster page

Vocabulary

Means of Transportation

6 **Use the words from the box to label the pictures.**

airplane	bus	car	coach	horse
motorcycle	ship	speedboat	train	

1. 
____

2. 
____

3. 
____

4. 
____

5. 
____

6. 
____

7. 
____

8. 
____

9. 
____

10. 
____

7 **In pairs, read about other means of transportation and check (✓) the ones you have in your city.**

1. ☐ A **cable car** is a type of cable railway used for public transportation in which the carriages are pulled by a cable moving continuously at a constant speed.
2. ☐ A **ferryboat** is a vessel that transports people, cars, and freight over water.
3. ☐ A **truck** is a motor vehicle designed to transport goods, carry special cargo, or do other useful work.
4. ☐ The **subway** is an underground railroad system used to transport a large number of passengers in urban and suburban areas.

Travel-related Words

8 **In pairs, complete the sentences with the words from the box. Then listen and check.** 46

baggage claim area	boarding pass		
delayed	gate	luggage	route	take off

1. Oh, no! I will have to wait at the airport again. My flight is _______________.
2. My _______________ is at terminal 2.
3. The GPS gave me the wrong _______________. Now I don't know where I am.
4. I have too much _______________! I will need at least four suitcases!
5. The plane will _______________ in 30 minutes, and we will land in São Paulo in four hours. Great!
6. Where is the _______________? I have to pick up my luggage.
7. I need to have my _______________ issued. Where's the check-in counter?

9 **Research two travel-related verbs or expressions and use them in meaningful sentences. Write them in your notebook.**

*We all need to **go through passport control** when we leave or enter a country.*

Reading

1 Match the pictures to the types of travel.

1. A trip to the beach
2. A trip to the city
3. A cruise
4. A cultural trip
5. A trip to the mountains

a. 
b. 
c. 
d. 
e. 

2 MAKING PREDICTIONS. In pairs, read the title of the article and predict what it is about. Then read the article and check your predictions.

Tourism Every...

http://www.tourismeverydaytoday.org

Different Perspectives on Tourism

People often associate tourism with relaxation and pleasure. We are not saying that this is not true. But there are different ways to have fun and relax. If you want to know more about it, read on and find out.

Inclusion is not new in society. What does it mean to be inclusive in tourism?

An inclusive tourism business or destination tries to provide positive travel experiences for people with different needs by looking at things from different perspectives and offering design and service solutions that aim to accommodate as many different groups as possible.

Tourists can make a big difference in small towns. When you visit these small towns and villages, you help their economy and show tourists places and experiences they had not thought of. This could also be a nice cultural and educational experience in which the locals can sell their products and make their traditions known to the world.

Try ecotourism. This is about combining communities, environmental protection, and sustainable travel. It is based on principles such as:

- Respect for the environment and culture.
- Positive experiences for visitors and locals.
- Direct financial benefits to conservation, local communities, and the private sector.
- Respect for the rights and spiritual and cultural beliefs of all people in local communities.

Ecotourism is about enriching personal experiences, making a difference, and also learning and having fun.

3 SKIMMING. What are the different types of tourism mentioned in the text?

____

____

I can interpret an article about different perspectives on tourism.

e-Language Booster

4 **SCANNING. Read the text again and circle the best options to complete the sentences.**

1. Inclusive tourism focuses on **one group of tourists** / **different groups of tourists**.
2. Tourists **can't** / **can** make a big difference in small towns.
3. Trips can be cultural and **educational** / **boring**.
4. Ecotourism is about environmental protection and **sustainable** / **luxurious** travel.
5. Ecotourism is based on positive experiences for tourists and **travel agents** / **locals**.
6. She organized a trip with a group of friends and they **loved the place** / **didn't like the place**.
7. She was a tourist guide at **an important** / **a small** company.

5 **Imagine you work for a travel company. In small groups, make a list of ideas on how you could make tourism more inclusive in your city.**

Listening

6 **Listen and circle the correct options to complete the sentences.** 47

1. The lady has been a tourist guide for **eight years** / **three years**.
2. Three years ago, she **stopped working** / **started her company**.
3. Traveling **is always very expensive** / **can be cheap enough**.
4. She was stranded in the middle of a street when **a tourist** / **a local** helped her.
5. The experience was **positive** / **negative**.

Writing

7 **Work in groups. Research into ecotourism and make notes of the most relevant pieces of information you find.**

8 **Write a paragraph about ecotourism. Use the information in Activity 7 and read the script on page 160.**

#TIP

For your paragraph to convey a sense of cohesiveness, focus exclusively on a single idea, point, or argument being discussed.

I can write about ecotourism.

Language Booster page 42

#UNDERSTAND

Grammar

Zero Conditional

1 **Read the statements below and check (✓) the correct ones.**

If you visit small communities, **you help** their economy.
People strengthen small communities **if they buy** their products and learn about them.
If you respect communities and ecology, **you follow** the principles of ecotourism.

1. ☐ There are two parts in each statement.
2. ☐ The parts of the statements starting with *if* express a condition.
3. ☐ The result of the conditions in these sentences is not true.
4. ☐ We can say that the condition expressed in the zero conditional sentences always has the same result, no matter if it is present, past, or future time.

2 **Choose the correct option to complete the statements.**

1. The sentences in Activity 1 refer to facts that
   a. ☐ were probably true in the past, are true in the present, and will be true in the future.
   b. ☐ will only be true in the future.
2. In the *if* clause, we use
   a. ☐ the Simple Present.
   b. ☐ will.
3. In the main clause, we use
   a. ☐ the Simple Present.
   b. ☐ will.
4. The *if* clause
   a. ☐ goes before the main clause.
   b. ☐ can go before or after the main clause.
5. We use a comma when the *if* clause
   a. ☐ goes before the main clause.
   b. ☐ goes after the main clause.

3 **Work in groups. Can you complete these general truths?**

1. If it snows, ______________________________.
2. You need to spend a lot of money if ______________ ______________.
3. If you drive a car, ______________________________.
4. If you mix red and blue, ______________________________.

Prepositions with Means of Transportation

4 **Read the sentences and underline the prepositions related to travel and means of transportation.**

1. I met my friend on the bus.
2. There were many passengers on the *Titanic*.
3. Pets are welcome in my car.
4. I left my sunglasses in the taxi.
5. I like traveling by plane. It's much faster.
6. I went to the Bahamas by boat.

5 **Read the sentences in Activity 4 again and complete the rules.**

1. __________ is used when we are talking about general ways of travel or transportation.
2. __________ is also used for transportation environment or the surface.
3. __________ is used for vehicles where you can sit and can't stand up.
4. __________ is used when talking about a specific vehicle where you can stand or walk while the vehicle is in motion.

6 **In pairs, answer the questions with *in*, *on*, or *by*.**

1. How do you go to school?
   ____
2. How do you usually travel long distances?
   ____
3. What is your favorite way of traveling?
   ____

I can use the Zero Conditional and prepositions with means of transportation.

e-Language Booster

First Conditional

7 **Read the extracts from the video and check (✓) the true statements about them.**

If we organize everything, **we'll visit** her.
We'**ll visit** her if we **organize** everything.
If they say yes, **we'll start** planning the whole thing.
We'**ll start** planning the whole thing if they **say** yes.

1. ☐ These statements are about ongoing actions.
2. ☐ They refer to possible situations.
3. ☐ There's a condition in both of them.

8 **Look at the statements in Activity 7 again and answer the questions.**

1. How many parts do these sentences have? ________________
2. Do they refer to situations that are possible in the future? ________________
3. Are they general truths? ________________
4. Where is the comma? ________________
5. What tense do we use in the *if* clause? ________________
6. What tense do we use in the main clause? ________________

9 **Complete the sentences with the First Conditional.**

1. If it rains, ________________.
2. If I ________________, I'll go to the movies tonight.
3. If I ________________, I'll buy those jeans.
4. She'll be late if the plane ________________.
5. He'll miss his ride if ________________.
6. If I see her, ________________.

10 **In pairs, write two conditional questions to ask your classmate. Interview each other. Write down his / her answers.**

A: *Will you come to class tomorrow if it rains?*
B: *Yes, I will. I usually come by car.*

1. **A:** ________________
   B: ________________
2. **A:** ________________
   B: ________________

I can use the First Conditional.
Language Booster page 43

#DEVELOP

Listening

1 **Read the captions and match them to the icons.**

1. choose destination **2.** choose means of transportation **3.** download **4.** enter your location

a.  ☐

b. 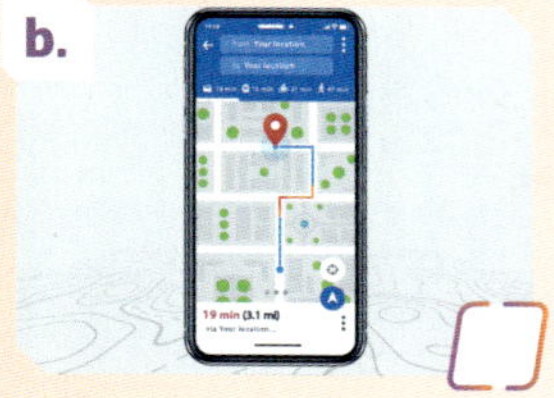 ☐

c.  ☐

d.  ☐

2 **LISTENING FOR GIST. Listen and check (✓) the topic of the audio.** 48

1. ☐ A description of a transportation app.
2. ☐ A comparison between transportation apps.
3. ☐ Instructions to use a transportation app.

3 **LISTENING FOR DETAILS. Listen again and number the steps in the correct order.** 49

☐ Select the option you want.
☐ Open the transportation app.
☐ Enlarge the map.
☐ Select the means of transportation.
☐ Tap and write a different address if necessary.
☐ Tap on the field on the top.
☐ Tap on the Start button.
☐ Write the destination address in the second field.

4 **Complete the table. Then listen again and check.** 50

On a PC	On a smartphone or tablet
There are different programs.	There are different [1] ________.
You click on a program icon with your mouse.	You [2] ________ on the [3] ________ / [4] ________.
You click on the + and – buttons to enlarge or reduce the map.	You use your [5] ________ to enlarge or reduce the map.

Pronunciation

5 **Practice saying these words. Pay attention to the sounds /æ/ and /ɑː/.** 51

	/æ/	/ɑː/
1.	cap	cop
2.	math	moth
3.	tap	top
4.	cab	cob
5.	jab	job

6 **Listen and circle the words you hear.** 52

1. sack / sock
2. band / bond
3. cap / cop
4. math / moth
5. jab / job

Speaking

7 **Record a voice message to send to a friend. Teach him / her how to use a travel app. Send the message to your friend.**

I can give instructions on how to use a travel app.
e-Language Booster

Use of English

8 **Listen and complete the dialogue with phrases used to make arrangements.** 53

Elsa: [1] ________________ next Sunday?

Bart: Yes.

Anna: Me too, why?

Elsa: [2] ________________ a picnic by the lake?

Bart: Great! [3] ________________ we meet?

Elsa: Is 11 o'clock OK? [4] ________________ go by bike.

Anna: Good! We need to take some food.

Bart: I'll buy some lemonade.

Elsa: OK, if you buy the lemonades, I can make the sandwiches.

Anna: And I'll take the fruit with me.

Bart: Great.

Elsa: So, [5] ________________ next Sunday at 11.

9 **In groups of three, role play the conversation in Activity 8. Then role play the conversation again using your own ideas.**

10 **Underline the correct options to complete the dialogue.**

A: Do you already have vacation plans for the summer?

B: Yes, I'm thinking of going to Georgetown for a week.

A: Georgetown? I've never been there. What's it like there?

B: It's pretty rural, so if you like big city life, you [1] **won't find / don't find** much there. But the countryside is very beautiful, and the people are always very friendly.

A: Have you been there before?

B: Yes, actually a couple of times.

A: And what are you going to do this time? Are you going to travel around or stay in one place?

B: I've rented a cabin. If the weather is nice, [2] **I'll go hiking / I go hiking** – Georgetown is in the Rocky Mountains.

A: Oh! That sounds exciting. If you [3] **will travel / travel** to the Rocky Mountains, you're in for some adventure! But not my thing — I prefer a relaxing vacation.

B: What about you, then? Do you have any plans?

A: Well, I'd like to go somewhere hot and just lie on the beach for a week. In fact, if I [4] **get / will get** the time off from work, I'll go anywhere!

B: Oh, gosh.

11 **Work in pairs. Write a short dialogue planning a trip with your classmate. Remember to use the Zero and First Conditionals. Then role play your dialogue.**

____

____

____

____

____

I can talk about travel arrangements.

Language Booster page 44

#CHALLENGE

Writing

1 **Read the statements and check (✓) the ones you think apply to writing factual articles.**

1. ☐ Using facts.
2. ☐ Writing in scientifc language.
3. ☐ Using paragraphs.
4. ☐ Choosing clear headlines.
5. ☐ Expressing personal opinions.

2 **Read the article and underline the true statements about it.**

Inclusive Traveling

1 Countries have their own laws and regulations regarding accessibility and discrimination against people. These include ramps for wheelchairs and people with physical disabilities, and elevators in some subway stations.

2 In many airports, train stations, and bus stations, the announcements are loud but not very easy to understand. It is necessary to have written information available as well. Some airports and train stations have announcements in Braille. There are also employees who are ready to help those who need extra help.

3 In some countries, women feel more comfortable traveling in female-only subway trains. These countries offer a way to overcome this problem. On trains, there are carriages for women. They are easy to recognize because they are pink.

4 Travel has changed. Today it is possible for everyone to travel if certain conditions are met. It is necessary to make governments aware that inclusion should be part of our everyday life.

1. There are facts in this article.
2. The writer has included personal opinions.
3. The first paragraph introduces the topic.
4. The second paragraph describes problems for people with mobility issues.
5. The third paragraph shows a way to protect women.
6. The last paragraph is a conclusion.

3 **Read the article again and match the paragraphs to the pictures. One paragraph does not have a corresponding picture.**

a.

☐

b.

☐

c.

☐

4 **Complete the chart about the article.**

Paragraph	Key Information
1	
2	
3	
4	

I can interpret a factual article about inclusive tourism.
e-Language Booster

Prepare to Write

5 You are going to write a factual article about inclusive tourism in your town or city. Complete the chart with the information you want to include in your text.

Paragraph	Key Information
1	
2	
3	
4	

Write

6 Write your factual article. Use the information in Activity 5 and the text in Activity 2 as a model.

NEW TAB

Check and Change

7 Read your article and make sure you included:

- ☐ a catchy headline.
- ☐ a clear introduction.
- ☐ facts and / or figures.
- ☐ a conclusion.

8 Edit your text. Make sure all the items in Activity 7 are included. Then choose a picture for your article.

Publish

9 Write a clean version of your factual article.

Speaking

10 Work in groups. Read your classmates' articles. Then give your opinion about them. How can they improve their articles?

I can write a factual article.

Language Booster page 45

SUSTAINABLE DEVELOPMENT GOALS

Project: A Travel Newsletter

#DIGITAL LITERACY

Search online for travel newsletters and look at some examples. There are also templates online that you can use for your travel newsletter. Newsletters should be short, straight to the point, and include pictures to make them more attractive to your audience.

Step 1 Think

1 Work in groups. Do some research to answer the questions.

1. What is a newsletter used for?

____

2. What are the elements of an effective newsletter?

____

2 Read the travel newsletter and underline the best option to complete the statement about it.

The travel newsletter is about **selling a hot air balloon ride package** / **a free-of-charge hot air balloon ride for two**.

Hot Air Balloon ...

Hot Air Balloon Ride For Two Giveaway

It's a one-of-a-kind sensation to drift silently above trees or hills, as if you're floating in the air. With flights flying up to thousands of meters into the sky, hot air balloon tours provide a unique perspective of the area below. Most rides depart before sunrise, when the wind is calm and the temperatures are cool, although sunset trips are also available depending on the location.

Follow us on social media and tag at least two friends to participate!

The lucky winners will be announced this coming Saturday.

Step 2 Plan

3 In groups, decide on the topic for your travel newsletter. Choose one and make notes of the things you would like to include in your newsletter. Use your notebook. Read the suggestions below.

1. Inclusive tourism.
2. Ecotourism.
3. Local tourism.

I can recognize features of a travel newsletter and plan to write one.

Step 3 Research

4 **Research into travel newsletters and the topic you chose in Activity 3. Make notes.**

____

____

____

Step 4 Design

5 **Create your travel newsletter using a free online travel newsletter template. Use the information from your research and the previous activities.**

- Check the text.
- Check the purpose.
- Check the organization.

#TIP STEP 4

Add pictures to your newsletter that will appeal to your audience.

Step 5 Present and Publish

6 **Work in groups. Present your travel newsletter to the class.**

#TIP STEP 5

1. You can practice the presentation and video record it.
2. Don't read out the descriptions.
3. Speak slowly and fluently.

Step 6 Evaluate

7 **Complete the evaluation table.**

★☆☆ More to learn | ★★☆ Good | ★★★ Excellent

Criteria	My Evaluation	Group Evaluation	Teacher Evaluation
Teamwork	☆☆☆	☆☆☆	☆☆☆
Language	☆☆☆	☆☆☆	☆☆☆
Design	☆☆☆	☆☆☆	☆☆☆

#SELF-ASSESSMENT

1 **Mark the learning objectives according to the key.**

★☆☆	★★☆	★★★
I don't understand.	I understand, but I need help.	I can do it!

Learning Objectives	Rating
To interpret a conversation about traveling.	☆☆☆
To talk about traveling.	☆☆☆
To interpret an article about different perspectives on tourism.	☆☆☆
To write about ecotourism.	☆☆☆
To use the Zero Conditional and prepositions with means of transportation.	☆☆☆
To use the First Conditional.	☆☆☆
To give instructions on how to use a travel app.	☆☆☆
To talk about travel arrangements.	☆☆☆
To interpret a factual article about inclusive tourism.	☆☆☆
To write a factual article.	☆☆☆
To recognize features of a travel newsletter and plan to write one.	☆☆☆
To create a travel newsletter and present it to the class.	☆☆☆

2 **Work in pairs. Discuss the questions.**

1. What did I find most interesting to learn? Why?
2. How did I learn it?
3. How can I use it in real life?

UT Language Booster page 46

ENTERTAINMENT TODAY

In this unit, you will learn how to:
- Talk about different kinds of entertainment.
- Write an art event review.
- Create a digital poster.

Say what you know:
- Cultural events.
- Favorite movies and songs.
- Women in entertainment.

#5 GENDER EQUALITY

Video

A Trip to the Museum

Before You Watch

1 **In pairs, make a list of four artists you know and write what they do.**

____

____

____

____

While You Watch

2 **Watch and check (✓). What is the conversation about?** ▷ 08

1. ☐ A new museum in town.
2. ☐ An amazing museum exhibition.
3. ☐ Different kinds of entertainment.

3 **Mark the sentences T (True) or F (False). Then watch the video again and check your answers.** ▷ 08

1. ☐ Emma loves going to different museums.
2. ☐ Luis doesn't like movies or concerts.
3. ☐ Emma doesn't like movies or concerts at all.
4. ☐ They must not eat or drink inside that museum.
5. ☐ They must not take pictures there.
6. ☐ They have to pay an expensive fee to go into the museum.

4 **Watch once again. Check (✓) the words related to art and entertainment that Emma and Luis mention.** ▷ 08

1. ☐ Exhibition
2. ☐ Movie
3. ☐ Concert
4. ☐ Novel
5. ☐ Museum
6. ☐ Work of art
7. ☐ Installation
8. ☐ Pictures
9. ☐ Sculptures
10. ☐ Paintings
11. ☐ Guided tour
12. ☐ Theater

After You Watch

5 **Go back to your list in Activity 1 and the items in Activity 4. Can you make your list longer?**

____

____

____

____

____

____

____

____

____

____

I can demonstrate an understanding of a conversation about entertainment.

e-Language Booster

Vocabulary

Music, Movies, and TV

6 Read the captions. Then copy the chart below in your notebook and complete it. Some can go in more than one column.

1.

comedy

2.

romantic story

3.

rock music

4.

classical music

5.

TV series

6.

news program

7.

reality TV show

8.

pop music

9.

thriller

10.

documentary

Different forms of entertainment			
Movies	TV Shows	Books	Music

7 Listen to the descriptions and number the words. 54

- [ ] A cartoon
- [ ] A documentary
- [ ] A thriller
- [ ] Pop

8 In groups, complete the sentences. Use the words from the box.

broadcast cable TV cooking show episodes season sitcom soap opera

1. The show is about to be ________________.
2. This famous chef has his own ________________ on Channel 5.
3. A ________________ is a television show that has a regular cast of characters in a variety of funny situations.
4. A ________________ is a radio or television series that focuses on home circumstances and is typically melodramatic.
5. ________________ channels are more interesting than regular TV.
6. This amazing series has ten ________________.
7. That drama series is so successful! They are in their 10th ________________.

I can talk about different kinds of entertainment.

Language Booster page 47

Reading

1 Work in groups and discuss the following questions.

1. How are gender stereotypes harmful?
2. How can we build a more inclusive and accepting society?

2 MAKING AND CONFIRMING PREDICTIONS. The picture in Activity 1 is related to the article. Predict what the article is about. Then read and check.

World Matters

http://www.worldmatters.com

Famous people can have a great influence on others. Emma Watson is one who has worked to break down stereotypes, particularly in relation to gender equality.

She is an ambassador for the United Nations' HeForShe campaign, which promotes gender equality. She defines feminism this way: men and women should have the same rights and opportunities. She has already inspired thousands of people around the world. She believes that men and boys should participate in this movement for gender equality. Feminism is not a movement by women for women.

Other celebrities have also contributed to thinking about stereotypes. Margot Robbie has a successful career as an actress and has millions of fans. She is often asked by journalists about her personal life. "Why don't you have children?" Her answer is simple: this cliché "if you get married, you have to have children" is really annoying. The point is that this is not a question for married men.

Another cliché says that a man should be taller than his wife and also older. Two celebrities show that this is not true. Adam Levine, the musician, is shorter than his wife, and actor Chris Hemsworth is seven years younger than his wife.

These are some examples that show how important it is to break stereotypes. If we do that, we will take a big step closer to equality.

3 SCANNING. Read the article again and choose the best title.

1. ☐ Fashion and stereotypes
2. ☐ Breaking stereotypes
3. ☐ Celebrities love stereotypes

4 SKIMMING. Read the article once again and check (✓) the best summary.

1. ☐ Stereotypes are part of our everyday life and affect us all. However, this is not the case with celebrities. This article describes why celebrities and stereotypes have nothing to do with each other.
2. ☐ Celebrities are known all over the world. This article shows that they can help deconstruct stereotypes. These stereotypes can violate rights and equality.
3. ☐ This article shows a negative aspect of celebrities. They sometimes do strange things because they want to shock people and become more famous.

5 Work in small groups. How do you think we can break stereotypes? Have a discussion and make notes of your ideas.

____

____

____

____

____

____

____

____

I can interpret an article about stereotypes.

e-Language Booster

Listening

6 **Listen and check (✓) the possible inferences or conclusions.** 55

1. ☐ Dan has a lot of followers.
2. ☐ Dan wears jeans and a T-shirt.
3. ☐ Dan posts ridiculous selfies.
4. ☐ Dan is a good citizen and likes helping others.
5. ☐ Dan doesn't care about what people think of influencers.

Writing

7 **Work in groups. Research into digital influencers and how they influence young people. Make notes of the most relevant information.**

____

____

____

____

____

____

#TIP

You can look for the Top Ten influencers across social media, if you don't know any.

8 **Write a short text about digital influencers. Use the information in Activity 7.**

I can write about digital influencers.

Language Booster page 48

Grammar

Must not to Express Prohibition in the Present

1 Read the text, and then circle the correct options to complete the statements.

Kensington is an artist. Her works are fantastic, but she **must not** show them in some countries. She **must** be careful in those countries. She can participate in interviews, but she **must not** talk about her works of art. Interviewers **must not** ask her questions about her works.

1. *Must* shows **possibility** / **obligation**.
2. *Must not* shows **obligation** / **prohibition**.
3. *Must* and *must not* **change** / **don't change** form with different pronouns.

2 Read the paragraph below and complete the sentences. Use the words from the box. There is one extra word.

ability advice obligation
permission prohibition

In my city, we **can** ride our bikes, but we **must not** use the pedestrian area. We **must** ride our bikes in the bike lanes. We **have to** be careful. We **have to** wear a helmet, that's very important. We **should** also use sunblock to protect our bodies.

1. *Can* indicates ________________.
2. *Must* indicates ________________.
3. *Have to* indicates ________________.
4. *Should* indicates ________________.
5. *Must not* indicates ________________.

3 Work in groups. Complete the prohibitions below.

1. In the street, we must not ________________.
2. At home, I must not ________________.
3. At school, we must not ________________.
4. On a plane, we must not ________________.
5. When we use the Internet, we must not ________________.

Sense Verbs and Adjectives

4 Read and match the sensation to the corresponding icon.

1. It smells like jasmine.
2. Can you hear the music? It sounds nice!
3. Touch it. It feels very soft.
4. It looks beautiful.
5. I think it tastes nice, too, but I won't eat it!

a.  [ ]

b. 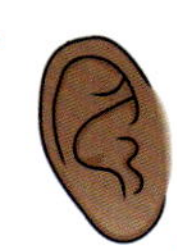 [ ]

c.  [ ]

d. 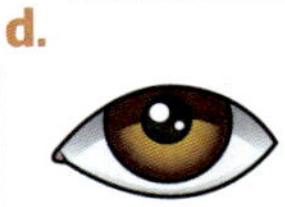 [ ]

e.  [ ]

I can use *must not* to express prohibition.

5 **Complete these statements. Use the adjectives from the box.**

beautiful	delicious	fresh	good	old	soft	strong	weird	wonderful

1. Broccoli tastes ______________ and it looks ______________.
2. This table looks ______________ and ______________.
3. This is a porcupine. It looks ______________.
4. This cake tastes ______________. It smells ______________, and it looks______________.
5. This blanket feels ______________.

6 **Work in small groups. Look at the art pieces and describe them using the sense verbs from the box and adjectives of your own.**

feel	look	smell	sound	taste

A: *This piece of art* ***looks*** *really* ***unique****.*
B: *I agree with you. It* ***looks*** *kind of* ***weird****, too.*

1.

____
____
____

2.

____
____
____

3.

____
____
____

7 **Work in groups. Describe something using the sense verbs and adjectives for your classmates to guess.**

A: *It* ***looks nice****,* ***feels cold****, and* ***tastes refreshing****.*
B: *Is it ice cream?*

I can use sense verbs and adjectives to describe sensations.
Language Booster page 49

Listening

1 **Read the captions and match them to the pictures.**

1. Digital media
2. Banned media
3. Print media
4. Traditional media

2 **LISTENING FOR GIST. Listen to the audio and check (✓) what it is about.** 56

1. ☐ Social media
2. ☐ Human rights today
3. ☐ The media and human rights

3 **LISTENING FOR DETAILS. Listen again and circle the correct option.** 57

1. Freedom of opinion is **a human right** / **an obligation**.
2. TV is a **traditional** / **new** form of media.
3. Social media **has created conflict** / **has helped** important social movements.
4. Some governments want to control the media and **the way people get information** / **to allow more freedom of expression**.
5. This podcast is for **the media** / **everybody**.
6. The speaker is **in favor of** / **against** the media.

Pronunciation

4 **Practice saying these words. Pay attention to the stress. Then listen and repeat.** 58

1. Control
2. Entertainment
3. Exhibition
4. Museum
5. Prohibit
6. Prohibition
7. Stereotypes

Speaking

5 **Work in groups. Think about different media, traditional and digital. What useful information can you get from them? What should you be aware of?**

I can interpret a podcast about the media.

Use of English

6 Listen, read, and underline the phrases that describe sensations about works of art. 59

In an Art Gallery

Guide: This is an abstract painting. What do you feel when you look at it?
Tourist 1: I feel empty, I do not know. It has no effect on me.
Tourist 2: I don't feel like that at all. To me, these lines look like waves, like ocean waves. I can almost hear the waves breaking on the beach.
Tourist 3: I feel inspired by this painting. It's so colorful, so cheerful. It cheers me up.
Tourist 4: I find this artwork so dramatic. It has a great depth. I am amazed by it.
Guide: Well, I think it's time for lunch break! Let's go back!

7 Work in groups of five. Listen again and role play the conversation. 60

8 Work in pairs. Match the critiques to the works of art.

1. Wow! There are so many of them. They are so colorful and cheerful. Look at that! In the middle it looks like a flower with lots of petals. I love all the different patterns!
2. It's kind of weird. I feel weird looking at it. It's also a little retro. It looks old and worn.
3. They're beautiful. There are different layers with different colors. I would love to have one of these ceramic jars at home.

a.  ___

b.  ___

c.  ___

9 In small groups, critique the artwork in the picture. How does it make you feel?

____

____

____

____

____

I can talk about how I feel about art.
Language Booster page 50

#CHALLENGE

Writing

1 **How much do you know about reviews? Check (✓) the true statements.**

1. ☐ Reviews focus on strengths and weaknesses.
2. ☐ Reviews do not use evidence to support ideas.
3. ☐ Reviews state a personal opinion with confidence and authority.
4. ☐ Reviews draw conclusions about whether something will be useful or interesting to their audience.

2 **Read the review of a documentary film and go back to your answers in Activity 1. Then mark the sentences T (True) or F (False).**

1. ☐ The review is about a documentary movie.
2. ☐ This is a negative review.
3. ☐ The movie is about gender equality.
4. ☐ A woman directed this documentary.
5. ☐ The movie is too serious and not entertaining.

3 **Read the review again and check (✓) the information you find.**

1. ☐ Description of the movie.
2. ☐ Positive and negative points.
3. ☐ Reasons why you shouldn't watch the movie.
4. ☐ Writer's opinion.

"This Changes... +

"This Changes Everything" Must Be Watched

This fascinating documentary aims to highlight the problems women face in achieving equality with their male counterparts.

After seeing children's entertainment on TV and being astonished by how few females were portrayed in these shows and cartoons, Geena Davis launched the Institute on Gender in Media.

The fact that *This Changes Everything* was directed by a guy, Tom Donahue, is an intriguing component of all of this. Given the subject matter, some may argue that this picture, in particular, should have been directed by a woman.

This is a very important, but also entertaining movie that contains many movie clips and historical information. It is worth watching for anyone who wants to learn more about gender inequality that unfortunately still exists.

Do you plan on watching *This Changes Everything?* Click here and let us know what you think.

4 **Complete the chart about the review.**

Topic	Information
Introduction	1 ______
Weakness	2 ______
Writer's opinion	3 ______

I can interpret a movie review.
e-Language Booster

Prepare to Write

5 You are going to write a review of an art event. Do some research. Then complete the chart with information you want to include in your text.

Topic	Information
Introduction	
Information about the event	
Your opinion	

#TIP

When using search engines:

1. Make your keywords precise.
2. Use two or more keywords.
3. Pay attention to spelling.
4. Try different search engines.

Write

6 Write the review. Use the information in Activity 5 and the text in Activity 2 as a model.

____

____

____

____

Check and Change

7 Read the review and make sure you included:

- ☐ an introduction.
- ☐ information about the art event.
- ☐ strengths and weaknesses.
- ☐ your opinion.

8 Edit your text. Make sure all the items in Activity 7 are included. Then choose a picture for your review.

Publish

9 Write a clean version of your review.

Speaking

10 Work in groups. Read your classmates' reviews. Then give your opinion about them. How can they improve their reviews?

I can write a review.

Language Booster page 51

Project: A Digital Poster

#DIGITAL LITERACY

For digital posters you should:

1. Maximize graphics over text.
2. Be dynamic and move between different screens.
3. Use animation to emphasize the message.

Step 1 Think

1 Work in groups. Do some research to answer the questions.

1. What information can you post on a digital poster?

____

2. How can you organize the information?

____

2 Read the posters and check (✓) the correct statements about them. Do you think the posters are effective in conveying their message?

1. 

a. ☐ The poster is about women learning to drive.
b. ☐ The poster is about women fighting for the right to vote.

2. 

a. ☐ The poster is about cooking.
b. ☐ The poster is about a coronavirus disease prevention measure.

Step 2 Plan

3 **In groups, decide on the topic for your digital poster. Choose one and make notes of the things you would like to include. Read the suggestions below.**

1. Gender inequality in your school.
2. Gender inequality in entertainment.
3. A gender inequality timeline.

Step 3 Research

4 **Research into digital posters and the topic you chose in Activity 3.**

Step 4 Design

5 **Create your digital poster using a free online tool. Use the information from your research and the previous activities.**

- Check the text.
- Check the purpose.
- Check the organization.

Step 5 Present and Publish

6 **Work in groups. Present your digital poster to your group.**

Step 6 Evaluate

7 **Complete the evaluation table.**

★☆☆ More to learn · ★★☆ Good · ★★★ Excellent

Criteria	My Evaluation	Group Evaluation	Teacher Evaluation
Teamwork	★★★	★★★	★★★
Language	★★★	★★★	★★★
Design	★★★	★★★	★★★

#TIP Step 4

There are several free online tools you can use to create your poster. Try different ones and find out which one suits your needs best.

#TIP Step 5

1. You can practice the presentation and video record it.
2. Don't read out the descriptions.
3. Speak slowly and fluently.

I can create a digital poster and present it to the class.

#SELF-ASSESSMENT

1 Mark the learning objectives according to the key.

★☆☆ I don't understand.	★★☆ I understand, but I need help.	★★★ I can do it!

Learning Objectives	Rating
To demonstrate an understanding of a conversation about entertainment.	☆☆☆
To talk about different kinds of entertainment.	☆☆☆
To interpret an article about stereotypes.	☆☆☆
To write about digital influencers.	☆☆☆
To use *must not* to express prohibition.	☆☆☆
To use sense verbs and adjectives to describe sensations.	☆☆☆
To interpret a podcast about the media.	☆☆☆
To talk about how I feel about art.	☆☆☆
To interpret a movie review.	☆☆☆
To write a review.	☆☆☆
To recognize features of a digital poster and plan to create one.	☆☆☆
To create a digital poster and present it to the class.	☆☆☆

2 Work in pairs. Discuss the questions.

1. What did I find most interesting to learn? Why?
2. How did I learn it?
3. How can I use it in real life?

UT Language Booster page 52

UNIT EIGHT 8

CRIME AND JUSTICE

#16 PEACE, JUSTICE AND STRONG INSTITUTIONS

In this unit, you will learn how to:

- Talk about crime and justice.
- Write an opinion essay.
- Create an online bulletin board.

Say what you know:

- Crimes and criminals.
- Punishments.
- Obligations and responsibilities.

#DISCOVER

Video

Wrongdoings

Before You Watch

1 **In pairs, make a list of your school rules. Then answer the questions.**

____

____

____

1. Have you ever broken any school rules?

____

____

2. What happens if you break the rules?

____

____

While You Watch

2 **Watch and check (✓) the alternative that best describes the video.** ▷ 09

1. ☐ They discuss problems at school. Emma and Luis disagree.
2. ☐ They discuss a classmate's wrong actions at school. Luis disagrees with Emma at first.
3. ☐ They discuss crimes in society. Emma disagrees with Luis at first.

3 **Watch the video again and write Brandon, Emma, or Luis.** ▷ 09

1. __________ starts a video call.
2. __________ sent a text message.
3. __________ can't go to school for three days.
4. __________ first thinks that the punishment is excessive.
5. __________ thinks that everyone must follow the rules.
6. __________ wants support from his classmates.

4 **Watch the once video again and answer the questions.** ▷ 09

1. What did Brandon do wrong?

____

____

____

2. What was Brandon's punishment?

____

3. What does Brandon want Emma and Luis to do?

____

After You Watch

5 **Go back to the list in Activity 1 and answer the question in groups.**

What should be the consequences for each of the wrongdoings?

I can demonstrate an understanding of a conversation about wrongdoings at school.

e-Language Booster

Vocabulary

Crimes and Criminals

6 **Match the crimes in the pictures to the corresponding definitions.**

a. 
burglary [ ]

b. 
shoplifting [ ]

c. 
mugging [ ]

d. 
assault [ ]

e. 
vandalism [ ]

f. 

fraud [ ]

g. 

terrorism [ ]

h. 
murder [ ]

1. Hitting and injuring a person physically.
2. Breaking into a home, car, etc., to steal things.
3. A lie or deception with the objective of financial or personal gain.
4. Attacking and robbing a person in a public place.
5. The act of killing a person.
6. Using intimidation or violence for political reasons.
7. Destroying people's or public properties.
8. Stealing something at a store.

7 **In pairs, associate the words from the box with the crimes in Activity 6. Then listen and check.** 61

attacker burglar fraudster mugger murderer shoplifter terrorist vandal

a. ____________ e. ____________

b. ____________ f. ____________

c. ____________ g. ____________

d. ____________ h. ____________

8 **Circle the correct words to complete the definitions below. Use a dictionary if necessary.**

1. **Community service** / **Sentence**: unpaid work to help the community in a particular area.
2. **Innocent** / **Guilty**: responsible for a crime.
3. **Innocent** / **Guilty**: not responsible for a crime.
4. **Parole** / **Sentence**: the punishment and duration of that punishment as ordered by a court or fixed by law.
5. **Innocent** / **Juvenile delinquent**: a young offender.
6. **Guilty** / **Parole**: release from detention before the sentence is complete if the prisoner has shown very good behavior.
7. **Offender**: **Community service**: a person who has committed a crime, a criminal.

I can talk about crimes and criminals.

Language Booster page 53

Reading

1 **MAKING AND CONFIRMING PREDICTIONS. Look at the pictures. What do you think the article you are going to read is about? Read the article below and check your guesses.**

2 **Choose one of the options below for the title of the article.**

1. Crimes, Criminals, and Punishment
2. Society and Detention
3. Young Offenders and Crime Prevention

3 **SCANNING. Read the article again and answer the questions.**

1. What crimes do young offenders usually commit?

____

2. What crimes do adult offenders usually commit?

____

4 **SUMMARIZING. Read the article again and check (✓) the alternative that best summarizes it.**

1. ☐ Sometimes young offenders commit less serious crimes, but they can become habitual offenders and commit serious crimes. The best way to change this is through education.
2. ☐ Young offenders must understand they have committed a crime and have to go to prison. This way, they will learn that our actions have consequences.
3. ☐ Young offenders and adult offenders commit different crimes, but they are all dangerous to society. One way to solve this problem is to talk about crimes and punishment at school.

World Matters

http://www.worldmatters.com

Do young offenders always commit petty crimes? Some people may argue that this is usually the case. For this reason, these juvenile offenders should not be institutionalized. In these institutions, it is argued they usually learn more about crime than they do at home. But that does not mean they should not receive punishment. They need to learn that all our actions have consequences.

There are several problems associated with young offenders. They start committing minor crimes. But statistics show that many young offenders become habitual criminals and have long criminal careers. Young offenders commit certain crimes, such as graffiti, assault, and car or motorcycle theft, more frequently than adults. Adult offenses tend to be fraud, traffic offenses, and more serious or violent crimes.

There are several risk factors for juvenile crime. Some of these include living in bad neighborhoods, family problems, and school difficulties. Young offenders are generally absent from school quite frequently. They do not study or do anything outside of school. There are strategies to prevent this. One of them is to reduce the risk of these young people slipping into delinquency. This is related to education: families need to be educated, and kids need to learn to stop and think before they do something.

Young offenders are a problem for society and for themselves. Therefore, it is necessary to help these young people and their families. The best way to do that is by showing them that they are responsible for their actions and by educating them.

I can interpret an article about young offenders and crime prevention.

e-Language Booster

Listening

5 Listen to an interview and answer the questions. 62

1. Why did Dana start smoking?
2. What did Jezz want?
3. What did she do to the boy?
4. Why did she end up in an institution?
5. How does she contribute to society now?

Writing

6 Work in groups. Research into juvenile delinquency in your own country. Use the questions to guide you. Make notes.

1. At what age is a person considered a juvenile?
2. Are there special detention institutions for juveniles? Which ones?
3. What crimes do juveniles usually commit?
4. What factor causes juvenile delinquency?

#TIP

Make sure you look for reliable information on websites that are credible. Check the domain name and the source.

7 Write a short text about juvenile delinquency in your country. Use the information in Activity 6.

I can write about juvenile delinquency in my country.

Language Booster page 54

Grammar

Indefinite Pronouns

1 **Read the paragraph and complete the table.**

Everybody knows that we have to follow rules everywhere. When somebody breaks a rule, we have to do something. If we don't do anything, we set a bad example. Nobody likes bad examples.

	People	Objects	Places
1. Every...			
2. Some...			
3. No...			
4. Any...			

2 **Read the table in Activity 1 again and circle the correct words to complete the statements below.**

1. We use indefinite pronouns with *some* and *any* to describe **definite** / **indefinite** and incomplete quantities.
2. We use indefinite pronouns with *every* to describe **a complete** / **an incomplete** quantity.
3. We use indefinite pronouns with *no* to describe **abundance** / **absence**.
4. We often use indefinite pronouns with *any* in **affirmative** / **negative and interrogative** sentences.
5. We often use indefinite pronouns with *some* in **affirmative** / **negative and interrogative** sentences.
6. We often use indefinite pronouns with *no* in **interrogative** / **affirmative** sentences with a negative meaning.

3 **Underline the correct options to complete the paragraph.**

I saw [1] **anybody** / **somebody** in the street yesterday. It was dark [2] **nowhere** / **everywhere** and I couldn't see [3] **anything** / **nothing** clearly. I heard a noise. *Is there* [4] **anybody** / **everybody** *there?* I asked. No answer. I was a little scared. I walked on, and then [5] **no one** / **somebody** said with a strange voice, *Hi, Ava!* I turned round and I saw [6] **somebody** / **nothing** in the dark. It was my brother. He wanted to play a trick on me.

4 **Complete the sentences about the paragraph in Activity 3.**

1. Something I liked about the story was ______________________________.
2. Something I didn't like about the story was ______________________________.

5 **In pairs, create your own story based on the story in Activity 3. Use indefinite pronouns.**

____

____

____

____

Relative Pronouns

6 **Read the paragraph, pay attention to the underlined words, and circle the correct alternative.**

The person <u>who</u> commits a crime is an offender or criminal. Offenders have to be responsible for the crimes <u>which</u> they commit. Justice is the system <u>that</u> determines the punishment for criminals.

1. *Who* refers to the **person** / **crime**.
2. *Which* refers to **offenders** / **crimes**.
3. *That* refers to **criminals**/ **the system**.
4. Who refers to **people** / **things** whereas *which* and *that* refer to **people** / **things**.

7 **Complete the sentences in your own words.**

1. I love people **who** ______________________.
2. A book **which** surprised me was ______________ ______________________.
3. The best movie **that** I have seen is ______________ ______________________.

So for Results and Consequences

8 **Read the end of the story from Activity 3 and circle the best option to answer the question.**

My brother did something silly, **so** my parents talked to him. He understood he was wrong, **so** he apologized to me. I love him very much, **so** I gave him a kiss. He promised not to do it again.

What does **so** indicate in the paragraph?
Reason. / **Result or consequence.**

9 **Work in groups. Discuss different results or consequences for each situation and write your ideas.**

1. The students broke a school rule, so ______________ ______________________.
2. The teacher was absent, so ______________ ______________________.
3. The new students didn't know about the rule, so ______________________.

Adverbs of Manner

10 **Read the paragraph and check (✓) the best alternative to complete the sentences.**

Mr. Briggs is a good person. He often behaves very <u>nicely</u> and <u>carefully</u>, but yesterday, he didn't act <u>well</u>. His neighbor threw trash into his garden, and he reacted <u>angrily</u>.

1. The underlined words indicate ______________.
   - ☐ the reason people do things
   - ☐ the way people do things
2. We ______________ add *-ly* to the adjectives to form adverbs of manner.
   - ☐ *usually* ☐ *always*
3. *Well* is the adverb of manner for ______________.
   - ☐ bad ☐ good

11 **Change the adjectives below into adverbs of manner. Then choose four of them to complete the sentences from the box.**

1. calm: ______________
2. careful: ______________
3. polite: ______________
4. angry: ______________
5. good: ______________
6. nice: ______________

When there's an accident, we should act ______________ and ______________.

If you're angry, think ______________.

Talk to others ______________.

I can use relative pronouns, so for results and consequences, and adverbs of manner.
Language Booster page 55

#DEVELOP

Listening

1 Read and check (✓) the offenses that affect your city.

1. ☐ Corruption
2. ☐ Cybercrimes
3. ☐ Drug abuse
4. ☐ High levels of violence
5. ☐ Human trafficking
6. ☐ Violence against women

2 LISTENING FOR GIST. Listen to the audio and check (✓) its main idea. 63

1. ☐ The woman works for UNDOC and is in charge of the violence against women section.
2. ☐ Violence against women happens all over the world, and the women's organization works to prevent crimes against women.
3. ☐ The woman is an expert in international crime prevention. Her organization works to protect women and girls against violence.

3 LISTENING FOR DETAILS. Listen again and answer the questions. 64

1. What is UNDOC interested in?
____
2. Why are gender-sensitive approaches a problem?
____
3. How does society feel about law enforcement?
____
4. Where is there violence against women?
____
5. Why aren't there reports of violence against women in some cultures?
____
____
6. How can we all help?
____
____
____

Pronunciation

4 Listen, pay attention to the stressed words, and repeat the sentences. Then check (✓) the correct statement about sentence stress. 65

The **kids** are at the **store.**
Do you **have** any **brothers** or **sisters?**
Why aren't you **working?**
He **bought** a **white car** for his **dad.**
I am **Brazilian.**
We are **not familiar** with this **new law.**
The **athlete ran quickly** in the **race.**
They do **not know** the **answer.**

1. ☐ Content words such as nouns, verbs, adjectives, and adverbs, as well as negative words, are stressed because they affect the meaning of the sentence.
2. ☐ Short words such as articles, prepositions, and conjunctions should always be stressed because they affect the meaning of the sentence.

Speaking

5 Work in groups. Go online and find information about movements in favor of the protection of women. Make notes. Talk to your classmates about your findings and describe the advantages and disadvantages of joining such movements.

I can interpret an interview about offenses against women.
e-Language Booster

Use of English

6 **Listen, read, and check (✓) what the underlined parts refer to.** 66

Matt and Tiff discuss a program for prisoners.

Matt: This program has many benefits. It combines education, sports, values, and reflection.

Tiff: Is it for everybody? I mean, can all prisoners participate?

Matt: It is not mandatory. If they want to participate, they have to learn to play team sports and value cooperation and collaboration. Something else that's very positive, is that when they leave prison, they tend not to reoffend.

Tiff: I see what you mean, but there's also a downside.

Matt: You think so? I can't think of anything. What disadvantages can you think of?

Tiff: It's not for everyone in prison. It shows discrimination.

Matt: I don't think it does. Some people are not willing to learn or reflect. I don't think that's a disadvantage, but a very good point!

Tiff: OK. What do they have to study?

Matt: See? Here is another advantage. They can finish elementary or secondary school, and when they finish it, they can go into any profession. They get support all the way through.

Tiff: That's great.

1. ☐ Results and consequences.
2. ☐ Certainties and doubts.
3. ☐ Advantages and disadvantages.

7 **Work in pairs. Listen and role play the dialogue in Activity 6.** 67

8 **Underline the indefinite pronouns in the dialogue in Activity 6.**

9 **Work in pairs. Choose one of the crimes you learned about. Think about the advantages and disadvantages of a community program for these kinds of offenders. Write about such a program. Use adverbs of manner, indefinite and relative pronouns, and so for results and consequences in your text.**

____

____

____

____

____

10 **In pairs, present your program to your classmates.**

I can describe advantages and disadvantages.

Language Booster page 56

#CHALLENGE

Writing

1 **Read and check (✓) the correct statements about opinion essays.**

1. ☐ An opinion essay starts with an introduction to the topic.
2. ☐ In an opinion essay, the writer shows agreement or disagreement.
3. ☐ In an opinion essay, the writer never shows agreement or disagreement.
4. ☐ There's a conclusion in an opinion essay.
5. ☐ In an opinion essay, the writer justifies his / her opinions.
6. ☐ In an opinion essay, there must be images.
7. ☐ In an opinion essay, there's more than one paragraph.

2 **Read this opinion essay and check your answers in Activity 1. Then underline the correct options to complete the sentences.**

1. This text is **formal** / **informal**.
2. The first paragraph **introduces the topic** / **presents an advantage**.
3. The second paragraph **describes different crimes** / **shows the relationship between crimes and breaking rules at school**.
4. The third paragraph shows **a different perspective** / **another advantage**.
5. The fourth paragraph **describes a good point** / **shows a disadvantage**.
6. The last paragraph **considers the importance of education** / **describes different types of content**.

3 **Read the text again and answer.**

1. What are crimes?
2. What happens if students violate a regulation?
3. Why is reflection necessary?
4. Why are classmates important?
5. Besides content, what else should students learn at school?

Crime Prevention and Education

Crime has become one of the most troubling aspects of society. If society and governments want to prevent crime, education should play an important role.

Crimes are defined as illegal activities that must be punished. In education, there are regulations that students sometimes violate. So if they violate a regulation, they should be responsible for it and suffer the consequences.

Reflection is also necessary. Students need to think about the consequences of their behavior. They and other people are affected when they break a rule. If they do not think about it, the consequences will be negative. They may think that they will be punished if they do something wrong and that there is nothing else to do. This may be shocking to some, but we can make a comparison. In a way, this shows what happens to prisoners who are serving their sentences. Some come out of prison and commit crimes again.

Another benefit of crime prevention education is the cooperation between classmates. Classmates can play a very important role because they can help those who are about to break a rule. They can also serve as a support system. During adolescence, groups are of the utmost importance.

Some believe that classes should focus only on content. Content is very important, but learning to be a good citizen is as important as learning facts. Students can access information in different ways. So it's very clear that education is a key to crime prevention.

I can interpret an opinion essay about crime prevention.

Prepare to Write

4 **You are going to write a short opinion essay about one of the topics discussed in this unit. Decide on the topic and complete the chart with the information you want to include in your text.**

Paragraph	Key Information
1	
2	
3	
4	

#TIP

1. Introduce the issue and express your point of view.
2. Justify your position in each paragraph of your essay.

Write

5 **Write a short opinion essay. Review the features in Activity 1 for help. Then use the information in Activity 4 and the text in Activity 2 as a model.**

____

____

____

____

____

____

____

____

____

____

Check and Change

6 **Read your opinion essay and make sure you included:**

- [ ] an introduction.
- [ ] advantages and disadvantages.
- [ ] your opinions.
- [ ] a conclusion.

7 **Edit your text. Make sure all the items in Activity 6 are included.**

Publish

8 **Write a clean version of your opinion essay.**

Speaking

9 **Work in groups. Read your classmates' opinion essays. Then give your opinion about them. How can they improve their essays?**

I can write an opinion essay.
Language Booster page 57

Project: An Online Bulletin Board

#DIGITAL LITERACY

Online bulletin boards help remote groups collaborate online. To work on your project, add all your digital sticky notes to a collaborative online whiteboard. It's much easier to sort ideas and notes when they are all in the same place.

Step 1 Think

1 **Work in groups. How can you organize the information on an online bulletin board? Research online if necessary.**

Step 2 Plan

2 **In groups, start planning your online bulletin board. Answer the questions below.**

1. What rules do students usually break at school?

____

____

____

____

2. How can families help prevent students from breaking rules?

____

____

____

____

____

3. How can teachers and the whole school staff work to reduce rule breaking?

____

____

____

____

4. How can you and your classmates contribute to a wrongdoing-free school environment?

____

____

____

I can recognize features of an online bulletin board and plan to create one.

Step 3 Research

3 **Research and brainstorm different answers to the questions in Activity 2.**

1. ______________________________
2. ______________________________
3. ______________________________
4. ______________________________

Step 4 Design

4 **Create your online bulletin board using a free online tool. Use the information from Steps 2 and 3.**

- Check the text.
- Check the purpose.
- Check the organization.

Step 5 Present and Publish

5 **Present your online bulletin board to your classmates.**

Step 6 Evaluate

6 **Complete the evaluation table.**

★☆☆ More to learn — ★★☆ Good — ★★★ Excellent

Criteria	My Evaluation	Group Evaluation	Teacher Evaluation
Teamwork	☆☆☆	☆☆☆	☆☆☆
Language	☆☆☆	☆☆☆	☆☆☆
Design	☆☆☆	☆☆☆	☆☆☆

#TIP Step 4

1. Play around with different fonts to show different meanings and ideas.
2. Use different images and icons to clarify meaning.

#TIP Step 5

1. Practice the presentation and video record it.
2. Don't read out the information.
3. Speak slowly and fluently.

I can create an online bulletin board and present it to the class.

e-Language Booster page

#SELF-ASSESSMENT

1 Mark the learning objectives according to the key.

★☆☆ I don't understand.	★★☆ I understand, but I need help.	★★★ I can do it!

Learning Objectives	Rating
To demonstrate an understanding of a conversation about wrongdoings at school.	☆☆☆
To talk about crimes and criminals.	☆☆☆
To interpret an article about young offenders and crime prevention.	☆☆☆
To write about juvenile delinquency in my country.	☆☆☆
To use indefinite pronouns.	☆☆☆
To use relative pronouns, so for results and consequences, and adverbs of manner.	☆☆☆
To interpret an interview about offenses against women.	☆☆☆
To describe advantages and disadvantages.	☆☆☆
To interpret an opinion essay about crime prevention.	☆☆☆
To write an opinion essay.	☆☆☆
To recognize features of an online bulletin board and plan to create one.	☆☆☆
To create an online bulletin board and present it to the class.	☆☆☆

2 Work in pairs. Discuss the questions.

1. What did I find most interesting to learn? Why?
2. How did I learn it?
3. How can I use it in real life?

UT FT Language Booster page 58

INTEGRATE

Learn to Learn

Reviewing Bloom's Taxonomy

1 **Review Bloom's action verbs and read the definitions. Check (✓) the one that summarizes the taxonomy.**

1. ☐ Bloom's Taxonomy is the way the cognitive skills are taught to students according to their learning objectives.
2. ☐ Bloom's Taxonomy is a hierarchical ordering of cognitive skills used to classify educational learning objectives into levels of complexity and specificity.
3. ☐ Bloom's Taxonomy is a hierarchical complexity of cognitive skills that educational learning uses to specify objectives into levels.

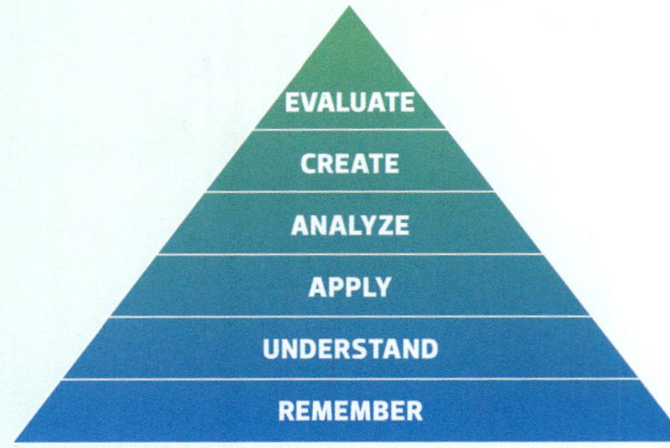

2 **Explain how the taxonomy was applied to the learning sequence below.**

1. Remember

What is this?

2. Understand

Where does milk come from?

3. Apply

What are the uses of milk?

4. Analyze

What are the different milk by-producs?

5. Create

What recipes can you create with milk by-products?

6. Evaluate

Which recipe is the best?

3 **Now follow the action verbs from the taxonomy and design your own activity.**

1. Remember	2. Understand	3. Apply

4. Analyze	5. Create	6. Evaluate

4 **Compare your activities with your classmates'.**

5 **Evaluate your own work and make any changes you want.**

6 **Develop a final activity based on Bloom's Taxonomy.**

7 **Was it easy to identify and include all the categories from the taxonomy in your activity?**

Video

About Online Courses

Before You Watch

1 **What do you remember from the video in the #Discover section? Answer the questions and share them with a classmate.**

1. What are Luis and Emma talking about?

____

____

2. What are the courses they discuss?

____

____

3. Who likes Game Design, Emma or Luis?

____

____

4. Who likes the Great Classics Trap?

____

____

5. In which course are there four assignments?

____

____

6. Which course is practical?

____

____

While You Watch

2 **Watch the video again and check your answers to Activity 1.** ▷ 01

3 **Who said it? Write L (Luis) or E (Emma).**

1. ☐ I like the first course best.
2. ☐ I love games.
3. ☐ I'm tired after school.
4. ☐ I enjoy doing things.
5. ☐ Would you like to take the second one?

After You Watch

4 **In pairs, you are going to create a video to talk about and compare two different courses. Complete the chart.**

	Course 1	Course 2
Name		
Topic		
Duration		
Weekly study		
Activities		
Your opinion		

5 **Record your video and share it with your classmates.**

1. Write the conversation. Use the information in the chart. You can use the video as a model. Remember to include:
   - adjectives ending in *-ed* or *-ing*.
   - comparatives and superlatives.
   - *like / love / hate* + *-ing* forms.
   - *would like* for requests and offers.
2. Role play the conversation.
3. Make the video and share it.

6 **In groups, provide feedback to your classmates about their video.**

Vocabulary	
Information	
Presentation	

Learn to Learn

Celebrations Around the World

1 Match the pictures to the correct descriptions.

a. 
Carnival in Rio [ ]

b. 
Dia de los Muertos, Mexico [ ]

c. 
Chinese New Year [ ]

d. 
Kwanzaa [ ]

1. It is a celebration that reunites the living and the dead in Mexico.
2. A secular festival by African-Americans to celebrate their cultural heritage and traditional values.
3. An annual Brazilian festival that happens before Easter. It has music and dance.
4. It is the celebration of a new year and the most important event in China.

2 Compare the celebrations in the previous activity. How similar / different are they?

3 How would you relate your favorite festivities with the traditions of your family or country?

4 How would you explain your traditions to a foreign visitor?

5 Make a calendar with the most popular celebrations or festivities. Include some brief information about them.

6 How would you summarize your favorite celebration or festivity?

7 What points do you consider when summarizing?

Video

About Looks and Fashion

Before You Watch

1 **What do you remember from the video in the #Discover section? Answer the questions and share them with a classmate.**

1. What are Luis and Emma talking about?

____

2. Who can they see on the screen?

____

3. Is this person a boy or a girl?

____

4. What is the singer promoting?

____

5. What's the connection between LC and the campaign?

____

6. Do Emma and Luis want to help?

____

While You Watch

2 **Watch the video again and check your answers to Activity 1.** ▷ 02

3 **Summarize the video in your own words.**

____

____

____

____

____

____

____

____

After You Watch

4 **You are going to create a video in which you show how you're transforming clothes. Complete the chart.**

Clothes	Problem	Transformation
T-shirt	*Stains*	*Patches*

5 **In pairs, make your video and share it with your classmates.**

1. Write the script, using the information in the chart. Check the example below.
Here's a T-shirt. I don't like it, and it has stains. I can use patches and transform it.
2. Practice saying the lines. Use prompts: real clothes or drawings / pictures.
3. Record the video and share it.

6 **In groups, provide feedback to your classmates about their video.**

Vocabulary	
Information	
Presentation	

Learn to Learn

Wiki

1 List the collaborative tools you know of. Try to remember what you have been using with this book.

____

____

____

____

____

2 Explain what a wiki is. Use bullet points to summarize how it works.

3 You are going to create a wiki. Organize your group and plan what each member will do.

Who will be responsible for:

- creating the wiki page?
- looking for free images?
- writing the bullet points?
- making the bullet points into a complete text?
- designing the page?

4 Discuss and agree on the following:

1. A famous person you'll write about.

____

2. The kind of information you will include.

____

3. The number / kind of images.

____

5 Create your wiki and share it with your classmates.

6 Evaluate your own wiki based on your classmates' production.

7 How can collaborative work help all the members of a group for a successful outcome?

Video

About Food

Before You Watch

1 **What do you remember from the video in the #Discover section? Complete and compare answers with a classmate.**

1. Luis and Emma are talking about ________.
2. They have ________ cartons of milk.
3. They collected ________ packs of pasta.
4. There are ________ cans of vegetables.
5. They need ________ of rice.
6. They also need packs of ________.

While You Watch

2 **Watch the video again and check your answers to Activity 1.** 03

3 **Write the words from the box in the correct column.**

cookies crackers milk pasta
peas peaches rice soup

Fruit	Vegetables	Meal	Snack	Drink

After You Watch

4 **You are going to create a video for the Global Food Bank Network to convince people to donate. Explain what people can donate, where they can donate, and why it is important.**

Food you need	Quantity	What you have collected

5 **In pairs, make your video and share it with your classmates.**

1. Write the script. Use the information in the chart. Use the dialogue in the video as a model.
2. Practice saying the lines. Use prompts: real / empty cartons, cans, etc., or use pictures.
3. Make the video and share it.

6 **Work in groups. Give feedback to your classmates about their video. Use the chart below.**

Language	
Information	
Visual aids	

Learn to Learn

Virtual Pets

1 **List** the virtual pets and games you know.

2 Read about a digital pet and **compare** it to the pets you listed in Activity 1.

Tamagotchi is a pocket-sized virtual pet that requires constant care and attention. If not taken care properly, it dies. Just as any real pet would.

3 **Complete** the sentences with your own opinion.

1. Digital pets are ________________________.
2. We can learn to ________________________ by having a virtual pet.
3. A virtual pet is not the same as a real one because ________________________.

4 Research more about digital pets and **examine** their functionalities and characteristics.

5 **Invent** a virtual pet. Give it a name and indicate its features.

6 **Provide feedback** on your classmates' virtual pets.

7 How did the process of building a virtual pet help you understand how it works?

Video

About Past Inventions

Before You Watch

1 What do you remember from the video in the #Discover section? Answer the questions and share them with a classmate.

1. What are Luis and Emma talking about?

____

2. When do they have to submit the assignment?

____

3. Who does Luis want to write about?

____

4. Does Emma like the idea?

____

5. What inventions does Luis mention?

____

____

While You Watch

2 Watch the video again and check your answers to Activity 1. ▷ 04

3 What other invention does Emma mention? Check (✓) the correct alternative.

1. ☐ Mona Lisa
2. ☐ Life raft
3. ☐ The Vitruvian Man

After You Watch

4 You are going to create a video to tell an anecdote. Explain what happened to you while you were doing something in connection with a machine, a device, or a gadget. Complete the chart.

Once I was charging my cell phone when it exploded in my hand. I had to go to the hospital...

Activity in progress in the past	Complete activity

5 In groups, make your video and share it with the class.

1. Write the script. Use the information in the chart.
2. Practice saying the lines. Use facial expressions and body movement.
3. Record the video and share it.

6 In groups, provide feedback to your classmates about their video.

Anecdote	
Presentation	
Use of body and facial expressions	

Learn to Learn

A Robot

1 **Choose** some characteristics of a good friend.

bossy	generous	respectful
calm	helpful	rude
dishonest	kind	smart
easy-going	lazy	stubborn
extroverted	reliable	unhappy

2 How can you **show** you are a good friend? Write the things you do.

____

____

____

____

3 Imagine you can build a smart robot that will be your friend. **Choose** the characteristics it should have.

4 Now **plan** what your robot will look like. Think about the physical characteristics.

5 **Design** your robot friend. Illustrate the characteristics you chose for it and give it a name.

6 **Evaluate** your classmates' robots and **redesign** any characteristics of your robot you'd like to.

7 What other way would you plan your sketch?

Video

About Technology and Innovation

Before You Watch

1 What do you remember from the video in the #Discover section? Complete the sentences.

1. Jaime lost his ___________ last week.
2. Jaime is starting a training ___________.
3. ___________ are doing Jaime's job now.
4. Jaime is going to be trained to become a ___________ engineer.
5. The program lasts ___________ years in total.

While You Watch

2 Watch the video again and check your answers to Activity 1. ▷ 05

3 Answer the questions according to the video.

1. Has the company fired Jaime?

____

2. Is Jaime going to get paid?

____

After You Watch

4 You are going to present a gadget and make predictions about similar gadgets in the future. Write a script using *will* to express predictions.

*In the future, all cars **will** be able to work on their own without a driver. They **will probably** be controlled by a GPS and...*

____

____

____

____

____

5 In groups, record your video and share it with your classmates.

1. Check the script. Have you used expressions to make predictions?
2. Practice saying the lines. Use pictures if necessary.
3. Make the video and share it.

6 In groups, provide feedback to your classmates about their video.

Language	Information	Visual aids

Learn to Learn

Game Time

1 **List** some endangered species you have learned about. Add some more to the list.

Panamanian Golden Frog

____

____

____

____

____

____

2 **Discuss** with your classmates and **compare** your lists.

3 From your lists, **discover** nine of the most endangered animals. In your notebook, write a fact file for each of them. Use the model below.

Name: ______________________________

Location: ______________________________

Why it's endangered: ______________________________

4 **Categorize** the animals you talked about. In your notebook, create mind maps similar to the one below.

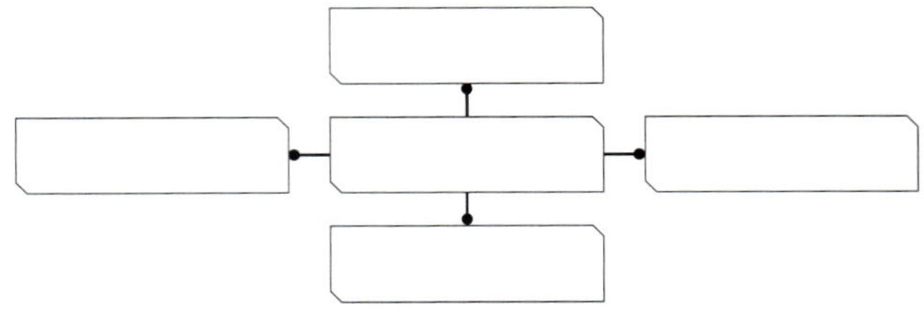

5 **Design** a new Bingo game!

6 **Decide** if Bingo is the best game to learn new words.

7 How can creating a vocabulary game help you learn?

Video

Endangered Animals

Before You Watch

1 What do you remember from the video in the #Discover section? Answer the questions.

1. Are Emma and Luis at school?

____

2. What are they talking about?

____

3. How many pandas are estimated to be left in China?

____

4. Why are they in danger of extinction?

____

5. Why does Emma think we should have stricter laws everywhere?

____

While You Watch

2 Watch the video again and check your answers to Activity 1. ▷ 06

3 Summarize the video in your own words.

____

____

____

____

After You Watch

4 You are going to create a video. In this video, you will talk about an amazing aspect of animals. Look back through the unit and find examples. Complete the chart.

Topics	Information

5 In groups, make your video and share it with your classmates.

1. Write the script. Remember to use the information in the chart in Activity 4.
2. Practice saying the lines. Use pictures. You can also use slides.
3. Make the video and share it.

6 Work in groups. Give feedback to your classmates about their video. Use the chart below.

Language	
Information	
Visual aids	

Learn to Learn

Going Around

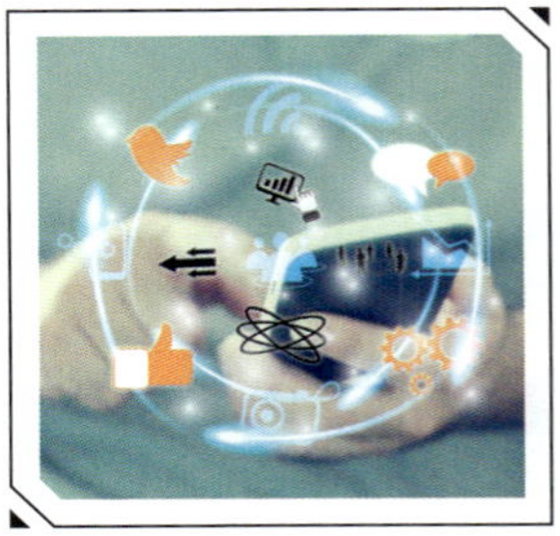

1 Explain what a social network is.

____

____

2 Interview your classmates and fill out the chart below.

Student	Does he / she have a social network?	Networks he / she uses	Profiles he / she follows

3 Demonstrate what characteristics make good professional profiles. Write them in your notebook.

4 Select the characteristics from Activity 3 and adapt them to a travel profile.

5 Collaborate with your classmates to create a travel profile on a social network of your choice. Write on a separate sheet of paper.

6 Vote on the best three profiles in class.

7 How can social media be a tool for learning?

Video

Traveling Together

Before You Watch

1 **What do you remember from the video in the #Discover section? Complete with Emma or Luis.**

1. ____________ finishes a video call.
2. ____________'s grandma lives in Natureville.
3. ____________ doesn't like educational trips.
4. ____________ doesn't know about ecotourism.
5. ____________ has two brothers.
6. ____________ wants to go to Natureville.
7. ____________ doesn't need a passport.
8. ____________ wants to run a bike race.

While You Watch

2 **Watch the video again and check your answers to Activity 1.** 07

3 **Summarize the video in your own words.**

____

____

____

____

____

____

____

____

____

____

After You Watch

4 **You are going to create a video. Talk about interesting features of your city. Complete the chart with information about the topics.**

Topics	Information
Places to visit	
Interesting activities	
Typical food and drinks	
Transportation	

5 **In groups, make your video and share it with your classmates.**

1. Write the script. Remember to use the information in the chart in Activity 4.
2. Practice saying the lines. Use pictures. You can also use slides.
3. Make the video and share it.

6 **Work in groups. Give feedback to your classmates about their video. Use the chart below.**

Language	
Information	
Visual aids	

Learn to Learn

Lip Dab Challenge

1 **Select** ways to practice new English sounds.

1. ☐ listening to music
2. ☐ singing
3. ☐ reading
4. ☐ talking to people
5. ☐ looking at phonetic symbols
6. ☐ repeating
7. ☐ other: ______________

2 Do you **compare** the mouth and tongue movements in the different sounds of the English language?

3 Look at the images. Can you **explain** which sounds they are?

/θ/	/i/

Thing	Beach
Think	Meet

4 **Adapt** the pronunciation practices into a lip dab challenge.

5 **Organize** a lip dab challenge. List the songs you think are the best for the challenge and justify your choices.

6 **Decide** on the songs for your lip dab challenge. Then have fun!

7 How can lip dab help you with your English pronunciation?

Video

A Trip to the Museum

Before You Watch

1 **What do you remember from the video in the #Discover section? Put the statements in order.**

- ☐ Emma describes a work of art.
- ☐ Emma talks about the collection at the museum.
- ☐ They enter the museum.
- ☐ Luis says what form of entertainment he likes.
- ☐ They discuss the guided tour.

While You Watch

2 **Watch the video again and check your answers to Activity 1.** ▷ 08

3 **Summarize the video in your own words.**

____

____

____

After You Watch

4 **You are going to create a video about entertainment in your city. Complete the chart.**

Topics	What can you say about it?
Form of entertainment 1	
Form of entertainment 2	
Form of entertainment 3	
Form of entertainment 4	

5 **In groups, make your video and share it with your classmates.**

1. Write the script. Remember to use the information in the chart in Activity 4.
2. Practice saying the lines. Use pictures. You can also use slides.
3. Make the video and share it.

6 **Work in groups. Give feedback to your classmates about their video. Use the chart below.**

Language	
Information	
Visual aids	

Learn to Learn

Bloom's Taxonomy Revisited

1 **Choose** the correct order of the action verbs below, according to Bloom's taxonomy. Circle the correct option.

1. Remember, Understand, Analyze, Apply, Create, Evaluate
2. Understand, Remember, Apply, Analyze, Create, Evaluate
3. Understand, Remember, Analyze, Apply, Evaluate, Create
4. Remember, Understand, Apply, Analyze, Create, Evaluate

2 How would you **summarize** Bloom's taxonomy?

____

____

3 **Explain** to a classmate how Bloom's Taxonomy can help you as a learner.

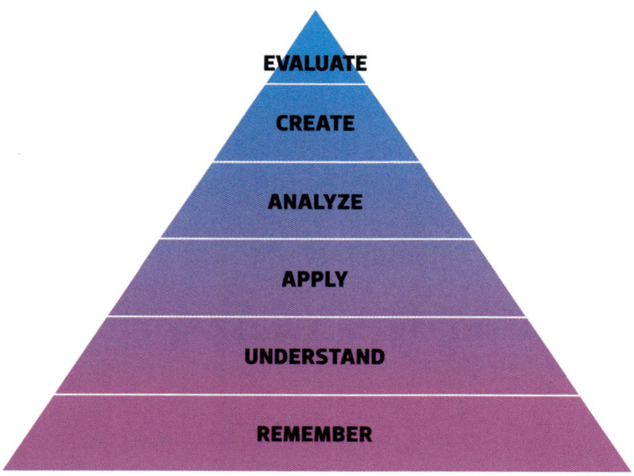

4 **Select** one of the paths to build a study plan.

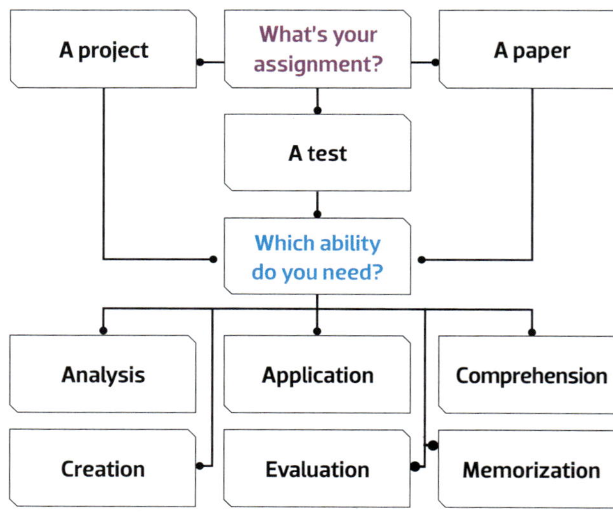

5 **Create** your own study plan based on Bloom's taxonomy.

6 What kind of activity would you use to **assess a student's** understanding of the taxonomy?

7 How can this task help you understand Bloom's taxonomy better?

Video

Wrongdoings

Before You Watch

1 **What do you remember from the video in the #Discover section? Read and mark the sentences T (True) or F (False).**

1. ☐ Emma starts a video call with Luis.
2. ☐ Brandon has done something wrong at school.
3. ☐ Brandon has received no punishment.
4. ☐ Brandon's attitude was correct.
5. ☐ Emma and Luis agree in the end.
6. ☐ They have to stop the video call because Emma's busy.

While You Watch

2 **Watch the video again and check your answers to Activity 1.** ▷ 09

3 **Summarize the video in your own words.**

____

____

____

After You Watch

4 **Write about three regulations at your school and how students might break them. What would be the consequences?**

Topics	Describe the consequences
Example 1	
Example 2	
Example 3	

5 **In groups, make your video and share it with your classmates.**

1. Write the script. Remember to use the information in the table in Activity 4.
2. Practice saying the lines. Use pictures. You can also use slides.
3. Make the video and share it.

6 **Work in groups. Give feedback to your classmates about their video. Use the table below.**

Language	
Information	
Visual aids	

#VIDEO & AUDIO TRACKS

Unit	Tracks	Page	Activities
Video Tracks			
0	01	10	2, 3, and 4
		137	2
1	02	24	2, 3, and 4
		139	2
2	03	38	2, 3, and 4
		141	2
3	04	52	2, 3, and 4
		143	2
4	05	66	2, 3, and 4
		145	2
5	06	80	2, 3, and 4
		147	2
6	07	94	2, 3, and 4
		149	2
7	08	108	2, 3, and 4
		151	2
8	09	122	2, 3, and 4
		153	2
Audio Tracks			
–	01	–	Introduction
0	02	13	5
	03	14	5
	04	15	9
	05	16	3
	06	16	4
	07	16	5
	08	17	7
	09	17	9
1	10	25	1
	11	25	3
	12	25	4
	13	27	5
	14	29	7
	15	30	3
	16	30	4

Unit	Tracks	Page	Activities
Audio Tracks			
1	17	30	5
	18	30	6
	19	31	8
2	20	39	6
	21	41	5
	22	44	3
	23	44	4
	24	44	5
	25	45	7
3	26	53	7
	27	55	5
	28	58	2
	29	58	3
	30	58	4
	31	59	5
	32	59	7
	33	59	8
4	34	69	5
	35	72	2
	36	72	3
	37	72	4
	38	72	5
5	39	81	7
	40	83	5
	41	86	2
	42	86	3
	43	86	4
	44	86	5
	45	87	7
6	46	95	8
	47	97	6
	48	100	2
	49	100	3
	50	100	4
	51	100	5

Unit	Tracks	Page	Activities
Audio Tracks			
6	52	100	6
	53	101	8
7	54	109	7
	55	111	6
	56	114	2
	57	114	3
	58	114	4
	59	115	6
	60	115	7
Audio Tracks			
8	61	123	7
	62	125	5
	63	128	2
	64	128	3
	65	128	4
	66	129	6
	67	129	7

UNIT ZERO

Video Script 01

L: Luis **E:** Emma

L: Let's do our homework.

E: Right. Have you checked the links?

L: Yes. I like the courses, they look amazing.

E: I like the first course best, Game Design. It's longer than the others, but I think it's the most interesting. I love games. Would you like to take the second one? It's short, and it has a lot of activities.

L: Clothes DIY?

E: No, Great Classics Trap.

L: I don't know. There's a lot of extra work and you must read a lot and complete four assignments. I'm tired after school, and I'd like an easier, more practical course. I enjoy doing things.

E: Then, food? OK, I'll try to contact @healthyfoodathome and see what they say.

L: Great. When do we have to submit the report on the online course?

E: At the end of the month. We have four weeks.

L: Oh, OK! Thanks! Talk to you later!

E: Bye!

Audio Scripts

Activity 5 02

Welcome to Great online courses! We have practical courses about different topics. The most popular courses this month are: *Great civilizations*. A course about ancient history and the consequences of great civilizations at present. Learn fun facts about the Egyptians, the Greeks, and the Romans. A four-week course and you'll need about five hours a week to watch videos, read articles, and you may take part in live seminars where you can talk to your teachers (plural) and classmates.

Interested in food and health? So don't miss *Food medicine*. This course will help you eat healthily and enjoy your food. You don't need any cooking experience. You'll learn how to combine food. A two-week course. All you need is two or three hours a week to cook and prepare your healthy food. We offer recipes and cooking basics for a great start.

Activity 5 03

L: Luis **E:** Emma

E: Check out this online course about outdoor sports. Do you like sports, Luis?

L: I like sports, but I don't like practicing them. So, I think this is a great course for me. Lots of videos.

E: Not for me. I really hate sitting in front of a screen for hours!

L: Oh!

Activity 9 04

L: Luis **E:** Emma

E: Would you like some help with your homework, Luis?

L: Yes, please! I can't decide on a course, and I have to finish the assignment.

E: Of course. Would you like to see my paper?

L: I'd like that, yes. It would be great!

E: OK, here it is!

Activities 3 and 4 05 and 06

Hi, I'm Kelly from Mexico City. I wanna be an architect, and I'm taking online classes on design. Really interesting, and I love doing the assignments.

Hello from Bangalore. My name's Rajesh. I'm doing a course on Space Science, and I'm satisfied with it. I have to submit my first assignment next week, and I'm excited. I'm using different resources. I like learning online. You meet students from all over the world and learn about their cultures.

UNIT ONE

Video Script 02

L: Luis **E:** Emma

L: Look at this photo.

E: Who's that? I don't recognize her.

L: Not her... It's LC.

E: The rapper? With a dress on?

L: Come on, Emma! It's not a dress; it's an oversized and very long T-shirt with patches. But he could be wearing a dress without any problem, right?

E: Sure... I was just wondering, you know.

L: Anyway, he does volunteer work for an NGO, and this is part of their new campaign. He's collecting old clothes and accessories to transform them into nice outfits.

E: That's an interesting initiative. Repurposing old clothes is a great way to recycle. Did you know this is called upcycling?

L: I didn't know, but it's a great idea, right?

E: Totally. Whenever we change something old in a way that makes it better or more valuable than it was before, we can call it upcycling. It's very common in the fashion industry.

L: Cool! I didn't know that. Look, there's a link here, let's find out what he needs and how we can help.

E: Yeah, let's see! I have a bunch of clothes I can donate...

Audio Scripts

Activity 8 11

Farah's wearing jeans, brown boots, a sweater, and a red jacket. It's cold, and she's also wearing a scarf and gloves. She's carrying a purse.

Tony's wearing black pants, sneakers, and a T-shirt. He's carrying a backpack, too.

Activity 9 12

Carry a backpack	Wear pants
Wear boots	Carry a purse
Wear flip-flops	Wear a scarf
Wear gloves	Wear a sweater
Wear a jacket	Wear sneakers
Wear jeans	Wear a T-shirt

Activity 5 13

T: Tony F: Farah

T: I'm finding out more about how we can help. People are asking some very interesting questions.

F: OK.

T: For example, "Can we buy studs and patches?" That's a yes, right?

F: Yes, and when you contact them, please invite them to join us.

T: OK. This one's disappointing. "I like the clothes in the photos. Can I buy them?"

F: Yes, disappointing. Forget about it. Is there another one?

T: Yes! Listen to this one. "Can we help you make new clothes? My family sells fabric and we can use it."

T: Wow! We have to consider that. Some people like making clothes, and they can donate their time.

T: True. I'll write to this person... Maggie D.

F: Great.

Activity 7 14

W: Will M: Mel

W: Hi, Mel. These are the questions in the form. One. Who has some free time?

M: Jim, Sandy, and I.

W: And me! Two. Who can help in the organization?

M: Sandy and I. Jim is studying this week.

W: OK. Who can you help?

M: Mmm, I can help some people in my community.

W: Of course. What can you donate?

M: Clothes and accessories.

W: OK. Five. What is interesting about the campaign?

M: It's easy to help.

W: True. The last one, what do you like doing?

M: Oh, lots of things. That's very general!

W: Hahahaha.

Activities 3 and 4 15 and 16

B: Bea V: Vic

B: Vic, do you follow trends in fashion?

V: Sometimes, Bea. I don't like oversized clothes, and they're in fashion now.

B: Do you wear tight clothes?

V: No, just the right size, but it's difficult to find them when they're not in fashion. What about you?

B: I usually wear the colors in fashion for T-shirts. But then I wear jeans and black or blue sneakers. When they're not the latest fashion, they're cheaper.

V: That's a benefit, for sure.

B: Yeah. Jeans and sneakers are never out of fashion. But I've read about the clothes campaign, and I am checking my clothes to see what I can donate.

V: Me too, this is a great campaign.

UNIT TWO

Video Script 03

L: Luis E: Emma

L: Do you have the list, Emma?

E: Yes, I do. We've collected a lot of food for the Global Food Banking Network! We don't need any more milk or pasta. There are 50 cartons of milk and 60 packs of pasta.

L: Great! What about cans of vegetables? How many do we have?

E: Ten, I think. Peas, but we also have peaches.

L: Yummy! I love peaches. My mom makes the best peach cobbler in the world! I'm not a big fan of peas, though.

E: I love pea soup. We eat it every week. My dad is the cook at home, and we try to keep healthy eating habits. We always go together to the farmer's market to get fresh fruits and veggies. I love it!

L: I know! Your dad makes awesome barbecue with grilled vegetables! It's a pity we can't donate fresh food...

E: No, we can't. But we need a lot of rice, beans, and lentils.

L: Exactly! I think we need to ask for a variety of grains that provide a more balanced diet.

E: You're right. So... Do we need any packs of cookies or crackers?

L: Yes! This food donation needs to be as complete as possible! This is going to be great!

E: Right! OK, I need to go now, talk to you later. Bye!

L: Bye!

Audio Scripts

Activity 5 21

T: Tom **S:** Sam

T: Interesting article, right, Sam?

S: Yes, I love ceviche. Soooo tasty. Don't you think, Tom?

T: I don't like savory food, I prefer sweet food.

S: Do you like key lime pie?

T: I do, but I prefer chocolate cake.

S: Me too. And a combination of chocolate and strawberries is the best!

T: Oh, yes! What's your favorite food?

S: Mmmm, pizza and hamburgers.

T: Do you eat that every week?

S: No, not every week.

T: They're not very healthy.

S: No, but they're delicious!

Activities 3 and 4 22 and 23

V: Vic **B:** Bea

V: We have to write a report on eating habits, Bea.

B: OK, Vic. Here's a good habit. You must have a big breakfast. It's the most important meal of the day.

V: Oh, is it? I usually just have a cup of tea and two cookies for breakfast.

B: That's not healthy. You shouldn't eat cookies for breakfast. Nor any junk food like hamburgers and hot dogs. Eat fruits and vegetables.

V: I know, but I love them. But when I have a hamburger for lunch, I have fish or chicken and a salad for dinner.

B: Yes, I think it's a question of balance.

V: Here's another good habit. Drink a lot of water — not soda, tea, or coffee.

B: And here's another one. Don't watch TV while you eat.

V: No?

B: No, it's not healthy. Look at this! There's something about soup. It's OK, but as a snack. Not a very healthy dish.

V: At home we eat chicken soup with lots of vegetables.

B: I think that's different then. It has a lot of vitamins.

V: Anything about ice cream? I love having ice cream on the weekend.

B: Let me check. I need to find some information about that....

UNIT THREE

Video Script 04

L: Luis **E:** Emma

E: For this assignment, we have to make a list of the most sustainable inventions and gadgets. We have to submit it by Friday.

L: I know. We also have to choose a great inventor and write about him.

E: Why him? Some great inventions were created by women! For instance, the life raft, the dishwasher, the car heater, among others. I was watching a video about Grace Hopper the other day. Have you ever heard about her?

L: No! Who is she?

E: In 1944, Grace Hopper and Howard Aiken designed Harvard's Mark I computer, a five-tonne, room-sized machine. She also had the idea for the terms *bug* and *debugging* when she was removing moths from the device, can you believe that? Now, try to think what the world would be like without the invention of programming.

L: Wow! No... I can't imagine life without computer programming!

E: There are so many more like Ada Lovelace, Marie Curie, Melitta Bentz, and... Maria Telkes who invented the 100% solar-powered house!

L: Wow, that's cool! I was browsing online for some ideas, too... So far I have these inventions on my list: desert refrigerator, reusable bags, and electricity generating soccer ball.

E: You have a great list there! Can you share it with me, please?

L: Sure!

E: I want to write about a woman inventor. There are some women shaking up the tech world like María Alexandra Tamayo, a 24-year-old Colombian inventor who was seeking to democratize access to drinking water in her country.

L: Really? That's very interesting! It's so difficult to choose! I think I'll write about Leonardo da Vinci.

E: He was a great inventor, too!

L: Well, let's get started then.

Audio Scripts

Activity 7 26

1. A device is a machine or tool that does a special job.
2. Digital refers to a system that uses numbers, typically zeros and ones, to record and send information electronically.
3. A gadget is small and useful. It can be a machine, a device, or a tool cleverly designed.
4. Invention is a general word. An invention is a useful machine, gadget, etc. Anything that is invented, is not a part of nature.
5. A machine is a piece of equipment with moving parts. It uses power such as electricity to do a job.
6. Technology is the application of scientific knowledge in everyday life to solve problems or invent useful tools.

Activity 5 27

A: What's the best invention for you?

B: Mmm, it's difficult to decide, but I'd say the smartphone.

A: Why?

B: With a smartphone, you don't need a camera, or a computer, or a device to play music.

A: Yes, it's true. It's useful for lists and notes.

B: I don't use it to make lists or take notes, I prefer the old, traditional way. But I use it as a GPS!

A: Do you drive?

B: No, I don't, but it's excellent for public transport and to walk or ride a bike, too. I use it all the time when I ride my bike.

A: Do you use it as a phone?

B: Of course I do! But I don't like talking on the phone, I prefer texting.

A: Yeah! Me too.

Activities 28 and 29

This is George and welcome to Pod-Tech, your podcast about technology. Today I'm going to explain to you about technology for different generations.

Generation X includes people who were born between the mid-60s and mid-80s. They had phones in their homes (yes, landline phones) and that's how they communicated with others. They also had computers in their homes, but they were very limited. There was nothing smart about them.

Generation Y or Millennials are people who were born between 1981 and 1996, and technology is part of their everyday lives. But they weren't born into technology; they had to migrate into the digital world.

Generation Z or Centennials are people who were born between the late 1990s and the early 2010s. They came into this world with a smartphone under their arm. The Internet is part of their identity: it's at home, at school, everywhere.

Those born between 2010 and 2025 are Generation Alpha. They, too, came into the world with a smartphone and a tablet under their noses, but for them artificial intelligence and virtual reality are part of their everyday lives. They have access to all the information they want at the click of a mouse or the tap of a finger. They're constantly connected and use their smartphones just about everywhere. Their social life takes place mainly on social media. So what will the next generation be called?

UNIT FOUR

Video Script 05

L: Luis E: Emma

L: Good luck today – I know you'll be awesome! Let me know how it goes when you can.

E: Who are you wishing good luck to?

L: Oh, my cousin Jaime. He lost his job last week.

E: Oh, no. So, he's going to an interview today?

L: No, he's starting a training program. You see, he used to work at a factory, but a multinational company bought the factory and they automated a lot of processes. Jaime worked in packaging; he selected the products from the shelves to be sent to customers. But now they have a new barcode system: robots scan the barcode and pick up the product.

E: Robots?!

L: Yes, but small ones. More like robotic figures. Look, it's like an arm.

E: Oh, right. I was thinking about that movie with Will Smith, iRobot, you know, the robots that are like people.

L: That's what I thought! Anyway, Jaime's job doesn't exist anymore. But they didn't fire him – the company offered to train him to be a robotics engineer. They need people to fix the automated processes if something goes wrong.

E: Wow! That's so cool!

L: Yep. His training program starts this week. It's a six-week intensive program at the community college, and then he's going to work in the company as a trainee. He's going to spend three days working and two days studying. The program is three years in total. He is really looking forward to it!

E: Cool! And is he going to get paid?

L: Of course! That's the best part — when he's qualified, he'll earn a lot more money!

Activity 5 34

T: Teo C: Chiara

T: Hi, my name is Teo, and this is my idea for a better future with technology. Electric cars without drivers. Electric cars aren't new, but these cars will be intelligent and won't need a driver. That means there will be no accidents because satellites will send information to the car's computer. The computer will also regulate the speed. So many advantages: no pollution, no accidents, and you will save time because you won't have to drive anymore. Thank you!

C: Hello! I'm Chiara, and I'd like to share my idea with you. A special chip that can read your mind. You don't have to write reports or answers or take notes at school; you think and the chip does the rest. Is it dangerous? No, it can only read your mind. It's linked to your DNA or fingerprint, so you can't read other people's thoughts. It can help you save time. Ecological? Not really, but I think it'll make our future easier. Thanks!

Audio Scripts

Activities 2, 3, and 4 35, 36, and 37

1. I think we won't need roads. People will fly with their cars. Airplanes will be necessary for longer distances. Flying

bicycles? No, bikes are good for exercising. I think people love to ride their bikes in a park just to work out. But we will need flying buses. We won't have teletransportation, I don't think that's possible.

2. I think in 20 years people will be living on other planets because there won't be enough room for all of us. Of course, houses will look different because there isn't enough oxygen on other planets. Well, the problem isn't oxygen, but the atmosphere, I think. We'll have robots to do all the housework. That's fascinating! Then I won't have to do the dishes after dinner or clean up my bedroom. I know, I'm too lazy!
3. In the future, technology will make our lives easier. We'll have more free time because computers will do many things. Our health will also be better. But there are limits, of course. People need human contact, and computers won't replace that. I think we'll want to go out with our boyfriend or girlfriend. Humanity has changed a lot, but love still exists, don't you think?

Activity 5 38

1. I want you to turn off the TV.
2. Take out the trash, please.
3. Let's hang out in the park tomorrow.
4. I forgot my log in for this e-mail account.
5. I really liked my work out at the gym today.
6. And the pilot said: "Prepare for take off, and turn off your cellphones."

UNIT FIVE

Video Script 06

L: Luis E: Emma

L: Hi, Emma!

E: Hi, Luis. Everything OK?

L: Yeah, just one thing. Have you seen the documentary for our science class?

E: Which one? The one about endangered animals?

L: Yes! It is so interesting! You should watch it!

E: I am going to watch it tonight. Have you ever seen an endangered animal, Luis?

L: No, I have never seen one. Only in the documentary. The giant panda is one of them. They are so cute!

E: That's sad! Everyone loves pandas. I heard that there are fewer than 2,500 left in China.

L: That's right. The movie shows that they are in danger of extinction because of habitat loss and poaching.

E: So sad! I hope we can save the remaining animals.

L: Me too. They show that China is now taking stricter measures to protect the pandas.

E: That's great! I think we should have stricter laws everywhere to protect endangered species.

L: I think so, too! Well, I have to go now. We should meet after you watch the documentary and do our assignment together. We can help each other.

E: Sure! I'll call you again tomorrow.

L: Bye!

E: Goodbye! Take care!

Audio Scripts

Activity 7 40

When I was in Indonesia, I was invited to see dragons. I thought it was a joke. You find dragons in children's stories. But the Komodo dragon is a real animal. It's a reptile, about ten feet long. It's the largest lizard in the world. It has a long head and short legs. It is a carnivore and eats all kinds of animals, from the biggest to the smallest. Their reproduction is very interesting. There are male and female dragons, and female dragons usually lay about 30 eggs. But the female dragon does not need the male dragon to reproduce. It has male and female chromosomes and can reproduce asexually.

Activities 2, 3, and 4 41, 42, and 43

Today's podcast is about habitats. Habitats are the natural environments in which animals live. Let's learn about them.

1. Grasslands receive more rain than deserts, but less rain than forests. Most plants are grasses. There are grasslands on every continent except Antarctica. One quarter, or 25% of the Earth, is covered by grasslands. Two-legged and four-legged animals live in the grasslands.
2. There are two polar habitats, at the north pole and at the south pole. It's very cold, but the polar habitats have two seasons, summer and winter. In the summer, the sun shines 24 hours a day, and in winter it's completely dark. The weather is ice-cold.
3. Deserts are the driest places on Earth, but there are plants and animals there. In some deserts, it rains in one day, and it doesn't rain again for months or years.
4. Forests don't have extreme temperatures and are full of green-leaved trees. It's warm in the summer and cold in the winter, and sometimes it snows. There's even enough rain in the forest for the plants, so there are many trees there.
5. The rainforest is a warm, humid habitat. The trees grow very tall and form a kind of roof, the canopy. Most animals live in the canopy, which is the upper part of the trees, the part with the leaves.

UNIT SIX

Video Script 07

L: Luis **E:** Emma

L: Ready to go?

E: Just a moment, I have to finish a video call with my grandma. I have to go, Grandma, but I'll see you soon!

L: Is your grandma coming for spring break?

E: No. If we can get everything organized, we'll go see her.

L: Cool! Where does she live?

E: In Natureville, a very small and picturesque village. We'll go by car; it's cheaper than the train or the bus. There are five of us in our family.

L: What can you do there?

E: A lot of fun activities! We usually ride our bikes to the lake and go swimming. Then we hike on the hills and have picnics in the woods. There are also educational trips.

L: Educational field trips? Like at school?

E: Don't worry about it. They're really fun and you learn a lot. If you participate, you'll learn how to survive in different places, how to find your way if you get lost, how to enjoy and protect the environment... very useful skills.

L: It sounds interesting.

E: It is. This village is one of the best places for ecotourism.

L: Ecotourism? I've never heard of that before.

E: You should read about it. And it's also about inclusive tourism. I'll tell you what: Do you want to come with us? You can share a room with my two brothers.

L: I'd love to! I'm going to ask my parents right now!

E: If they say yes, we'll start planning the whole thing.

L: Do I need my passport?

E: No! Natureville is in this country, about seven hours from here.

L: Great!

E: I'm sure they'll be OK with the idea. I'll go get my bike and race you to the club.

L: Deal!

Audio Scripts

Activity 6 47

M: How long have you been a guide?

W: For eight years. But three years ago it all changed. That's when I started the company Inclusive Tourism.

M: What kind of company is it?

W: It's about giving us all the opportunity to travel, learn, and have a good time. You do not have to travel long distances or spend a lot of money.

M: How did you start the company?

W: I was driving my car from my house to the capital when it stopped and would not start. I was in the middle of a small street. No stores, no gas stations, nothing! And no cell phone reception. An old woman riding a horse came to me and offered to help. She took me to her village and offered me food and drink. She and her family showed me the village. It was beautiful. A blue lake, flowers, and plants... a paradise! And all the locals were so helpful and friendly... And it was only two hours away from my house. That changed my mind. I organized a trip with a group of friends, and they loved the experience. So I stopped working for a big travel company and started my own. It's about ecotourism, inclusion, beautiful experiences, and learning.

M: That's fantastic! Now tell me...

Activities 2, 3, and 4 48, 49, and 50

I'll help you, Mom, don't worry. Go to the transportation app icon and open the app. You'll see two fields on top of each other. The first one shows your current location. If you wanna change it, tap on it and enter the address. Then tap on the second field and enter your destination address. If the app shows different options, read them all and tap on the one you want. Next, tap on the mode of transportation. You'll see a number of options. They all indicate how long it may take. Tap on the option you want. You'll see the map with the route. Zoom in on it with your fingers. When you're ready, tap the Start button and you're done.

UNIT SEVEN

Video Script 07

L: Luis **E:** Emma

L: Promise it'll be fun?

E: Of course. You'll see, the exhibition is amazing.

L: I think I'd still rather go to the movies or a concert.

E: Those are fun too, but you'll like this museum.

L: OK, if you say so... Look, there's a tour at 6 o'clock.

E: And here are some rules for getting into the museum... We must not eat or drink inside the museum.

L: Oh! I'll eat this one later.

E: We must not take pictures. That's a pity! I wish I could take some of these beautiful images home with me.

L: We can buy prints at the souvenir shop at the end of our visit. You know that the intense light of camera flashes can hurt paintings and the surface of ancient and delicate objects.

E: That's interesting. We should be careful with the artwork in the museum so that more and more people can visit and see them.

L: Exactly. It's our responsibility as visitors in a museum.

E: We don't have to pay a fee to get in, it's free!

L: That's great! Let's go in then.

E: Wow, I love all these paintings and sculptures. Let's start by the sculptures section.

L: That sculpture there looks strange. Can you tell what it is?

E: It's a wooden statue. It looks like two people dancing, don't you think?

L: True! You know what? I'm kind of enjoying this visit. Thanks for inviting me.

E: I'm glad you liked it, Luis. I just love visiting different museums...

Audio Scripts

Activity 7 54

1. It is the kind of music that produces the most popular hits. They are usually short songs that are easy to sing. They usually have a good rhythm.
2. It could be a book or a movie. There is a lot of suspense. Sometimes there is action.
3. There is information about real life events.
4. It's an animated movie. There are no people, only pictures.

Activity 6 55

A: Thank you very much for this interview, Dan. We know you're very busy.

B: Haha, yes, but I always have time for interviews.

A: You're very young and a big influencer. How do you feel about that?

B: I think it's a big responsibility. A lot of young people watch my videos and read my posts, and I know they follow my ideas.

A: That's right.

B: In general, people think that we don't do anything positive, that we post ridiculous pictures and videos, and that we're not intelligent at all. I want to change people's ideas about influencers. Two months ago, I started a campaign to raise money for a little girl who needed surgery. We raised enough money for the surgery, and the girl is now OK.

A: You say "we raised money", but it was you.

B: No, it was the people. Everybody helped.

A: Oh!

Activities 2 and 3 56 and 57

The Universal Declaration of Human Rights states that we all have the right to freedom of opinion and expression. This means that we are free to have our own opinions. We also have the right to seek and receive information and ideas through any media anywhere in the world.

Media includes traditional media. These include television, radio, movies, newspapers and magazines. But new, digital media have also emerged: social media, e-mail, and the Internet. It is impossible to imagine our world without them. Currently, people get more information from the Internet and social media than from traditional media. As a result of social media, many movements such as Black Lives Matter or the women's rights movement have spread.

Some governments believe that the right to freedom of opinion and expression can be dangerous for them. Therefore, they try to control the media to influence people. This control runs counter to our freedom of expression. Thanks to social media, it is currently more difficult for governments to control this. But we should not forget that there are countries where people do not have the right to express their own opinions. They also cannot get information from different sources. It's our duty as citizens to work together and ensure that right.

UNIT EIGHT

Video Script 09

L: Luis **E:** Emma

L: Hi, Emma

E: Hi, Luis. What's up?

L: Well... Did you get the text message from Brandon?

E: Let me check... yes, here it is. Wow, too long for a text message. What happened?

L: Brandon got into trouble at school, and now he is suspended for three days!

E: You know he was dishonest more than once, and he should be responsible for his actions. I think that's OK.

L: Well, I don't! It's not like he committed a serious crime.

E: Well, he didn't steal anything or do drugs, I agree. But he did act dishonestly, and that's a violation of school policy. So the school has to punish him.

L: I am sorry to disagree, but that's too much.

E: Actually, there were two offenses. First, he cheated because he turned in a report that was not his. Then he lied when the teacher asked him.

L: Well, yeah, but...

E: No buts! The rules are clear and everyone must follow them. If you don't follow the rules, you are punished. That's how it happens in our society, right? If you act dishonestly, steal something for example, you're going to be punished, in jail!

L: I think that's a good point.

E: Thank you! Back to his message, what is he telling us?

L: He wants us to speak up for him.

E: I can speak up for him because he's a good, helpful classmate, but not because of his cheating. I cannot agree with that.

L: You're right. I have to go now. Talk to you later!

E: Bye!

Audio Scripts

Activity 5 62

M: Man **G:** Girl

M: Thank you for this interview, Dana. We know it's difficult.

G: Yes, but I think my experience is important for other young people.

M: What would you like to tell us?

G: When I was 12, three years ago, I started smoking. I didn't like it, but I wanted to make my mother angry.

M: Oh, I see.

G: Then I got into bad company. One day when we were hanging out, we saw a boy carrying a backpack. Jezz, the leader of the group, said, "I bet you can't get that backpack for me." I was too stupid and I jumped onto the poor boy. I went from a backpack to a smartphone and then to a motorcycle. The police arrested me, and I ended up in an institution.

M: That was horrible, I can imagine.

G: Yes, but my family helped me a lot. They visited me every day and showed me that I had their support and they wanted to help me. After eight months, I was released. I got psychological help. Since then I haven't committed any crimes. At school I started a campaign against juvenile delinquency. Everybody is helping. We also visit other schools and juvenile detention centers. I think we can help young offenders.

M: I think thank you isn't enough. You're very brave and a role model for society.

Activities 2 and 3 63 and 64

M: Man **W:** Woman

M: We are pleased to speak with Ms. Marsh, an expert in international crime prevention. Tell us a little about your organization.

W: We have a long history of working with UNDOC, the United Nations Office on Drugs and Crime. One of their interests is violence against women. There are several problems here. Sometimes the police or the judiciary do not know gender approaches, and that's terrible for the victims. Another problem is that society feels it cannot trust law enforcement, which is very sad.

M: I can understand that.

W: Violence against women and girls is our priority. It happens everywhere in the world, in rich and poor countries, in developed and underdeveloped countries. We have to deal with physical violence, but also psychological violence. It can be terrible for the victims. The statistics are alarming. One in three women around the world has experienced violence. In some cultures, certain forms of violence against women are not considered serious crimes, so there are no reports to the police or the justice system. We need to work hard to change that.

M: How can we help?

W: In many ways. One way is to inform society that this is a serious problem. Another way is to give women and girls the protection they need and allow them to report any kind of problem. If they get help, they will be willing to report any form of violence.

M: I see your point.

NOTES

NOTES

PICTURE CREDITS

Front cover (A) F8 Studio/Shutterstock/Shutterstock / (B) Supphachai Salaeman / Shutterstock/Shutterstock / (C) StockStyle/ Shutterstock/Shutterstock / (D) the_rocket_booster / Shutterstock/Shutterstock / (E) Good Job/Shutterstock/Shutterstock / (F) Meliun/Shutterstock/Shutterstock / (G) OrangeVector/ Shutterstock/Shutterstock; Page 09 insta_photos/ Shutterstock/Asset Library; Page 10 Evellean/Shutterstock/Asset Library; Page 11 (A) Dinis Tolipov/123rf/123RF / (B) Alice Nerr/Shutterstock/Asset Library / (C) fizkes/shutterstock/Shutterstock / (D) Lightspring/Shutterstock/Asset Library / (E) SpeedKingz/Shutterstock/Asset Library / (F) Bilal Kocabas/shutterstock/Shutterstock; Page 12 Meryll/Shutterstock/Asset Library / (B) julynx/ 123rf/Asset Library / (C) julynx/ 123rf/Asset Library / (D) julynx/ 123rf/Asset Library; Page 13 Sasha Ka/Shutterstock/Asset Library; Page 15 (A) Wavebreak Media Ltd/123rf/123RF / (B) PHOVOIR / Alamy Stock Photo/Alamy / (C) Vadim Guzhva/123rf/123RF / (D) selinofoto/Shutterstock/Asset Library; Page 16 (A) Erdal Bayhan/Shutterstock/Asset Library / (B) fizkes/Shutterstock/Asset Library / (C) Lbeddoe/shutterstock/Shutterstock / (D) Prostock-studio/Shutterstock/ Asset Library; Page 17 SeventyFour/shutterstock/Shutterstock; Page 20 mindscanner/123rf/123RF; Page 23 iordani/123rf/123RF; Page 24 (A) Fotinia. Shutterstock/Asset Library / (B) TZIDO SUN. Shutterstock/Asset Library / (C) mangostock. Shutterstock/Asset Library; Page 25 (A) tanatat. Shutterstock/Asset Library / (B) theapflueger. Shutterstock/Asset Library / (C) denisfilm/123RF/123RF / (D) Jaromir Chalabala/123RF/123RF / (E) atlasfoto/123RF/123RF / (F) Maria Savenko. Shutterstock/Asset Library / (G) artman1. 123rf.com/Asset Library / (H) Cheuk-king Lo. Pearson Education Asia Ltd/Asset Library / (I) Vitaliy Mateha. 123rf.com/Asset Library / (J) moskalenko1julia/123RF/123RF; Page 26 (A) Iurii Golub/123RF/123RF / (B) Mynameislisenok/shutterstock/ Shutterstock / (C) 101imges. Shutterstock/Asset Library / (D) Claudia Mora. 123rf.com/Asset Library; Page 27 SeventyFour/Shutterstock/Shutterstock; Page 28 (A) Sasha Ka. Shutterstock/Asset Library / (B) RimDream. Shutterstock/Asset Library / (C) Natalia Duryagina/shutterstock/Shutterstock; Page 29 (A) belchonock/123rf.com/Asset Library / (B) Jane0606. Shutterstock/Asset Library; Page 30 (A) Iryna Gyrych/123RF/123RF / (B) Felix Mizioznikov/Shutterstock/ Shutterstock / (C) lithian. 123rf.com/123RF / (D) Jordi Salas/123RF/123RF; Page 31 (A) mangostock/Shutterstock/Asset Library / (B) Sylvie Bouchard/ Shutterstock/Shutterstock; Page 32 (A) Vector Dude. Shutterstock/Asset Library / (B) skvalval. Shutterstock/Asset Library / (C) soloway/123RF/123RF; Page 33 101imges. Shutterstock/Asset Library; Page 37MJTH/shutterstock/Shutterstock; Page 38 (A) Ian Allenden/123rf/Asset Library / (B) Oliver Shirra/123rf/123RF / (C) Moving Moment/Shutterstock/Asset Library / (D) Gts/Shutterstock/Shutterstock / (E) dmitrievmike/123rf/123RF / (F) tandav/123rf/123RF / (G) Celso Pupo/Shutterstock/Asset Library / (H) canjmh/123rf/123RF; Page 39 (A) 546601/Shutterstock/Asset Library / (B) Fotonic. Shutterstock/Asset Library / (C) PixaHub. Shutterstock Asset Library / (D) morgenstjerne/Shutterstock/Asset Library / (E) dionisvera. 123rf.com/Asset Library / (F) Valentina Razumova/Shutterstock/Asset Library / (G) Akane1988/shutterstock/Asset Library / (H) s-ts/Shutterstock/Asset Library / (I) Mathee saengkaew/Shutterstock/Asset Library / (J) akiyoko/Shutterstock/Asset Library; Page 40 (A) 5 second Studio/Shutterstock/Asset Library / (B) Marie C Fields/ Shutterstock/Asset Library / (C) 2164064/Shutterstock/Asset Library / (D) jazz3311/Shutterstock/Asset Library / (E) 324493/Shutterstock/Asset Library / (F) vm2002/Shutterstock/Asset Library / (G) Foodio/Shutterstock/Asset Library / (H) Sergii Koval/123rf/123RF; Page 41(A) Ildi Papp. Shutterstock/Asset Library / (B) helen bird/ Shutterstock/Asset Library / (C) dolga777 / 123RF/Asset Library; Page 43 (A) twinsterphoto/123rf/Asset Library / (B) Iakov Filimonov/123rf/123RF / (C) romk123rf/123rf/123RF; Page 44 (A) Flashon Studio/Shutterstock/Asset Library / (B) Peter Bernik/123rf/Asset Library / (C) maxsheb/123rf/123RF / (D) Shutterstock/Asset Library/Asset Library; Page 45 Jon Barlow/ Pearson Education Ltd/Asset Library; Page 46 Song_about_ summer/Shutterstock; Page 48 (A) photka/Shutterstock/Asset Library / (B) chsherbakova yuliya/Shutterstock/Asset Library; Page 51 pasiphae/123rf/123RF; Page 53 (A) Seregam/Shutterstock/Asset Library / (B) Kitch Bain/Shutterstock/Asset Library / (C) Savanevich Viktar/Shutterstock/Asset Library / (D) Maksym Dykha/Shutterstock/Asset Library; Page 54 (A) evkaz/Shutterstock/Asset Library / (B) Forgem/Shutterstock/Asset Library / (C) FabrikaSimf/Shutterstock/ Asset Library / (D) Valentyn Volkov/Shutterstock/Asset Library / (E) Hal_P/Shutterstock/Asset Library / (F) Agarianna76/Shutterstock/Asset Library / (G) fad82/shutterstock/Shutterstock / (H) dpa picture alliance / Alamy Stock Photo/Alamy / (I) Phil Crean A / Alamy Stock Photo/Alamy; Page 55 Syda Productions/ Shutterstock/Shutterstock; Page 57 (A) Pei Ting Hung/123rf/123RF / (B) Andrii Bicher/123rf/123RF / (C) ammentorp/123rf/123RF / (D) Stock-Asso/ Shutterstock/Asset Library; Page 58 (A) YanLev/Shutterstock/Asset Library / (B) KAY4YK/Shutterstock / (C) Shutterstock/Asset Library / (D) Vlad Teodor/ Shutterstock/Asset Library; Page 60 Myper/Shutterstock/Asset Library; Page 62 (A) ClassyPictures/shutterstock/Shutterstock / (B) trailexplorers/ Shutterstock/Asset Library / (C) comussu/Shutterstock/Asset Library; Page 65 ALPA PROD/shutterstock/Shutterstock; Page 66 Wright Studio/Shutterstock/ Asset Library; Page 67 (A) andreypopov/123rf/123RF / (B) mashiki/123rf/123RF / (C) Jon Barlow. Pearson Education Ltd/Asset Library / (D) DuxX/shutterstock/ Shutterstock / (E) Dmytro Vietrov/123rf/Asset Library / (F) Halfpoint/shutterstock/Shutterstock / (G) Tommaso Altamura/123rf/Asset Library / (H) Marcin Balcerzak/Shutterstock/Asset Library; Page 68 (A) Anton Starikov/Shutterstock/Asset Library / (B) vetasster/Shutterstock/Asset Library / (C) Elena Zajchikova/ Shutterstock/Asset Library / (D) LesPalenik/Shutterstock/Asset Library; Page 69 (A) Scharfsinn/Shutterstock/Asset Library / (B) Billion Photos / Shutterstock/ Asset Library; Page 70 Suwin/Shutterstock/Asset Library; Page 71Toria/Shutterstock/Asset Library; Page 72 (A) merlin74/123rf/123RF / (B) Costazzurra/ Shutterstock/Asset Library / (C) liakoltyrina/123rf/123RF / (D) insta_photos/shutterstock/Shutterstock; Page 73 BigganVi/shutterstock/Shutterstock; Page 74 Lutsina Tatiana/Shutterstock/Asset Library; Page 75 Dmytro Zinkevych/shutterstock/Shutterstock; Page 76 (A) PDQ Digital Media Solutions Ltd./Pearson Education Ltd/Asset Library / (B) phipatbig/Shutterstock/Asset Library / (C) PDQ Digital Media Solutions Ltd. Pearson Education Ltd/Asset Library; Page 79 Michele D'Ottavio / Alamy Stock Photo/Alamy; Page 81 (A) Lee Yiu Tung/Shutterstock/Asset Library / (B) Hristo Vitanov Avramov/Shutterstock/Asset Library / (C) Menno Schaefer/Shutterstock/Asset Library / (D) Bildagentur Zoonar GmbH/Shutterstock/Asset Library/Asset Library / (E) Benny Marty/Shutterstock/ Asset Library / (F) David Carillet/Shutterstock/Asset Library; Page 82 (A) Arm001 / Shutterstock/Asset Library / (B) Brandon Cole Marine Photography / Alamy Stock Photo/Alamy; Page 83 GUDKOV ANDREY/shutterstock/Shutterstock; Page 85 Rawpixel.com/shutterstock/Shutterstock; Page 86 (A) Virrage Images/ Shutterstock/Asset Library / (B) Rudy Lopez Photography/Shutterstock/Asset Library / (C) softlight69/123rf/Asset Library / (D) Wojciech Wandzel/ Shutterstock/Asset Library / (E) Wim Hoek/Shutterstock/Asset Library; Page 87 AndreAnita/Shutterstock/Asset Library; Page 88 Tom Wang/Shutterstock/ Asset Library; Page 90 apinan/123rf/123RF; Page 93 Neirfy/shutterstock/Shutterstock; Page 94 gorillaimages/shutterstock/Shutterstock; Page 95 (A) Sergey Skleznev. 123rf.com/Asset Library / (B) Milkovasa. Shutterstock/Asset Library / (C) nerthuz/123rf/Asset Library / (D) phive. Shutterstock/Asset Library / (E) Kirill Cherezov. 123rf.com/Asset Library / (F) Rob Wilson. Shutterstock/Asset Library / (G) Sergiy Kuzmin. Shutterstock/Asset Library / (H) Rowena/Shutterstock/ Asset Library / (I) fckncg. 123rf.com/Asset Library / (J) N ON NE ON/shutterstock/Shutterstock; Page 96 (A) Shutterstock/Asset Library / (B) ohrim/ shutterstock/Shutterstock / (C) Natalia Deksbakh. 123rf.com/Asset Library / (D) Jes2u.photo. Shutterstock/Asset Library / (E) rcaucino. 123rf.com/Asset Library; Page 97 Hemis / Alamy Stock Photo/Alamy; Page 99 antoniodiaz. Shutterstock/Asset Library; Page 100 (A) blankstock. 123rf.com/Asset Library / (B) PST Vector / Shutterstock/Asset Library / (C) olessya.g. Shutterstock/Asset Library / (D) yupiramos/123rf/123RF; Page 101 haveseen. Shutterstock/Asset Library; Page 102 (A) leungchopan. Shutterstock/Asset Library / (B) Cathy Yeulet. 123rf.com/Asset Library / (C) BalazsSebok/shutterstock/Shutterstock; Page

104 totophotos. Shutterstock/Asset Library; Page 107 guruXOX/shutterstock/Shutterstock; Page 108 godrick/Shutterstock/Asset Library; Page 109 (A) RedlineVector/ Shutterstock/Asset Library; Page 109 (A) RedlineVector/ Shutterstock/Asset Library / (B) Studio Romantic/Shutterstock/Asset Library / (C) LightField Studios/Shutterstock/Asset Library / (D) Stokkete/Shutterstock/Asset Library / (E) VasiliyBudarin/Shutterstock/Asset Library / (F) Images By Kenny/ Shutterstock/Asset Library / (G) Georg Berg / Alamy Stock Photo/Alamy / (H) Andrey N Bannov/Shutterstock/Asset Library / (I) pixelbliss/123rf/Asset Library / (J) fivepointsix/Shutterstock/Asset Library; Page 110 (A) spotmatik/ Shutterstock/Asset Library / (B) MRP / Alamy Stock Photo/Alamy; Page 111 Iren_Geo/ shutterstock/Shutterstock; Page 112 (A) cowardlion/shutterstock/Shutterstock / (B) AKIllustration/Shutterstock/Asset Library; Page 113 (A) Ninell/ Shutterstock/Asset Library / (B) Idea tank/Shutterstock/Asset Library / (C) Ultrashock/Shutterstock/Asset Library / (D) Robyn Mackenzie/Shutterstock/Asset Library / (E) Africa Studio/Shutterstock/Asset Library / (F) Ragne Kabanova/Shutterstock/Asset Library / (G) Repina Valeriya/Shutterstock/Asset Library / (H) fazon/123rf/Asset Library; Page 114 (A) corgarashu/Shutterstock/Asset Library / (B) Iurii Kiliian/Shutterstock/Asset Library / (C) macrovector/123rf/123RF / (D) Ella Grynko/123rf/123RF; Page 115 (A) belchonock/123rf/Asset Library / (B) Tancha/Shutterstock/Asset Library / (C) MongPro/ Shutterstock/Asset Library / (D) MIGUEL G. SAAVEDRA/Shutterstock/Asset Library / (E) paul prescott/Shutterstock/Asset Library; Page 116 Jacob Lund/Shutterstock/Asset Library; Page 118 (A) Sylvana Rega/Shutterstock/Asset Library / (B) SOPA Images Limited / Alamy Stock Photo/Alamy; Page 121 sebra/ 123rf/Asset Library; Page 122 Nenov Brothers Images/Shutterstock/Asset Library; Page 123 (A) LeventeGyori/Shutterstock/Asset Library / (B) Dmytro/123rf/123RF / (C) DmitriMaruta/ Shutterstock/Asset Library / (D) Frenzel/Shutterstock/Asset Library / (E) Formatoriginal/Shutterstock/Asset Library / (F) Rawpixel.com/Shutterstock/Asset Library / (G) justasc/Shutterstock/Asset Library / (H) Corepics VOF/Shutterstock/Asset Library; Page 124 (A) chalermphon_tiam/shutterstock/Shutterstock / (B) mundoview/Shutterstock/Asset Library / (C) sakhorn/Shutterstock/Asset Library / (D) Katarzyna Białasiewicz. 123rf.com/Asset Library; Page 125 antoniodiaz/Shutterstock/Asset Library; Page 126 Marek Uliasz. 123rf.com/Asset Library; Page 129 Jörg Carstensen. Pearson Education Ltd/Asset Library; Page 130 fizkes/shutterstock/Shutterstock; Page 132 Rawpixel.com/Shutterstock/Asset Library; Page 136 (A) Hurst Photo/Shutterstock/Asset Library / (B) Ernst Photography/Shutterstock/Asset Library / (C) MaraZe/Shutterstock/Asset Library / (D) Africa Studio / Shutterstock/Asset Library / (E) icemanj/ Shutterstock/Asset Library / (F) Billion Photos/Shutterstock/Asset Library; Page 138 (A) ARIMAG/Shutterstock/Asset Library / (B) Moab Republic/Shutterstock/ Asset Library / (C) Yiu Tung Lee/123rf/Asset Library / (D) Ailisa/Shutterstock/Asset Library; Page 140 Rawpixel.com / Shutterstock/Asset Library; Page 142 (A) Artyom Terechovitch/123rf/123RF / (B) Jarlath McDermott / Alamy Stock Photo/Alamy; Page 144 Ociacia/Shutterstock/Asset Library; Page 146 Justin Black/ Shutterstock/Asset Library; Page 147 San Hoyano/shutterstock/Shutterstock; Page 148 nopporn/Shutterstock/Asset Library; Page 150 (A) Amornchai Saengraksawong/123rf/123RF / (B) bearsky23/123rf/123RF / (C) bearsky23/123rf/123RF; Page 152 Rawpixel.com/Shutterstock/Asset Library

MÔNICA FIÃES **BICALHO**

HASHTAG ENGLISH 3
PRE-INTERMEDIATE

LANGUAGE BOOSTER

Pearson

Catalogue Publication Data

Hashtag English 3 Pre-intermediate Language Booster
Authors: Mônica Fiães Bicalho
Pearson Educación de México, S.A. de C.V., 2023
ISBN: 978-607-32-5684-1
Area: Schools
Format: 20,5 × 24,7 cm   Page count: 120

Product Vice President: Marianne Lewis ■ **ELT Director:** Marjorie Robles ■ **Product Managers:** Anita Heald, Priscila Marconi ■ **Product Developers:** Renata S. C. Victor, Carolina Andrade ■ **Editor:** Elaine Mendonça ■ **Art and Design Coordinator:** Anderson Ferreira ■ **Art and Design Editors:** Andréia A. Santa Rosa, Patricia Santos, Luiz Rubio ■ **Layout:** Casa de Ideias ■ **Illustrators:** MRS Editorial ■ **Cover & Interior Design:** Apis Design ■ **Cover Photo:** Shutterstock ■ **Digital Development Supervisor:** Isabel Silva ■ **Digital Content and Development Editors:** Rafaela de Mendonça, Fernanda Patucci, Lara Tasso, Mirella Armentano ■ **Digital Content Authors:** 2014 Solucões Editoriais, Ohana Editorial, Bella Szyszkowska ■ **Audiovisual Coordinator:** Lucas Domingues ■ **Audiovisual Editor:** Lucas Motta ■ **R&P Coordinator:** Maiti Salla ■ **R&P team:** Maricy Queiroz, Cristiane Gameiro ■ **Content Support:** 2014 Soluções Editoriais (Editors: Carla Maurício Coelho da Silva Vianna, Joyce Rocha Gomes, Marcos Carvalho Mendonça, Rebeca Pasqua de Andrade. Assistants: Cristine Zanela Monte, Elani Souza Gomes, Juliana Aga, Pedro Zanela) ■ **Proofreading:** 2014 Soluções Editoriais, Silva Serviços de Educação ■ **Picture Credits:** Pearson Asset Library, Shutterstock, 123RF, Alamy Stock Photo

Contact: soporte@pearson.com

First published, 2023

ISBN PRINT BOOK: 978-607-32-5684-1

Impreso en México. *Printed in Mexico.*

1 2 3 4 5 6 7 8 9 0 - 25 24 23 22

Avenida Antonio Dovalí Jaime #70
Torre B, Piso 6, Colonia Zedec Ed. Plaza Santa Fe
Delegación Álvaro Obregón, México, Ciudad de México, C. P. 01210

www.PearsonELT.com

Pearson

Pearson Hispanoamérica
Argentina ■ Belice ■ Bolivia ■ Chile ■ Colombia ■ Costa Rica ■ Cuba ■ República Dominicana ■ Ecuador ■ El Salvador ■ Guatemala ■ Honduras ■ México ■ Nicaragua ■ Panamá ■ Paraguay ■ Perú ■ Uruguay ■ Venezuela

LANGUAGE BOOSTER INDEX

The **LANGUAGE BOOSTER** is a separate book for you to review and practice the content of your Student's Book and engage in additional lessons in class and at home. The Language Booster is partially printed and partially worked on in the e-Language Booster, which consists of interactive consolidation activities. Each of the nine units in the print Language Booster follows the same structure as the Student's Book (Discover, Clarify, Understand, Develop, and Challenge). It also includes a page to reinforce the content covered in class (Assess). The additional pages at the end of the print Language Booster offer further practice. These are:

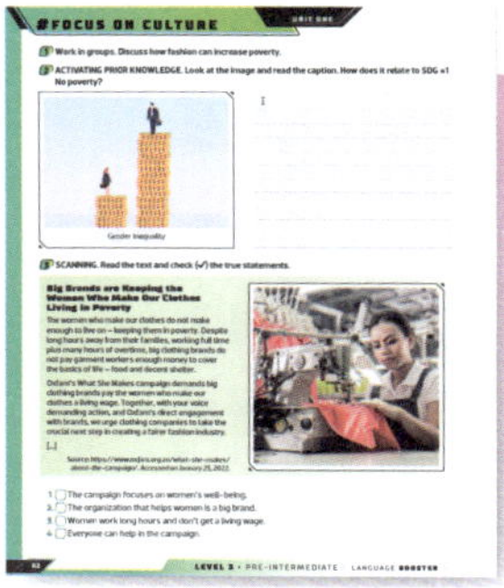

FOCUS ON CULTURE

This double-page section includes an authentic text, comprehension tasks, and a writing task.

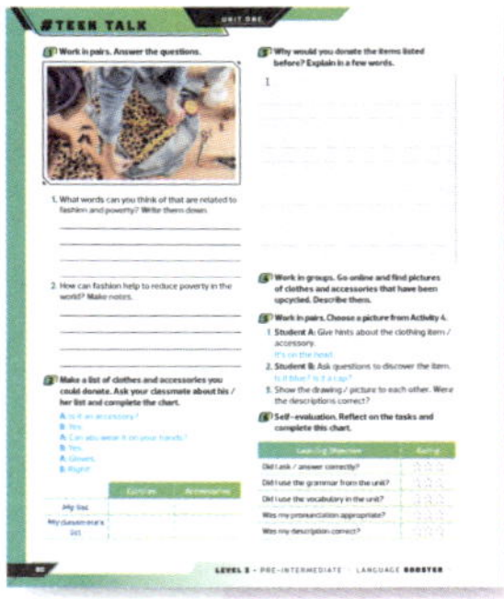

TEEN TALK

This single-page section contains communicative activities to practice the grammar and vocabulary of the unit. These activities include role-plays, information gap activities, interviews, and discussions.

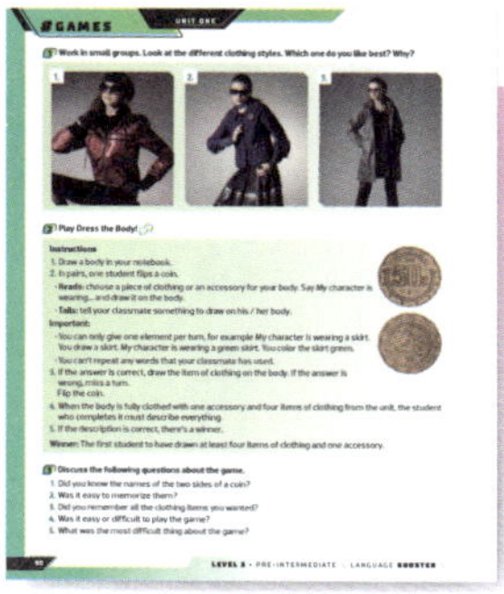

GAMES

The game pages contain nine games, one for each unit. These games review content in a fun way.

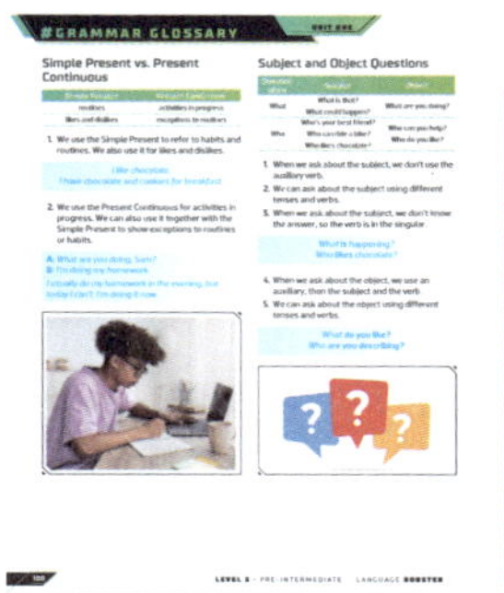

GRAMMAR GLOSSARY

The Grammar Glossary pages are designed for quick grammar reference and review.

The Language Booster also contains the audio tracks and the audio scripts from all the units.

Vocabulary

Adjectives with *-ed / -ing*

1 **Read the conversation and circle the correct option.**

Anne: Hi, Samuel! So, did you finally take that online course on how to fly a drone?

Samuel: Hi, Anne! I did, and I loved it! The course was [1] **amazing / amazed**. I was [2] **surprising / surprised** to see that a drone's not difficult to handle.

Anne: Good! You know, the course I was taking on photography was a little [3] **disappointing / disappointed**.

Samuel: Why is that?

Anne: The lessons were very [4] **confusing / confused**, and it made me feel [5] **exhausting / exhausted**. So I just gave up.

Samuel: You can certainly find a better one. There are many other options.

Anne: Yeah, you're right...

2 **Answer the questions about the text.**

1. How did Samuel feel about his online course?

____

2. How did Anne feel about her online course?

____

3 **Complete the sentences with your own ideas. Use adjectives ending in *-ed* or *-ing*.**

1. I watched a great soccer game last night. I felt really ______________________.
2. I can't believe she forgot my birthday. This is so ______________________.
3. My friend was ______________________ when she found out that I was going to quit my photography course.
4. I think data analysis is probably a / an ______________________ course.
5. My sister and I want to take some cooking classes with that chef. He is a / an ______________________ professional!

#CLARIFY

UNIT ZERO

Reading

1 **Listen to Danny and write down the kind of course he is looking for.** 02

____

2 **SCANNING. Read the text below. Can kids also take this course?**

____

Course...

Course Description

This online course will help young art students to be more confident.
Students will learn the basics of drawing.
They will also experiment with different areas of fine art.

Who is the course for?
Students who are 14–16 years old

All our online short courses include:

- Live online lessons.
- Live chats with students from around the world.

Course dates

April 4 to April 17	2:00 p.m. to 4:30 p.m.
May 2 to May 15	2:00 p.m. to 4:30 p.m.

Cost
$250.00

3 **SKIMMING. Read the article again and write T (True) or F (False).**

1. ☐ This is a course for those who want to learn how to draw.
2. ☐ This course has recorded lessons.
3. ☐ Students under fourteen can't attend the course.
4. ☐ The course is free of charge.
5. ☐ The course is offered on two different dates.

4 **Match the course to the description.**

☐ culinary
☐ photography
☐ drawing

1. Get to know the different kinds, find the right perspective, and try out the various photographic genres, such as portrait, art, documentary, and fashion.
2. Designed for aspiring painters, graphic designers, illustrators, and artists of all types, our series will teach you the foundation of art and design of all kinds.
3. Students begin by learning about some of the essential skills as well as the kitchen tools and how to use them in order to get the best results.

5 **If you had to choose one of the courses above, which one would you choose? Why?**

____
____
____
____
____
____
____

6 **Record your answer to Activity 5 in a voice message and send it to a classmate.**

Grammar

Comparatives and Superlatives
Hate, Like, Love + -ing Forms
Would like for Offers and Requests

1 Read the dialogue and write (C1) for Course 1 or (C2) for Course 2.

Jen: Tom, I want to take a photography course. Any recommendations?

Tom: Hmm... Here, look at this website. It shows two different courses. Course 1 is cheaper than Course 2, but I think Course 2 is more complete and interesting than Course 1.

Jen: I see... Look, Course 2 takes place in a city 100 miles from here, but Course 1 is in our city, so Course 2 is much further than Course 1.

Tom: Yes, but Course 2 offers a bigger space than Course 1 for you to practice and take photos. Some classes are in a very large area. Oh, and Course 1 offers private lessons with teachers, so the help you get is better than in Course 2.

Jen: You're right. Course 1 is better for me than Course 2.

Which course is better when we think about...

1. price? _______
2. quality? _______
3. short distance? _______
4. assistance from teachers? _______

2 Complete the sentences with the comparative form of the adjectives in the parentheses.

1. The course I want to choose is _______________ (expensive) than your course.
2. I try to be a good student, but Peter is a _______________ (good) student than me.
3. Is having photography classes outdoors _______________ (interesting) than in a classroom?
4. This course about soft skills is _______________ (short) than the course my school offers.
5. I find learning English _______________ (easy) than learning French. What about you?

3 Listen to Noah sending an audio message to some friends about summer courses. Then complete the sentences with one or two words. 03

1. Noah loves _______________.
2. Janice likes _______________.
3. Noah hates _______________.
4. Noah likes _______________, so he wants to learn to dance the tango.
5. Noah also likes _______________, and he wants Linda to join him in a course.

4 Write a sentence for each situation. Use would *like*.

1. Ask a classmate to help you with the homework.

____

2. Tell your teacher you would like her to read your paper.

____

Use of English

1 Complete the texts with the words from the box.

doing	I'd like to	learning
like	taking	Would you like

Jake

Hi Jake,
You know we have to choose an online course this semester and [1] ______________ take the one on photography. I really [2] ______________ taking pictures, and I think this could be interesting for my future. [3] ______________ to join me? I know you also love [4] ______________ pictures and it would be fun to study with you.

Hi bro,
Do you know if there are practical lessons? I love [5] ______________ new things, but I like [6] ______________ more practical things.

2 Complete the sentences about yourself.

1. I love ______________________________
______________________________.
2. I don't like ______________________________.
______________________________.
3. I'd like to ______________________________.
______________________________.

3 Record a message to a friend inviting him / her to join you in a course. Use the messages in Activity 1 as a model. Send the message to your classmate.

Writing

1 **Read the text and write T (true) or F (false).**

Hi, Jess!
I have seen the new task about the online course. I don't really like making things so the Vegetable Garden course is not interesting for me. Would you like to choose another one? I love reading and writing, and there is a course on comic book creation. That is much more exciting than gardening.
Best,
Ivan

1. ☐ Jess sent the note.
2. ☐ Ivan would like to take the Vegetable Garden course.
3. ☐ Ivan would like to do a course about comics.
4. ☐ Ivan prefers the gardening course.

Prepare to Write

2 **You are going to write a note to a classmate. Complete the chart with information about it.**

Initial greeting	
Explaining the situation	
Invitation	
Convincing	
Ending the note	

Write

3 **Write your note. Use the information in Activity 2 and the text in Activity 1 as a model.**

Check and Change

4 **Read the note and check that the sequence of the information is according to Activity 2. Are all the elements included in your note? Check the vocabulary and grammar. Use the information in this unit.**

Publish

5 **Write a clean copy of your note.**

6 **In pairs, write a conversation and role play it.**

Student A: You want to take an online course. Tell your classmate about the course, and invite him / her to join you.
Student B: Say what you don't like doing (in relation to the course), and suggest a different course.
Student A: Accept your classmate's suggestion.

#ASSESS

Vocabulary

1 Complete the sentences with the *-ed* or *-ing* form of the words in the box.

annoy	confuse	excite	impress	interest

1. This map is ____________! I don't know if I should turn right or left.
2. She is so ____________! Her birthday is today!
3. I am ____________ in the Arts course. I love painting!
4. My brother is ____________! He is always fighting with me.
5. The teacher is really ____________ with your test. You got the best grade!

Grammar

2 Read the sentences and circle the correct option.

1. In my opinion, the Design Thinking course is **more easy** / **easier** than the Photography course.
2. Is this class **more difficult** / **difficulter** than the digital content class?
3. I love **learning** / **learn** new things. That's why I take so many courses.

Reading

3 Read about a summer course and complete the sentences with one word.

Business for Teens

Would you like to learn about the business world, and how to think and act like a professional? This summer course is for you.
In 20 lessons, you can learn about being a leader and making your ideas reality. The course is for teenagers who are 13 to 17 years old. Click here to find out more.

1. The course takes place during the ____________.
2. The course has ____________ lessons.
3. During the Business for Teens course, you can learn to be a ____________.

Listening

4 Listen and circle the correct information. 04

1. Nancy and Elliot want to take a **future career course** / **language course**.
2. Elliot would like to take a **French** / **German** course.
3. Nancy prefers the **French** / **German** course.
4. Elliot would like to take the course on **Saturdays** / **Mondays and Wednesdays**.
5. They decide to start the course **at the end of the month** / **next month**.

Writing

5 Imagine that you have the chance to create an online course. Write a short description of the course.

____

____

____

____

____

____

____

____

Speaking

6 Record yourself speaking about the course you designed in Activity 5. Make sure you answer the questions below.

1. What is good about your course?
2. What don't you like very much about the course?
3. Why would you like to take this course?

Vocabulary

Clothes and Accessories

1 **Read the conversation and number the items according to the order they are mentioned.**

Donald: Hey, Alison. Check out my outfit for the party. I want to wear sweatpants and a tank top. What do you think?
Alison: To a party? Really? I know it is a simple party with our friends, but maybe you could wear something nicer.
Donald: Hmm... Like jeans?
Alison: Yes, maybe jeans and a T-shirt.
Donald: And what are you wearing?
Alison: Oh, I'm not dressed for the party yet, but I want to put on a dress and maybe brown boots.
Donald: OK... And I think your idea is good for my outfit, blue jeans and a white T-shirt.
Alison: Cool! See you there.

a.  [ ]

b.  [ ]

c.  [ ]

d.  [ ]

e.  [ ]

f.  [ ]

2 **Read the conversation again and check (✓) the items Donald decides to wear to the party.**

1.  [ ]
2.  [ ]
3.  [ ]
4.  [ ]
5.  [ ]

3 **Write the words from the box in the correct column.**

backpack	boots	flip-flops	gloves	jacket	jeans	pants	purse	scarf	sweater	T-shirt

Clothes	Footwear	Accessories

4 **Complete the paragraph with the correct form of the verbs *carry* and *wear*.**

Diana wants to travel to the mountains. She usually [1]__________ sneakers, but today she is [2]__________ her running shoes. She is also [3]__________ a backpack and her umbrella in case it rains. Because it is very windy there, she is also [4]__________ a warm jacket.

Reading

1 **Listen to the dialogue. What problem does Lara mention?** 05

____

2 **PREDICTING. Look at the website below. What is its purpose? Check the correct option.**

1. ☐ To find other uses for old clothes.
2. ☐ To donate old clothes.
3. ☐ To sell old clothes for a cheaper price.

Do you have...

newusefortheold.net

Do you have clothes that you aren't wearing anymore because they are too old? Are these clothes OK for donation? If they aren't, you can find a new use for them here.

1. Post a picture of your item on our website.
2. Explain what is wrong with it – why you can't donate it and want to find a new use for it.
3. Wait for other users to post ideas.
4. Enjoy!

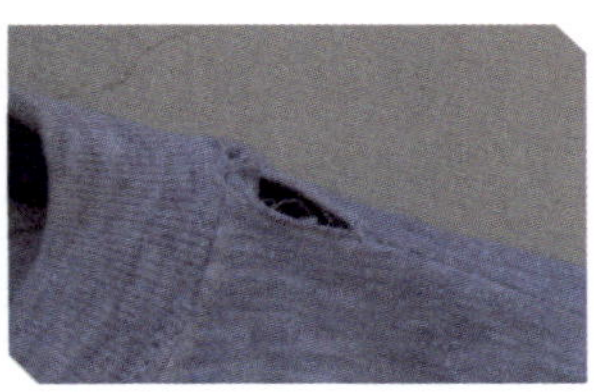

Here's my favorite shirt! There is a hole in it. I love the fabric, the color... What can I do? I want a new use for it.

Seth_Johnson41

Write your suggestions below:

Name: ______________________________

Suggestion: ______________________________

____

____

Name: Irene_LD36

Suggestion: I think you can turn it into a vest. You can remove the sleeves. It's simple! Right now I am wearing a vest that was a shirt in the past.

3 **SCANNING. Read the content of the webpage again and complete the sentences.**

1. This website is for users to give new ideas for old clothes when they are not in good enough condition ______________.
2. After you post the picture of the item, you need to write what is ______________ it.
3. After you finish posting, other users can post ideas of a ______________ for your clothes.
4. Irene_LD36 tells Seth to ______________ and transform his shirt into a vest.

4 **The items below were posted on the website. What new uses can you find for them?**

Jeans with large holes

A shirt with a ripped sleeve

Grammar

Simple Present vs. Present Continuous

1 **Read the dialogue between Lou and Mia and circle the correct options in the following sentences.**

Lou: Hey, Mia! Ready to go to the movies?
Mia: Yes, I am!
Lou: Err... Why are you wearing high heels? You never wear this kind of shoe.
Mia: I know. But I need to practice. It's difficult to walk in these shoes, and I have a wedding party to go to.
Lou: Oh, OK. But you are walking in a really funny way. Let me help you.

1. Mia **is** / **isn't** wearing the shoes she usually wears.
2. Mia's shoes are probably **comfortable** / **uncomfortable**.
3. Mia **is wearing** / **often wears** high heels.
4. Mia **is walking** / **often walks** in a funny way.

2 **Complete the sentences with one of the verbs from the box in the correct form.**

carry not like sing wear work

1. Andy never ____________ these shoes, but today is a special day, so he wants to wear his best shoes.
2. Carrie isn't home now because she ____________ at Janice's clothes store.
3. Oliver ____________ an umbrella. He is the guy in green jeans. Can you see him?
4. I ____________ to wear white clothes, but today is my wedding day, so I guess white is a good choice for my outfit.
5. Can you hear that? Someone ____________, but is completely out of tune.

3 **Answer the questions about yourself.**

1. What do you usually do on a weekday?

____

____

____

2. What are you doing today that is different from your usual routine?

____

____

____

Subject and Object Questions

4 **Listen to an interview with the creator of the website newusefortheold.net. Complete the questions the interviewer asks.** 06

1. ____________ on your website?
2. ____________ people look for your website?
3. ____________ on your website?
4. ____________ you offer the solution?

5 **Imagine you are the creator of a website. Answer the questions in Activity 4, and record yourself.**

#DEVELOP

UNIT ONE

Use of English

1 **Complete the sentences with the words from the box.**

affordable	appropriate	handmade	scruffy	stylish

1. My teenage friends often wear ________________ jeans and ________________ T-shirts.
2. Larry is buying a ________________ product for his wife because it's exclusive and unique.
3. I'm wearing high heels today because of the wedding. They're ________________ for the occasion!
4. I always follow trends in fashion by buying ________________ clothes at fast fashion stores.

2 **Read the sentences in Activity 1 again. Circle the verbs in the Simple Present and underline the verbs in the Present Continuous.**

3 **Complete the sentences with true information about you concerning fashion.**

1. I love to wear ________________.
2. I don't like to wear ________________.
3. I like to buy ________________.
4. I don't like to buy ________________.
5. I often wear ________________.
6. Today I'm wearing ________________.

4 **Complete the questions with a question word and an auxiliary verb when necessary.**

1. ________________ lives in your house with you?
2. ________________ you waiting for? Your mom?
3. ________________ people in your school like to wear uniforms?
4. ________________ you wear to a party?
5. ________________ chooses what you wear, you or your girlfriend?

5 **Answer the questions in Activity 4. Write complete sentences.**

____

____

____

Writing

1 **Read the text and underline the correct statements about it.**

According to research, making one pair of jeans uses 3,785 liters of water. Over 10 % of the world's population now does not have access to safe drinking water. Unfortunately, the driest nations suffer the consequences of the production of jeans. Pakistan, for example, has a big cotton sector, but suffers from a severe water shortage.

1. Producing one pair of jeans requires 378 liters of water.
2. Everybody has full access to clean water in the world.
3. Pakistan has a large cotton industry.
4. Pakistan is suffering from a water crisis.

Prepare to Write

2 **You are going to write a post about how jeans are made. Explain why they are not good for the environment. Research online and make notes.**

Write

3 **Write your post. Use the information in Activity 2 and the text in Activity 1 as a model.**

Check and Change

4 **Read your post and make sure you included all relevant information.**

5 **Edit your post. Check vocabulary and grammar. Use the information in this unit.**

Publish

6 **Write a clean version of your post.**

#ASSESS

Vocabulary

1 Complete the sentences using items of clothing, footwear, or accessories. The initial letters are given.

1. I'm buying f ____________ for Naomi, but I'm not sure they are her size.
2. I'd like to buy these white s ____________ for Nathan to go to school.
3. I bought this new red d ____________ today. How does it look?
4. I'm OK. My black j ____________ is really warm. And the s ____________ is an extra protection.

Grammar

2 Read the sentences and circle the correct option.

1. Thank you for your e-mail. I **apologize / am apologizing** for not replying sooner.
2. I **study / am studying** right now. I can't answer her call.
3. She **knows / is knowing** how you feel about that situation. She has a problem with that company, too.
4. Lauren **wears / is wearing** casual clothes on Fridays. But today she **wears / is wearing** appropriate clothes for a job interview.

Reading

3 Read the text below and complete the questions with *Who* or *What*. Then answer the questions.

Harry: I like to wear clothes that are in style now. I also follow blogs for tips on how to be more fashionable.

Melissa: My style is more punk, I guess. I like to wear chains, studs, and spikes. I hate old vintage clothes.

Leo: I am young, but I like wearing vintage clothes. Some people say that I am old-fashioned, but I think vintage clothes are never out of fashion.

1. ________ likes to wear fashionable clothes?
____
2. ________ thinks vintage clothes are fashionable?
____
3. ________ is Melissa's style?
____
4. ________ is your clothing style?
____

Listening

4 Listen to the conversation and mark the sentences T (True) or F (False). 07

1. ☐ Amós thinks the boots are affordable.
2. ☐ Lauren loves shoes with stains and holes.
3. ☐ For Amós, the boots are fashionable and stylish.
4. ☐ Lauren's style is old-fashioned.

Writing

5 Imagine you are creating your own collection for a fast fashion store. Write a short description of your collection. Describe a few items that you would like to be part of that collection.

Speaking

6 Record yourself. Talk about the collection you created in Activity 5.

Vocabulary

Fruit and Vegetables
Food Containers
Adjectives for Describing Food
Collocations – *Drink, Eat, Have*

1 **Read the conversation and answer the questions.**

Andrew: Let me check our list. We need to buy some vegetables, some fruit, two pots of ice cream, and yogurt. OK, let's start with the vegetables.

Abigail: Mom, Dad, can I help you get the vegetables?

Mary: Sure, Abby. We need some peas and an eggplant. You get the can of peas, and I'll get the eggplant.

Andrew: Do we need any lettuce? I don't think there's any lettuce at home.

Mary: Oh, right. Can you get a head of lettuce, please?

Andrew: Sure. Abby, can you do us a favor? We need yogurt. There isn't any at home anymore.

Abigail: OK, Dad. Look! You can buy six pots of yogurt, but you only pay for four. Can I get six pots of yogurt?

Mary: Here is an idea: We can get six pots of yogurt and give three pots to the food bank near our house.

Abigail: I like your idea, Mom. But we need to tell them that the yogurt expires soon.

Andrew: Well said, Abby. All right, we have vegetables and yogurt. Let's get the other items from the list.

1. What is on the family's shopping list?

___

2. What vegetables do they need to buy?

___

3. How much yogurt do they decide to buy?

___

4. What are they going to do with some of the yogurt?

___

___

2 **Write the words from the box in the correct column, according to the container.**

crackers ice cream milk orange juice peaches peas potato chips sugar tea yogurt

can	carton	bag	pot

3 **Think of a menu to follow every day and complete the meals with at least five options each. Use your notebook.**

1. Breakfast
2. Morning snack
3. Lunch
4. Afternoon snack
5. Dinner

4 **Write four sentences about your menu. Include adjectives from the box in your descriptions.**

bitter savory spicy sweet tasty

I have a tasty omelet for breakfast.

___

___

___

___

___

___

Reading

1 **Listen to the conversation. Then complete the sentences.** 08

1. Mia and Emily are looking at an ____________.
2. They talk about three options: ____________, ____________, and ____________.
3. At the end of the conversation, they decide to have ____________.

2 **PREDICTING. Look at the app below. What do you think people use it for? Read and check your predictions.**

____

____

Learn a bit and...

Learn a bit and eat it

★★★★★ 4.0

Learn a bit and eat it is an app where you learn about meals and place orders, too. You can learn about kinds of food from all over the world and find out what places near you offer them. Look at the highlights below.

Tacos Al Pastor

Al pastor (or tacos al pastor) is a traditional Mexican dish inspired by Lebanese immigrants. It is very popular in Mexico and the United States. It is made with seasoned and marinated pork and cooked vertically on a spit. Its cooking method results in crispy juicy tacos.

FIND RESTAURANTS

Fish and Chips

When people think of English food, they remember two dishes: the special English breakfast and fish and chips. Restaurants that offer fish and chips fry a portion of potatoes and a portion of fish. Then they put the portions together and serve. It's not a very healthy choice, but it is a very tasty snack to have sometimes.

FIND RESTAURANTS

3 **SCANNING. Now read the text again and write the name of the dish in each alternative.**

1. This dish is typical of Mexico:
____
2. This dish is not very healthy:
____
3. This is a crispy and juicy dish:
____

4 **Imagine you want to tell a friend about the *Learn a bit and eat it* app. What would you say about the things below?**

1. What you can do with the app:
____
2. How they know what restaurants are near you:
____

5 **The dishes below can also be found on the app. Read the information about them and answer the questions.**

Name	Ropa vieja	Key lime pie
Origin	Cuba	the United States
Main ingredients	meat, vegetables, spices	key lime juice, condensed milk, eggs

1. What typical dishes from your country are similar to these?
2. Which of these dishes would you like to try? Why?

Grammar

Countable and Uncountable Nouns Plural Nouns, Quantifiers, *How many*, *How much* Indirect Questions

1 Read the words and write C for countable or U for uncountable.

1. ☐ water
2. ☐ egg
3. ☐ lime
4. ☐ cream
5. ☐ hamburger
6. ☐ yogurt
7. ☐ milk
8. ☐ chips

2 Complete the sentences with *countable* or *uncountable*.

1. Juice is a / an __________ noun.
2. You can't count __________ nouns, for example, tea.
3. You can count __________ nouns, for example, apple.
4. __________ nouns have a plural form.
5. __________ nouns don't have a plural form.

3 Do the tasks below in your notebook.

1. Choose a dish you would like to cook.
2. List the ingredients you need. Use the exact amounts or *some* when you don't know the exact amount.

4 Listen to a man send an audio message to his wife and complete the sentences. 09

1. The man asks his wife __________ money she has with her.
2. He asks the woman to buy eight __________, some sweetened condensed milk, __________ sugar, __________ crackers, and some __________.
3. They don't need to buy __________ eggs or butter.
4. The man doesn't know __________ eggs he needs to make this pie, but he knows they have four at home.

5 Complete the questions with *how much*, *how many*, *some*, or *any*.

1. Do you know __________ money you need to buy your favorite drink?
2. __________ ingredients do you need to make your favorite dish?
3. Do you have __________ favorite desserts? What are they?
4. I'd love to learn how to make __________ desserts. Can you teach me?

6 Rewrite the questions using the prompts given.

1. What is there in this recipe?
   Do you know __________?
2. What are the ingredients?
   Can you tell me __________?
3. Is the supermarket closed?
   Do you know __________?
4. What time are we having dinner tonight?
   Would you mind telling me __________ __________?

7 Read the questions in Activity 5 again and answer them with your own information. Record yourself.

#DEVELOP

UNIT TWO

Use of English

1 **Read the conversation and put the sentences in the correct order.**

- ☐ Yes, please. I'd like a chicken salad and some orange juice.
- ☐ Oh, I'm sorry. There isn't any ice cream today. We have key lime pie and fruit salad.
- ☐ OK, so maybe some fruit salad. It's healthier, anyway.
- ☐ Here they are. A chicken salad, a glass of orange juice, and a fruit salad.
- ☐ Hello and welcome. Can I take your order?
- ☐ Thank you! It looks delicious!
- ☐ All right, a chicken salad and orange juice. We have a special price for desserts, too. Would you like any?
- ☐ Desserts? Yes, I'd like some strawberry ice cream.

2 **Read the conversation in Activity 1 in the correct order. Then answer the questions.**

1. What does the customer order at first?

____

2. Does the customer want dessert? What does she order at first?

____

3. What are the dessert options?

____

4. What dessert does the customer order in the end?

____

3 **Circle the correct options to complete the sentences.**

1. Lucas cooks **many** / **much** delicious dishes.
2. Please, stop by the supermarket and bring **any** / **some** pasta and **any** / **some** chicken. I'm cooking tonight!
3. **A: How many** / **How much** honey do you need for the pudding?
   B: Not many / **Not much**, just a small pot.
4. Leah doesn't want **any** / **some** cheese in her sandwich.
5. **A:** Do you have **any** / **some** carrots left? I want to make a carrot cake.
   B: Yes, I have **any** / **some** here. Take them!
6. **A: How many** / **How much** peaches are there in the refrigerator?
   B: There are **a lot of** / **any** peaches!

4 **You are in a restaurant. Read the instructions and write a short conversation between you and the server. Use the conversation in Activity 1 as a model.**

1. Order some food you like.
2. The server asks about drinks.
3. Order a drink you like.
4. The server says they don't have that drink. Order something different.
5. The server gives two dessert options.
6. Choose one of the options and thank the server.

____

____

____

____

____

____

Writing

1 Look at the text in Activity 2. What is the genre of the text? Where do you often find this genre of text?

____

Prepare to Write

2 Read the text and complete it with the words from the box.

any	cheap	delicious	drink	many	much

The WoW! Snacks +

The WoW! Snacks

4.0 ★★★★★

Address: 22 High Street, Phoenix – Arizona

Hours: 11:30 a.m. to 10:30 p.m.

User 1 ★★★★★

The restaurant is awesome. The decoration is new, and the food is [1] __________. The service is great, too. You can have a [2] __________ at the bar first, and then go to a table. It's not very [3] __________, but I think the prices are fair. When you go, try their special egg sandwich.

User 2 ★★★★★

I liked it, but not very [4] __________. They have good sandwich options, but they are all similar and they don't have [5] __________ choices for vegans. I really liked the drinks. They have more drink choices than sandwiches. The service is good, but there aren't [6] __________ servers.

3 Read the text again and number the items in the order they appear.

- ☐ Reviews people wrote about the restaurant.
- ☐ How people generally rank the restaurant.
- ☐ The name of the restaurant.
- ☐ Where to find the restaurant.

Write

4 Carry out research on a restaurant in your city that you would like to write a review about. Make notes. In your notebook, write your own review of that restaurant. Use the texts in Activity 2 as models.

Check and Change

5 Read your review and make sure you included:

- ☐ basic information about the restaurant.
- ☐ your ranking of the restaurant (stars).
- ☐ a description of your experience at the restaurant.
- ☐ food adjectives.
- ☐ quantifiers.

6 Edit your message. Make sure all the elements in Activity 5 are included.

Publish

7 Write a clean version of your review.

#ASSESS

Vocabulary

1 Write as many examples as you can remember for each category.

1. Fruits: ______________________________
2. Vegetables: ______________________________
3. Food containers: ______________________________
4. Adjectives for food: ______________________________

Grammar

2 Read the conversation and complete it with the words and phrases from the box.

any	do you know	how many	how much	some

Vicky: Walter, can you check [1]__________ eggs we still have? I need three to cook dinner.
Walter: Let me see... We have two eggs. But don't worry. I need to go to the supermarket. I think we need [2]________ vegetables, too. Right?
Vicky: Yes, please. We don't have [3]________. [4]______________ if they have any lactose-free yogurt in that supermarket?
Walter: I'm not sure, but I can check. [5]______________ yogurt do you need?
Vicky: Just two pots.
Walter: OK, see you later.

Reading

3 Read the conversation between a server and a customer. Then answer the questions in your notebook.

S: Server **C: Customer**
S: Hi, how can I help you?
C: Hi, can I have some ceviche, please?
S: Sure. Would you like something to drink?
C: Yes, a can of soda. Oh, and also a fruit salad, please.
S: OK, some ceviche, a can of soda, and a fruit salad. Would you like the fruit salad to come after you finish the ceviche?
C: Yes, please.
S: All right. I'll be right back.

Later...
S: So how was everything?
C: Just delicious! The ceviche was spicy, and I loved it!
S: I'm happy to hear that.
C: Can I have the check, please?
S: Of course. I'll be right back.

1. What does the customer order to eat at first?
2. What does the customer order to drink?
3. What does the customer order for dessert?

Listening

4 Listen to the audio review. Then complete the sentences. 10

1. The woman is talking about a restaurant in __________.
2. The restaurant serves special __________.
3. The woman's favorite sandwiches are the special __________ sandwich and the four-__________ sandwich.

Writing

5 Write a conversation between you and a server in a restaurant. Use Activity 3 as a model.

Speaking

6 Record yourself. Talk about a restaurant you like and what you usually order there. Then say why you recommend the restaurant.

Vocabulary

Gadgets and Inventions

1 **Match the words to the pictures.**

1.
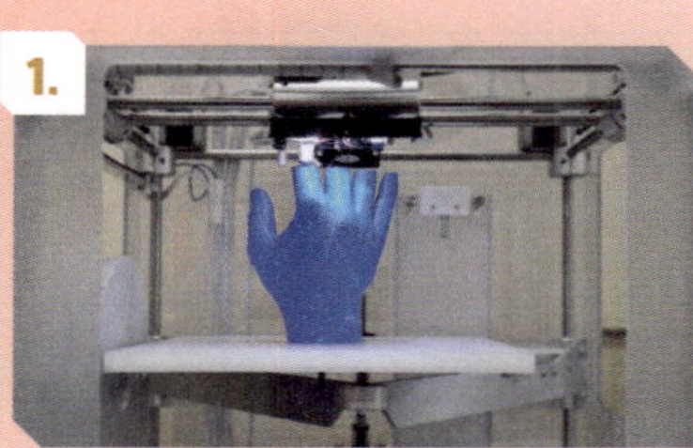

4.

2.

5.

3.

6.

- ☐ bluetooth headset
- ☐ dishwasher
- ☐ 3D printer
- ☐ drone
- ☐ electric car
- ☐ touchscreen smartphone

2 **Complete the table with the words from Activity 1. Some words can be used more than once.**

Machines	Devices / Gadgets

3 **Complete the table in Activity 2 adding one more item to each column.**

4 **Write an example of:**

1. A wireless device: ________________
2. A digital device: ________________
3. A technological machine: ________________

5 **It's your birthday and you can choose three devices or gadgets as a present. List them below.**

____

____

____

Reading

1 **Listen to Emily and Mia and write down the technological machine they are discussing.** 11

____

2 **MAKING AND CONFIRMING PREDICTIONS. Can you think of three other uses of drones in the future? Write them down. Read and check your predictions.**

____

____

3 **SCANNING. Now read the text and compare it to your predictions. Underline the different uses of drones in the text.**

Drones can go to places that humans cannot, and that will be very useful in the future. For example, in agriculture, they can monitor the health of crops and show where more water or fertilizer is needed. Costs can be reduced by focusing on areas that need attention.

Other potential opportunities include rescue missions. Drones will improve the safety of rescue workers.

Drones can also be an effective marketing tool. Drones will be used by real estate companies, resorts, schools, and a variety of other industries to show potential customers the facilities and infrastructure as well as the area.

4 **SKIMMING. Read the article again and mark the sentences T (True) or F (False).**

1. ☐ Drones can go where people can't.
2. ☐ Using drones in agriculture will make it more expensive.
3. ☐ Drones can make some missions less dangerous.

5 **Research into drones, their uses in the present, and their possible uses in the future. Make notes.**

____

____

____

____

____

____

6 **If you had the chance to own a drone, what would you use it for? Write down your answer. Then record it in a voice message and send it to a classmate.**

____

____

____

____

____

Grammar

Past Continuous

Simple Past and Past Continuous

1 **Mia had a school assignment to hand in on Monday. On Saturday she had a very busy morning. Read her diary entry and answer the questions.**

7:00 to 7:30	had breakfast
7:30 to 8:30	researched for the assignment
8:30 to 9:30	rode my bike
9:30 to 11:00	wrote the assignment
11:00 to 11:30	revised the assignment
11:30 to 12:00	talked to Emily
12:00 to 12:30	had lunch

1. What was Mia doing at 7:15?
____
2. What was Mia doing at 8:00?
____
3. What was Mia doing at 9:00?
____
4. What was Mia doing at 10:30?
____
5. What was Mia doing at 11:00?
____
6. What was Mia doing at 11:45?
____
7. What was Mia doing at 12:15?
____

2 **Complete the conversation between Mia and Emily with the correct form of the verb in parentheses.**

Emily: Hi, Mia! What's up?
Mia: Hi, Emily. Well, I was very busy this morning.
Emily: I called you at 9:00, but you didn't answer. What [1] _______ you _______ (do)?
Mia: I [2] _______ (ride) my bike to the park. Pete and Jane [3] _______ (skate) there, and I wanted to say hi.
Emily: I see. I called you because I [4] _______ _______ (test) my invention for the science project, and I needed your help.
Mia: Oh... Go ahead! What do you want to know?

3 **Listen to an interview with a history teacher about an inventor. Complete the questions below.** 12

1. What _______ Maria Telke invent?
2. How _______ Chloe become aware of Maria's work?
3. Why _______ Chloe _______ about solar energy?
4. What happened when she _______ her research?

4 **Listen to the interview one more time and answer the questions in Activity 3.** 13

#UNDERSTAND
UNIT THREE

Use of English

1 **Read the conversation and complete the blanks with the expressions from the box.**

I agree with this	I don't think so	
I see your point	Me neither	Me too

Sam: Leo, I was reading an article that said Generation Z is the most sustainable generation. Isn't it interesting?

Leo: Well, [1] ______________________.
This is the generation that buys a new smartphone every year. I don't think that's an especially sustainable habit.

Sam: [2] ______________________, but the article said that this generation prefers to buy sustainable brands. Hmm...
I [3] ______________________. More people buy brands that don't damage the environment.

Leo: [4] ______________________, but that is not exclusive to this generation. I think the world is changing and people in general are buying more sustainable brands. I am, at least.

Sam: [5] ______________________. I like to know that the brand I am buying understands their responsibility toward the environment.

2 **Rewrite the sentences below replacing the extracts in bold with the expressions in Activity 1.**

1. **I understand what you're saying**, but we can't change phones every year just because there is a new one in the market.
____
2. **I have the same opinion as you.** I don't change phones every year because of price, of course, but also because of sustainability.
____
3. **I don't change phones all the time either.** I always keep the same phone for at least two years.
____
4. **I also do that.** I usually keep my phone for two years or more. You can keep the same phone for five or six years.
____
5. **I don't believe you are right.** After two or three years your phone probably stops working.
____

3 **Read the conversation and circle the correct options.**

Noah: Hi Janice! So good to see you! What [1] **happened / was happening** last night? I [2] **was sending / sent** you three messages, but you [3] **didn't answer / weren't answering** me back.

Janice: Oh! Hi, Noah! I'm really sorry. Last night I was at Anna's, and I [4] **didn't see / wasn't seeing** your messages. We were very busy.

Noah: Wait! Are you friends again? Why were you busy? What [5] **did you do / were you doing** ?

Janice: I [6] **was helping / helped** her with the history assignment.

Noah: Oh... I see... friends again.

Writing

1 **Read the biography of Grace Murray Hopper and answer the questions.**

Who Was Grace Murray?

Grace Murray Hopper was an American mathematician. She was born in New York in 1906. She worked for the U.S. Navy.

In the early 1950s, Hopper developed the Universal Automatic Computer (UNIVAC I), the first commercial electronic computer. While working on this invention, Hopper had the idea of automatic programming and decided to explore new ways to use computers for programming. She had a major impact on the development of computers. For example, Hopper was the first person to use the word *bug* to talk about a computer error. This happened when a moth got into the circuitry of the automatic calculating machine she was developing.

Hopper continued to work for the U.S. Navy for a very long time. She died in 1992, but people still remember her as an important person in the development of computers.

1. What did Hopper develop in the 1950s?

   ____

   ____

2. When did Hopper have the idea of automatic programming?

   ____

   ____

3. What is the history of the term *bug* when referring to a computer failure?

   ____

   ____

4. What was Hopper's professional life like after the invention?

   ____

Prepare to Write

2 **You are going to write about the inventor of an item of your choice. Read the questions and go online to find the answers. Write them in your notebook.**

1. What is the item and who invented it?
2. When and where was the person born?
3. What can you say about the use of this invention?
4. What can you say about the history of this invention?

Write

3 **Use the information you researched in Activity 2 to write a biography of the inventor.**

Check and Change

4 **Read your biography and make sure you included:**

- ☐ The name of the inventor
- ☐ When and where the person was born
- ☐ The use and importance of the invention
- ☐ How it was invented

5 **Edit your biography. Make sure all the elements in Activity 4 are included.**

Publish

6 **Write a clean version of your biography.**

#ASSESS

Vocabulary

1 **Write five inventions that you think are relevant today.**

____

____

Grammar

2 **Read and complete the story with the verbs in parentheses in the Simple Past or the Past Continuous.**

Two days ago, I [1] ______________ (walk) in the street when I [2] ________ (see) this amazing smartphone. Because my smartphone was old and [3] ______________ (not work) very well anymore, I [4] __________ (decide) it was time to buy a new one, so I [5] __________ (buy) it. It was hundreds of dollars, but I [6] ______________ (not care). And I'm glad I have this new phone now.

Reading

3 **Read about the history of an invention that didn't become very popular. Then mark the sentences T (True) or F (False).**

The Wink glasses are an invention of the Japanese company Masunaga. When they were working on it more than ten years ago, they thought people would love this invention. Basically, these are glasses for people who spend a lot of time in front of the computer and have to remember to blink. The glasses have a sensor that detects when you don't blink for six seconds or more. Then the glasses create a kind of "fog" and force you to blink to see again. The glasses weren't very popular at first, but after some time Masunaga improved the technology and more and more people bought the glasses.

1. ☐ The glasses were a success from the beginning.
2. ☐ The glasses force people to blink.
3. ☐ The sensor is programmed to detect when the person doesn't blink for more than five minutes.
4. ☐ When you don't blink for some time, you can't see because of the fog.
5. ☐ After some time, more people started buying the glasses.

Listening

4 **Listen to Matthew and Rebecca talking about a gadget they bought, but that they don't use anymore. Then write M for Matthew and R for Rebecca.** 14

1. ☐ Bought the gadget because of a new activity.
2. ☐ Got a recommendation to buy the gadget.
3. ☐ Was impressed with the gadget at the store.
4. ☐ Realized you can go online to use the functions of the gadget.
5. ☐ Got the news from a family member that the gadget wasn't necessary.

Writing

5 **Think of a gadget you had in the past, but you don't have anymore and write about it. You should include:**

1. The name of the gadget, the brand (if you know), and its use.
2. How it made your life better.
3. If you think there is a new one that does better things.

____

____

____

Speaking

6 **Record yourself. Talk about a gadget or machine you bought, but stopped using after some time.**

Vocabulary

Phrasal Verbs

1 **Read the conversation and answer the questions.**

Agnes: Can I borrow your tablet? The battery of my cell phone is dead.
Mandy: Sure, just don't forget to put it away later. What do you need my tablet for?
Agnes: I want to search a new recipe for tomorrow's dinner.
Mandy: Why? You can order a pizza, can't you? It's just dinner with your friends, a group of people socializing.
Agnes: I know... But I always order pizza or hamburgers. This time I want to do something different. Jane took care of my dog on my last trip, so I want to thank her with a nice dinner.
Mandy: All right. I give up trying to talk you into ordering a pizza. Let's see... Hmm... Maybe you can cook lasagna.
Agnes: I don't know how to make lasagna...
Mandy: That's what the Internet is for! Let's see if we can learn how to make lasagna.
Agnes: OK, we have ten minutes. Then I want to work out at the gym. My workout starts in 15 minutes.
Mandy: Maybe in the future, people can invent a machine that can make any recipe they want...
Agnes: Haha! I'd love that!

1. In which sentence does Mandy ask Agnes to return a gadget to its correct place?
____
2. Which sentence shows that Agnes doesn't want to try to do something anymore?
____
3. In which sentence does Agnes show her intention to exercise?
____

2 **Rewrite the sentences from the conversation in Activity 1 and replace the words in bold with a phrasal verb from the box in the correct form. There is one extra option.**

find out **hang out** **look after** **look for** **set up**

1. I want to **search** a new recipe to make for tomorrow's dinner.
____
2. It's just dinner with your friends, a group of people **socializing**.
____
____
3. Jane **took care of** my dog on my last trip.
____
4. Let's see if we can **learn** how to make lasagna.
____

3 **Write about the following subjects.**

1. A device you wanted to learn to use, but you gave up (or almost gave up). Why did you want to give up?
____
2. Someone you hang out with who uses a device too much. How do you feel about it?
____
3. What features will people look for in a smartphone or virtual assistant in the future?
____

Reading

1 **Listen to Aiden's voice message. What are his plans for Saturday?** 15

____

____

2 **SKIMMING. Read the conversation and answer: Are Aiden and Xavier going to hang out on Sunday? Why (not)?**

____

____

Chat

Today

Hey, Aiden. What's up?

Hi! Sorry, I can't hang out on Sunday. I'm meeting Sheila. It's our second anniversary.

Wow! Congratulations!

I want to ask you something. Do you have any suggestions about phones that I can pass on to my grandpa? He wants my help, but I don't know what to tell him.

Hmm... I'm thinking of a great phone, but the price is a little high... You don't want something too expensive, do you?

Nope.

OK. I'll send you a link. Let's see what you think of this one.

3 **SCANNING. Read the conversation again and answer the questions.**

1. How does Aiden respond to Xavier saying that he is meeting Sheila on Sunday?

____

2. What does Aiden want Xavier's help with?

____

3. Why isn't Xavier's first idea of a phone good for Aiden?

____

4. What is Xavier going to do next in the conversation?

____

4 **Answer the questions below.**

1. What specifications are you going to look for the next time you buy a smartphone?

____

2. What innovative technology do you expect for phones in the future? Will they do anything that they don't do nowadays?

____

5 **Your friend wants your help with a technological gadget. Read his / her requests and replies, and write your part of the conversation. Try to be helpful!**

Your friend: Hey, there! Sorry for texting you so late, but I need your help.

You: 1 ____________________________________

Your friend: My sister asked for my help to set up her new smartwatch, but I can't do it.

You: 2 ____________________________________

Your friend: It's by a brand called WeWatch. I think it's a new brand.

You: 3 ____________________________________

Your friend: Hmm... That's a good idea. I'll try that. Thanks!

You: 4 ____________________________________

Grammar

Talking About the Future
Too and *Enough*

1 **Read the conversation between Aidan and his grandpa. Then mark the sentences T (True) or F (False).**

A: Aidan G: Grandpa SC: Store clerk

A: So Grandpa, these are the three best models there are: SP 2.5, SPX, and SPX Plus.

G: I like SPX Plus, but I don't have enough money to buy it. It's too expensive.

A: I know. How about the SP 2.5 model?

G: This phone isn't good enough. I want a smartphone with a great camera and the latest operating system, but this model has an older operating system.

A: Exactly, so let's rule out the SPX Plus. The quality is great, but it's too much money for a phone. SPX isn't too expensive. Do you think it's good?

G: Yes, I like it. But I came here to buy a great smartphone, not just a good one, so I want the best smartphone I can get.

A: OK, Grandpa. Listen, I don't want to pressure you, but we don't have much time. The store closes in 10 minutes and we can't be late for Aunt Alice's dinner. We're meeting everyone at the restaurant at 7:00, remember?

G: I know... Excuse me, can I see the specs of the SPX model again, please?

SC: Yes, of course.

A: I'm sure we're going to be late for dinner... Let me call Aunt Alice.

1. ☐ Grandpa needs more money to buy the SPX Plus smartphone model.
2. ☐ The word *too* in Grandpa's sentence "It's too expensive" means the same as *also*.
3. ☐ When you use *too* + adjective, you want to say that the quality is more than wanted.
4. ☐ When Grandpa says that "The phone is not good enough", he means that the phone is really bad.
5. ☐ You can use *enough* + noun or adjective + *enough*, as in "enough money" and "good enough".

2 **Read the message that Aidan sent Xavier telling him what happened at the store. Circle the correct options.**

So Xavier, let me update you on my grandpa's new phone. At the store, he couldn't choose a smartphone: one model was [1] **expensive enough / too expensive**, the other model wasn't [2] **good enough / enough good**... To be honest, I think that sometimes we have [3] **too many / enough** options and that makes our choice more difficult. I also think that Grandpa wants [4] **much enough / too much** from a smartphone, I don't know... Or maybe I am [5] **impatient enough / too impatient** sometimes. One thing I can say is: when you go shopping for a new smartphone, you always need to take [6] **enough money / too much money** with you.

3 **Listen to Joyce read an e-mail she got from Max. Then complete the sentences with the correct form of the verbs in parentheses.** 16

1. Max ________________ (be) in Cartagena on Tuesday.
2. Max's flight ________________ (arrive) at 4:20 p.m.
3. Max ________________ (meet) John for dinner that same evening.
4. Max thinks that John ________________ (be) at work before 7 p.m.
5. Joyce ________________ (pick) Max up at the airport until six o'clock.

Use of English

1 **PREDICTING. Look at the list of electronic devices Vivian wants to buy. Which items do you think she will buy?**

____

____

____

____

2 **LISTENING FOR GIST. Listen to Vivian talk to her friend Zack about her list and check your answers in Activity 1.** 17

3 **LISTENING FOR DETAILS. Listen again and answer the questions.** 18

1. What does Zack think of Vivian's list?

____

2. What does Vivian say about the SPX Plus smartphone model?

____

3. What does Zack think of the SPX Plus smartphone model?

____

4. What's Zack's opinion about Vivian's gift for Grandma?

____

5. What does Vivian say about her grandma?

____

4 **Think about the next smartphone that will be on the market. What features do you think it will / won't have? Write a list of at least four predictions. Use *will* or *won't*.**

____

____

____

____

Writing

1 **Read Daniel's e-mail to his friend from Canada and circle the best options to complete it. Is this e-mail formal or informal?**

CANCEL SEND

TO looper.daniel@mail.com / adams.patty@mail.com

SUBJECT Hello from Lima

[2] **Dear Patty, / Dear Ms. Patricia Adams,**

How are you? I'm at the school lab now and it reminded me of you.

[3] **I want to invite you / The purpose of this e-mail is to invite you** to my online birthday party. I know it sounds odd, haha. I've decided to throw an online party this year, as too many friends can't come to a physical party!

Can you join us? I'm going to send a small gift to everyone's house and then we can have fun together, even if we are far from each other.

[4] **Please confirm your presence by replying to this e-mail. / Please let me know.**

[5] **Kind regards, / Love,**
Dan

2 **Look at the format of the e-mail in Activity 1. Then number the parts of the e-mail in order.**

- ☐ Subject of the e-mail
- ☐ Recipient's address
- ☐ Main body
- ☐ Closing / Signature
- ☐ Greeting
- ☐ Body introduction

Prepare to Write

3 **Imagine that you are Patty, Daniel's friend. How would you reply to his e-mail? Make a list with your ideas.**

Write

4 **In your notebook, write an e-mail replying to Daniel. Use the information in Activity 3 and the text in Activity 1.**

Check and Change

5 **Read your e-mail and make sure you included:**

- ☐ a greeting.
- ☐ an introduction.
- ☐ a main body.
- ☐ a closing / signature.

6 **Edit your menu. Make sure all the elements in Activity 5 are included.**

Publish

7 **Write a clean version of your e-mail.**

#ASSESS

Vocabulary

1 Match the sentence halves.

1. When I finish working, I always put...
2. I went online to find...
3. I can't hang...
4. Drake needs you to help him set...
5. Miriam is looking...

- ( ) out where I could get that e-book from.
- ( ) up his new smartphone.
- ( ) out with you on Saturday. I have a course on digital health.
- ( ) my laptop away so my desk is neat.
- ( ) for a job, but it is hard to find one.

Grammar

2 Read the example sentences and complete the chart with the correct headings.

Arrangement **Plan / Intention** **Prediction** **Schedule**

1 ________	3 ________
This charger isn't powerful enough to charge the computer. It **will** shut down soon.	Laura **is traveling** with Mark on Saturday. They**'re flying** to Barcelona on vacation.
2 ________	4 ________
When I finish this semester, **I'm going to** take a course on innovation in digital marketing.	My bus **arrives** at 7:30 p.m. Please, don't be too late. Last time I had to wait for two hours.

Reading

3 Read an extract from an article and check (✓) the correct statements about it.

How Will Technology Shape the Future?

Technology is constantly evolving, and we feel like we never know enough about gadgets, tools, and platforms. People say that's not going to change, so we need to keep up with technological innovation. And one technological innovation that is part of our present and will be part of our future is Artificial Intelligence (AI). Today we use virtual assistants all the time, and in the future these assistants will also do much more for us. Another interesting aspect is that more people will have access to tech devices in the future. Some companies and institutions will invest in education and give children from different regions access to the digital world.

1. ( ) Sometimes we feel like we know too much about technology.
2. ( ) The extract says that it is important to continue learning about innovations in technology.
3. ( ) Artificial Intelligence is more present now than it is going to be in the future.
4. ( ) Virtual assistants are going to be part of our lives even more in the future.

Listening

4 Listen to some people answer the question *What is the next gadget you are going to buy?* and match the speakers to the statements. 19

Which speaker...

- ( ) is going to get a new gadget he / she wants from someone in his / her family?
- ( ) wants a gadget for reading?
- ( ) thinks people buy too many gadgets?
- ( ) says that he / she can't buy the new gadget until he / she has the money for it?
- ( ) says that a friend wants him / her to get a gadget to check the time more often?

Writing

5 Write an e-mail to a classmate about a new gadget you think will come out in 50 years' time.

Speaking

6 What is the next gadget you are going to buy? Talk about it.

Vocabulary

Endangered Animals
Compound Adjectives

1 **Read the conversation and check (✓) the picture that corresponds to the animal they are talking about.**

Ricky: Hey Mandy, what are you watching?
Mandy: A documentary about endangered species. It's really interesting! I want to play a part of it for you again. Check it out!
Ricky: Wow! There are so few of them around these days! That's sad. My dream is to travel to China one day and visit a sanctuary for them in Sichuan.
Mandy: I did not know there was a sanctuary for them! The documentary explains that one of the main reasons they are endangered is deforestation of the areas where bamboo grows. You know they eat bamboo, right?
Ricky: Right. I am aware of that as well.
Mandy: But tell me about the protected area.
Ricky: Oh... the place is huge, and it's also a sanctuary for other endangered species like the snow leopard and the clouded leopard.
Mandy: I would love to go there one day.
Ricky: I am not sure, but I think they have some volunteer programs.
Mandy: Let's find out!

1.  ☐
2.  ☐
3.  ☐

2 **Rewrite the sentences replacing the underlined expressions with a compound adjective. Then write the name of an animal that fits the description.**

1. You know they <u>eat bamboo</u>, right?
___
___
2. They <u>have black fur</u> and they are dangerous.
___
___
3. They <u>have big ears</u> and live in Africa.
___
___
4. They live in swamps and rivers and they <u>eat men</u>.
___
___
5. They <u>have large ears</u> and they are the second largest land animal.
___
___

3 **Choose an animal you like and write a short description of it. Don't forget to use at least one compound adjective in its description.**

___
___
___

#CLARIFY

UNIT FIVE

Reading

1 **Listen to an extract from a podcast and complete the sentences.** 20

1. Dr. Lasso is a specialist in ______________________ ______________________.

2. The ______________________ can live more than ______________________ years.

2 **SCANNING. Read the ad and answer: How many giant tortoises are there on the Galapagos Islands nowadays?**

____

Adopt a Giant...

www.galapagosstortoisess.com

Adopt a Giant Tortoise

Giant tortoises are not imaginary animals, as some think. Galapagos tortoises are native to the Galapagos Islands off the coast of Ecuador in South America. These herbivorous reptiles have an estimated average life expectancy of 150 to 200 years, but there are only about 15,000 of them left because they were hunted for food in the eighteenth and nineteenth centuries. By donating $50, you will help save these extraordinary animals, and you will receive a donation kit with a giant tortoise toy, a giant tortoise poster, and a donation receipt. Donate now with just one click!

3 **MONITORING COMPREHENSION. Read the ad again and mark the sentences T (True) or F (False).**

1. ☐ Giant tortoises are imaginary animals.
2. ☐ Giant tortoises can live to be two hundred years old.
3. ☐ Giant tortoises are an endangered species.
4. ☐ Donating money makes you the owner of a giant tortoise.
5. ☐ You can donate through the website.

4 **Rewrite the false sentences. Make them correct.**

____

____

____

____

____

____

5 **Imagine you have the opportunity to develop a website for helping protect endangered species. Research about an endangered species and write a brief description. Then create a campaign for the website. Use the model in Activity 2.**

____

____

____

____

____

____

____

____

____

____

Grammar

Present Perfect with *ever*, *never*, *for*, and *since*

1 **Read the conversation between Mora and Luis. Then check the table according to the animals they have heard about.**

Mora: Hi, Luis, can you help me with the project on unusual animals?
Luis: Sure! Which ones do you want to research?
Mora: I do not know... Have you ever heard of the Komodo dragon?
Luis: No, never. Even the name dragon is pretty unusual... LOL.
Mora: Yes, they seem very interesting. I think I can talk about them.
Luis: Why don't you do some research on the axolotl?
Mora: What is that? I have never heard of it!
Luis: It's a special kind of salamander.
Mora: I see... That's an idea. And what about the red-lipped batfish?
Luis: They are incredible! They look like they always have lipstick on.
Mora: I guess it will be the red-lipped batfish. Have you decided on your unusual animal?
Luis: Yeah, I am going to talk about the Tasmanian devil.
Mora: Creepy... I have never heard of it...

	Mora	Luis
Komodo dragon		
Axolotl		
Red-lipped batfish		
Tasmanian Devil		

2 **Use the table in Activity 1 to write sentences about Mora and Luis. Follow the example.**

Mora **has heard** about the Komodo dragon, but Luis **has never heard** about it.

1. ______________________________
2. ______________________________
3. ______________________________

3 **Luis was invited to record a podcast about his experiences in the city where he lives. Listen to the podcast, and then write sentences using the cues below.** 21

1. (live) Luis has lived in the city for five years.
2. (make good friends) ______________________________
3. (try) ______________________________
4. (organize) ______________________________
5. (be to the city museum) ______________________________

4 **You were invited to talk about your best experiences in the city where you live. Make notes about it.**

#UNDERSTAND

UNIT FIVE

#DEVELOP

UNIT FIVE

Use of English

1 Read the text. What is it? Check (✓) the correct option.

1. ☐ A text message.
2. ☐ An article.
3. ☐ An advertisement.

Best Friends

I am sorry, I do not think we should go on Sunday. The reason is that it will be too crowded then. In my view, Saturdays are usually quieter in the park. What do you guys think? Would Saturday be OK for you?

2 Read the text in Activity 1 again and identify the phrases used to justify an opinion. Write them down.

____

____

3 Match the parts that make sense together.

1. It's an endangered species.
2. Don't feed the wild animals.
3. In my opinion,
4. We should not go in the summer.

☐ There's evidence that this can make them sick.
☐ in the future, we will only see wild animals in protected areas.
☐ Because of that, it is placed in a special area.
☐ The reason is that there are more tourists in the parks.

4 Read the sentences below. Choose one and write a short paragraph explaining why you agree or disagree with it. Use phrases to justify your opinion and the Present Perfect with *ever*, *never*, *for*, or *since*.

1. I believe governments have to build sanctuaries for endangered species.
2. In my opinion, zoos can be a good place for some animals that are suffering.

____

____

____

____

____

____

____

____

____

Writing

1 **Read the sentences and check (✓) the ones that are true for articles.**

1. ☐ They have a headline.
2. ☐ They have the recipient's address.
3. ☐ They can include pictures.
4. ☐ They can be divided into paragraphs.
5. ☐ They do not need to have an introduction.

2 **Read the article and underline the sentence that introduces the topic and the conclusion.**

Saving the... +

www.galapagosstortoisess.com

Saving the Rainforest

Rainforests around the world are crying out for help, and we cannot turn our backs on the problem. Recently we have heard news about forest fires in Brazil, and it is important to understand that saving the Amazon rainforest is of global importance.

The fact that we need the rainforests to produce oxygen and clean the atmosphere so we can breathe is probably not news to anyone. Rainforests are a treasure to be preserved; they provide us with many valuable medicinal plants and can be a source of cure for some diseases.

Rainforests must be preserved, or we will lose our global fight against climate change.

Prepare to Write

3 **You are going to write an article about an animal habitat. Choose a habitat, do some research, and then make notes in your notebook. Try to answer the questions below.**

1. What is the habitat called?
2. What animals live there?
3. Are there any endangered species?

Write

4 **Write your article. Use the information in Activity 3 and the article in Activity 2 as a model.**

____

____

____

____

____

____

____

____

____

____

____

____

Check and Change

5 **Read your article and make sure you included:**

☐ a headline.
☐ a picture illustrating the topic.
☐ an introduction to the topic.
☐ a conclusion.

6 **Edit your article. Make sure all the elements in Activity 5 are included.**

Publish

7 **Write a clean version of your article.**

#ASSESS

Vocabulary

1 Label the pictures with the words from the box.

large-eared	long-tailed
red-eyed	yellow-feathered

1. 
____

2. 
____

3. 
____

4. 
____

Grammar

2 Look at the box with the life experiences Josh has had in his life (✓) and the ones he has never had (✗). Then write about them. Use the Present Perfect.

1. Go to a snowy forest.	✗
2. See a real giant panda.	✗
3. Research animal habitats.	✓
4. Visit an animal sanctuary.	✓

1. ______________
2. ______________
3. ______________
4. ______________

Reading

3 Read an extract from an article and answer: How long has the author had a passion for dolphins?

____

Teaching About the Environment Around us

The animal world has always fascinated me. I am thirty-three years old now, and when I was five years old, my grandmother gave me a book about dolphins, explaining how social and highly intelligent they are. To this day, I have a passion for dolphins and wildlife. At the time, I told my parents I wanted to be a veterinarian and take care of all the injured animals in the wild. I did not become a veterinarian, but as a science teacher, I have the opportunity to pass on my love of nature.

Listening

4 Listen to the conversation and check (✓) the correct sentences. 22

1. ☐ Josh is interested in the documentary about Antarctica.
2. ☐ Mia has never watched the documentary about grasslands.
3. ☐ Mia has seen the documentary about deserts.
4. ☐ Mia is not sure Josh will like the documentary about deserts.

Writing

5 Write a short article about an aspect of nature that fascinates you in your notebook. You can write about an unusual animal, a special habitat, etc. Make sure you choose a headline for your article and use an introductory sentence.

Speaking

6 Imagine you have the chance to choose a habitat to visit. Talk about it and audio record yourself. Use the questions below to guide you.

1. What habitat are you going to visit?
2. Why have you chosen it?
3. How far will you have to travel to visit it?
4. What animals do you expect to see there?

Vocabulary

Means of Transportation
Travel-related Words

1 **Read the conversation. What are the tickets the friends need to buy for the school trip?**

____

Scarlett: So Ethan, all set for the school trip next weekend?

Ethan: Nope, I haven't prepared anything, yet. Well, I have the train ticket, but that's about it.

Gianna: Just the train ticket? What about the bus ticket? We're taking the bus from the city to the campground.

Ethan: Yeah, I know, but I can buy the ticket there, right?

Logan: Uh... I don't think you can, Ethan. Besides, there are no more bus tickets.

Ethan: Man... What am I supposed to do now?

Logan: Can you go by car instead? You can ask someone to give you a ride, or maybe you can take a ride share service there.

Stella: No, you can't. Only the bus is allowed in that area. They want to make sure there aren't too many vehicles in the area.

Scarlett: I know there are bikes for rent there. Some people prefer to bike to the campground, so that's another alternative.

Ethan: Hmm... That sounds like a good idea. I'll see if I can get a ticket for the bus. If not, I'll just rent a bike.

2 **Read the conversation in Activity 1 again and complete the sentences with means of transportation.**

1. Ethan has a ____________ ticket for his school trip.
2. Ethan forgot to get a ____________ ticket.
3. Logan tells Ethan to go by ____________, but that is not an option.
4. The only option left is to rent a ____________.

3 **Look at the means of transportation below. Write a short paragraph explaining on which occasions people use them.**

People often travel to other cities by car.

____

____

____

____

____

____

____

____

Reading

1 **Listen to Caleb and Grace talk about Caleb's trip. Where is he going? How is he going to get there?** 23

____

2 **MAKING PREDICTIONS. Look at the title of the guide Grace sent to Caleb in Activity 3. What kind of information do you expect to find in it?**

____

____

3 **SKIMMING. Read and check your answers to Activity 2. Then answer: What are the best ways to get around the main areas of Singapore?**

____

A Guide to... +

A Guide to Getting Around Singapore

If you are a tourist in Singapore, transportation is not a problem. The island, which is considered a city, nation, and state, has many options to offer. Below are some of them.

MRT subway network: This is a very clean, efficient, and inexpensive means of transportation in the city center. The modern trains run every five minutes, and there are stations everywhere. You can buy a one-way ticket for about $1.20 to $2.40 or purchase a card with cheaper tickets.

Buses: Buses are cheaper than the MRT for short distances, and they are very convenient. If you want to go on a longer journey, the fare is higher, but it is still a good option if you want to get around without hassle.

Cabs: Yes, you can use ride-sharing apps in Singapore, but there are also cab services. You can call the cab companies and book a cab, but it's not a very cheap way to get around. Another disadvantage is that when it rains heavily, everyone wants a cab, and it is difficult to find one.

Car rentals: For some people this is an option, but public transportation in Singapore is so efficient that you do not really need to rent a car. Plus, it's expensive to get a driving permit, buy and park a car, and the tolls are not cheap either.

Bikes: Because of the heavy traffic, Singapore is not a good place to get around by bike. You will have to use the bus lanes.

On foot: Downtown Singapore is a place to explore on foot. It is not very big and there is a lot to see, so this is a good idea for visiting museums and Chinatown.

4 **SCANNING. Read the guide again and answer the questions with the corresponding means of transportation.**

Which means of transportation...

1. is cheap and ideal for short trips? ______________________________
2. is expensive and hard to find if the weather isn't good? ______________________________
3. is efficient, cheap, and very modern? ______________________________
4. can be dangerous if you don't use it in the right place? ______________________________

5 **Audio record your answers to the following questions.**

1. If you want to get around your city, what means of transportation are there?
2. What means of transportation do you recommend for someone visiting your city? Why?

Grammar

Zero Conditional
Prepositions with Means of Transportation
First Conditional

1 **Read the conversation between Caleb and Grace about the Singapore transportation guide. Then circle the correct options to complete the sentences.**

Grace: ... Now about your trip to Singapore, how can I help you?
Caleb: Well, I read the guidebook you sent me. It's great! I learned that you pay less for the ticket if you buy a card for the MRT network.
Grace: Yes, their subway system is really efficient. If you want to travel for a day, you need a day pass. There are also two-day and three-day passes.
Caleb: We want to go to Kranji Village, but it's in the countryside.
Grace: Oh, then you need a special bus. If you take the bus and stop at Kranji Marshes station, you can walk there in seven minutes. It's very close by. You can...

1. The guide says that tickets are cheaper if you **will buy** / **buy** a card for public transportation.
2. If your trip **is** / **will be** for two days, you should get the two-day pass.
3. Caleb needs to take a **regular bus** / **special bus** to go to the countryside.

2 **Read the conversation and the sentences in Activity 1 again. Then complete the rules for using the conditionals with the words from the box.**

expected	future	general	Simple Present

Zero Conditional

The tickets are cheaper if you buy a card.

1. We use the Zero Conditional to talk about ____________ results for certain actions.
2. The *if* clause is in the ____________ and the result / consequence clause is in the Simple Present, too.

First Conditional

Caleb will text Grace if he needs help.

1. We use the First Conditional to describe the ____________ future result for a specific situation.
2. The *if* clause is in the Simple Present and the result / consequence clause is in the ____________.

3 **Match the sentence halves. Then write Z for Zero Conditional or F for First Conditional.**

1. If you travel to other places, ...
2. If we don't get a train ticket, ...
3. If I get any extra money, ...

☐ we will rent a car. ______
☐ I spend it on traveling. ______
☐ you get to experience other cultures. ______

4 **Caleb posted a message on social media asking people for ideas for his trip. Think of ways you can complete the conditional sentences below.**

1. If you go to Clarke Quay shopping mall, ...
2. You will find a lot of places to go shopping if...
3. If you want to take pictures of outstanding landscapes, ...
4. If you like art, science, and history, ...

#DEVELOP

UNIT SIX

Use of English

1 LISTENING FOR GIST. Listen to the conversation between Michael and Marianne. What are the two subjects they talk about during the journey? 24

____

2 LISTENING FOR DETAILS. Listen again and answer the questions.

1. Why is Michael late?

____

2. Does Marianne think Michael will get to the Natural History Museum late?

____

3. What will Michael do if he forgets something during his presentation?

____

4. What does Michael do to remain calm if he has a presentation?

____

5. What does Marianne do if she has to take a passenger to another city?

____

3 Michael decides to ask Marianne to take him somewhere else after his presentation. Read the conversation and number the sentences accordingly.

Michael: Marianne, [1] ___________? My presentation is over at five, and I have to be at the mall by 6:15. If you don't have another client to drive, will you give me a ride?

Marianne: Yes, I'm free. [2] ___________?

Michael: Maybe 5:20?

Marianne: Hmm... [3] ___________? I have a daily fare at five, and it takes me about 30 minutes to get her home and back to the museum.

Michael: Sure! That's great! [4] ___________ outside the main entrance. [5] ___________?

Marianne: Perfect! 5:30 p.m., main entrance.

☐ Does that work for you
☐ Is 5:30 OK for you
☐ I'll be waiting for you
☐ are you available later this afternoon
☐ What time can we meet

4 Use the prompts to write Zero and First Conditional sentences.

1. you / arrive earlier / if / take the subway (First)

____

2. if / you / freeze water / turn into / ice (Zero)

____

3. if / people / sleep well / improve / quality of life (Zero)

____

4. we / not walk to school / if / rain / tomorrow (First)

____

Writing

1 **Look at the news below and check the correct statements about them.**

Christmas Travel Chaos: Airlines Cancel More Than 4,500 Flights

Five airlines accounted for the bulk of the cancelations: China Eastern canceled 474 flights, Air China 188, United canceled 177 flights, Air India 160, and Delta canceled 150 flights.

Delta said it had "exhausted all options and resources before canceling approximately 90 flights for Friday." The airline blamed the impact of the Omicron variant and weather conditions for the cancelations.

Travel Jobs Growing Across America

22 % - From 2010-2018, the number of jobs in the travel industry increased by 22 percent, compared to 17 percent in the rest of the private sector.

51 % - Number of states (including D.C.) where travel employment increased (2010-2017).

1. ☐ They are both fact-based and objective texts.
2. ☐ Their headings are long and uninteresting.
3. ☐ The first text is a fragment of a blog article.
4. ☐ The second text contains statistics (factual information).
5. ☐ Both texts show someone's opinion about something.

Prepare to Write

2 **You are going to write an introduction to a factual article. Think about what you would like to include in your text and make notes. Here are some suggestions.**

1. Inclusion in public transportation in my city / country.
2. Busiest holidays for air transportation in my country.
3. Environmentally friendly transportation in my city / country.

____

____

Write

3 **Write an introduction to a factual article. Use the information in Activity 2 and the texts in Activity 1 as models.**

____

____

____

____

____

____

____

____

Check and Change

4 **Read your article and make sure you included:**

- ☐ an interesting headline.
- ☐ a catchy introduction to the topic.
- ☐ travel-related words or expressions.

5 **Edit your text. Make sure all the elements in Activity 4 are included.**

Publish

6 **Write a clean version of your text.**

Vocabulary

1 Complete the sentences with the correct means of transportation.

1. Her car ride sharing app didn't work, so she decided to call a ____________.
2. Let's drive to Lima. If we go by ____________, we can enjoy the landscapes on the way.
3. There aren't many cycle lanes in my city, but I still like to go to school by ____________.

Grammar

2 Complete the sentences with the correct form of the verbs from the box. Use the conditional type in parentheses.

get	not leave	not pollute

1. If we go by car, we ____________ there more quickly. (First Conditional)
2. If you walk around downtown instead of driving, you ____________ the environment. (Zero Conditional)
3. We will miss our train if we ____________ soon. (First Conditional)

Reading

3 Read the text and mark the sentences T (True) or F (False).

What Are the Most Common Means of Transportation?

The website 10 Most Today has created a list of the ten most common means of transportation. Let us take a look at some of them!

The train is the most common means of transportation in the world. It is a unique means of transportation because it can cover long distances and takes much less time than, for example, ships. It is also quite cheap.

The second most common means of transportation is the car. Cars are most often used for personal use, and you can find them everywhere you travel.

In third place we have buses and trucks. Yes, trucks! Trucks can transport goods and buses can transport people, so they are both means of transportation. They are slower than trains, but still a very common option around the world.

1. ☐ Trains are the most common means of transportation, but they are often very expensive.
2. ☐ Cars are the most common means of transportation for private use.

Listening

4 Listen to two people talk about their preferences in transportation. Then complete the sentences with Jill or Lucca. 25

1. ____________ likes to cycle to places.
2. ____________ doesn't like to cycle to places.
3. ____________ likes to take the bus.
4. ____________ really likes walking.

Writing

5 Research three facts related to transportation in your country and write them in your notebook.

Speaking

6 Think of a very popular tourist destination in your country. Then use the questions below to talk about it. Record yourself.

1. How can people get there if they live in the same town?
2. How can people get there from other parts of the country?
3. How can the means of transportation there be better?

Vocabulary

Music, Movies, and TV

1 **Read the itinerary for a one-day trip to Wilmington, North Carolina, and complete the sentences with the words from the box. There are four extra words.**

One-day Itinerary...

One-day Itinerary in Wilmington, North Carolina (United States)

Here you will find some suggestions of what to see and do in Wilmington. Do not miss it!

Cape Fear Museum of History and Science:

Come and see "One Half of the People: Advancing Equality for Women", an exhibit about the history of women in the United States.

Click here for tickets.

River Walk along the Cape Fear River Waterfront

Walk along the pedestrian path, take lots of pictures of the beautiful view, and just relax.

Click here for tickets.

Tour of Old Wilmington

This is a guided tour where you'll learn more about the city's centuries of history. Do not forget your camera or smartphone to capture all the old buildings that tell the history of Wilmington.

Click here for tickets.

Thalian Hall Center for the Performing Arts

This theater offers all kinds of shows and artistic performances to showcase the diversity of people and interests in the area.

Click here for tickets.

At the end of the day, you can stay at one of our recommended hotels (click here to learn more) and relax with a comedy, a cartoon, or a romantic movie.

art installations **concert** **exhibition** **guided tour** **movies** **pictures** **sculpture** **theater**

1. The website recommends taking ________________ during the river walk and the Old Wilmington tour.
2. There is a / an ________________ about gender equality in North America's history in Cape Fear Museum of History and Science.
3. Thalian Hall is a ________________ where there are a lot of artistic shows.
4. Tour of Old Wilmington is a good choice if you want to go on a ________________.

2 **Imagine that you are traveling to another town or city for one day. What will you do there? Look at the list of activities and record a voice message to send a friend telling him / her about it.**

1. Go to a rock concert / a pop concert / a museum / a theater / an art gallery.
2. Go on a guided tour / a river walk.
3. See art installations / sculptures / paintings / exhibitions / a horror movie / a documentary about the city / a play.
4. Take pictures.

Reading

1 **Listen to a conversation between Amanda and Phil. What are they talking about? What are they going to do next?** 26

____

____

____

2 **SKIMMING. Read the text and answer: How does Zendaya's answer help fight stereotypes?**

____

____

____

____

____

Zendaya and...

Zendaya and Tom Holland Clear up "Silly Assumptions" about their Size Difference

BY SHEILA BROWN – DEC 15, 2021.

The pair responded to queries about the assumption that Zendaya's height is harming their love connection during an event in favor of their film Spider-Man: No Way Home. Tom said it was a silly assumption, and Zendaya demonstrated how common their size differences are saying that her mother is a couple of inches taller than her father.

Tom said there was no one in the tests who was shorter than him and added that it was possible Jon Watts, the director, made that decision because he was aware of the stereotype and wanted to destroy it.

3 **SCANNING. Read the text again and complete the sentences with one word.**

1. Zendaya and Tom Holland talked about their height difference during an ______________.
2. Tom is ______________ than Zendaya.
3. Tom Holland said that their height difference doesn't affect their ______________, and that it was a silly assumption.
4. Zendaya's mom is ______________ than her dad.
5. Tom said there was no one in the tests who was shorter than him, and he believes this was a way the director found to try to ______________ the stereotype.

4 **Audio record your answers to the questions below.**

1. What are other common stereotypes can you see in the media?
2. How can we play our part to start breaking stereotypes?
3. Are there stereotypes associated with your country? How are they referred to in the media?

5 **Imagine you want to send a message to a website that often promotes stereotypes. Think of ways you could complete the message.**

"Please, stop saying that it's not OK or strange ______________________________.

Also, stop promoting news about ______________ ______________________________.

______________________ I like your website, but we need to break these stereotypes."

Grammar

Must not to Express Prohibition in the Present
Sense Verbs and Adjectives

1 **Read the statements and complete them with the verbs from the box.**

feel confined	must not include
must reject	shouldn't judge

1. We ________________ all kinds of stereotypes, even the ones we have of ourselves.
2. Ads ________________ gender stereotypes.
3. We ________________ individuals based on our own prejudices.
4. I never ________________ by my sexual identity, labels, preconceptions, or cliches.

2 **Read the statements in Activity 1 again and answer the questions.**

1. Which verb in statement 1 shows that it is extremely necessary or mandatory to reject stereotypes?

____

2. Statement 2 shows something prohibited in marketing communications. What is the prohibition?

____

3. Which verb or verb phrase in statement 2 shows that it is a prohibition?

____

4. Does statement 3 also refer to a prohibition? Why (not)?

____

____

3 **Match the sentence halves.**

1. This article title, *Celebrities and their much older partners* sounds...
2. According to CAP Code Rules, you mustn't...
3. Anna, are you all right? You look...
4. CAP Code Rules also state that you must...

☐ be respectful to all kinds of people when creating your advertising.
☐ include gender stereotypes in advertising.
☐ so stereotypical, even disrespectful!
☐ upset. Is it because of that sexist news article?

4 **Listen to Allan tell his classmates his opinion about how stereotypes in TV shows and movies can impact people and complete the text.** 27

I read an article yesterday about how stereotypes in comedies, animations, and cartoons impact people. We must do something about it. Children, especially, can [1] ________________ when they [2] ________________ from the princesses and princes in movies. I think the media needs to start breaking stereotypes more. They must follow some rules, too. First, they [3] ________________ the notion that appearance is the most important thing for girls, for example. Secondly, they [4] ________________ gender stereotypes, saying that women usually [5] ________________. And finally, they must stop reinforcing the idea that men have to always [6] ________________.

#DEVELOP

UNIT SEVEN

Use of English

1 PREDICTING. Look at the picture of Ben at a theme park. Check all the sentences that you think are correct.

In this experience, ...

1. ☐ you must wear a VR headset.
2. ☐ you can see if planets look big, small, blue, red, etc.
3. ☐ you can feel hot or cold depending on the planet or star you touch.
4. ☐ you feel powerful, as if you could control the Solar System.
5. ☐ you feel scared.

2 LISTENING FOR GIST. Listen to Ben telling Heidi about the experience and check your answers to Activity 1. Then listen again and answer: How does Heidi feel about Ben's comment and about the experience? 28

____

3 LISTENING FOR DETAILS. Listen again and answer the questions. 29

1. What are the rules for the Solar System – the Big Bang Experience?

____

2. How does Ben feel about controlling the Solar System?

____

3. What does Ben say you can't do with the VR headset?

____

4. What does Heidi want to do? Why?

____

5. Why is Ben's comment offensive?

____

4 Imagine that you are going to the same theme park as Ben and Heidi and you want to check out the experiences. In your notebook, write a dialogue describing the experience to a friend. Follow the steps below.

1. Choose the kind of VR experience you are going to have and describe it.
2. Say what it feels like and what you can see.
3. After listening to you, what does your friend think the experience sounds like?

Writing

1 **Read part of a music festival review. Then complete the form.**

Sunset Melody Music Festival 2022 in LA

The two-day immersive festival welcomed all kinds of music fans from different parts of the United States to Los Angeles. There were four stages, each of them with a name of a color (Blue Stage, Yellow Stage, Green Stage, and Golden Stage) and a total of 92 artists. There was a DJ playing electronic music on the Green Stage and fans got a free T-shirt.
"It was just the best music festival of my life. The DJ made a huge difference!" says Ken Lyon Jones, 23.
The highlight of the festival was the pop band Dreamy-Dreamers. You could feel the crowd's energy. One thing is certain: You must not miss the next festival! Stay tuned to find out when it is going to happen.

Name of festival: [1] ______________________
____

Duration: [2] ____________

Location: [3] ______________________

Number of stages: [4] ______

Number of artists: [5] ______

Main attraction: [6] ______________________

2 **Read the music festival review again. Then check all the correct statements.**

1. ☐ The text has information about an event.
2. ☐ The writer compares previous events with this one.
3. ☐ The writer gives his / her opinions on the event.

Prepare to Write

3 **Think of an event or festival you have been to or know of. Make some notes about it and your opinion. You can also write other people's opinions.**

____

____

____

____

Write

4 **Write a review of an event or festival you have been to or know of. Use the information in Activity 3 and the text in Activity 1 as a model. Use your notebook to do so.**

Check and Change

5 **Read your review and make sure you included:**

☐ a description of the event / festival.
☐ your opinion.
☐ positive and negative aspects.

6 **Edit your text. Make sure all the elements in Activity 5 are included.**

Publish

7 **Write a clean version of your text.**

#CHALLENGE

UNIT SEVEN

#ASSESS

Vocabulary

1 Match the entertainment activities to the corresponding sentences.

1. a comedy movie
2. a documentary
3. a music festival
4. a musical
5. an art exhibition

☐ Check this out! *The Phantom of the Opera* is on. Let's buy some tickets!
☐ I love these paintings. They look so real!
☐ I want to learn more about the creation of virtual reality technologies.
☐ My favorite band will be there! Their songs are so cool!
☐ I need to laugh a little. Today was a hard day.

Grammar

2 Circle the correct words to complete the sentences.

1. If you work in advertising, you **must** / **must not** promote stereotypes or be offensive to any group of people.
2. Is this a picture of you at the music festival? You **look** / **sound** sad. Didn't you have fun?
3. I loved that experience with the Solar System and the VR headset. I **sounded** / **felt** powerful controlling all the planets.
4. You **must** / **must not** be more careful! Don't compare couple's ages like that.
5. Can you hear this song? It **sounds** / **tastes** familiar.

Reading

3 Read the text and answer the questions.

Two Ways to Deal with Stereotypes

Ignore Them

Stereotypes exist in every aspect of life. From sexual orientation to marriage expectations to lifestyle choices, society will always expect something of you, whether justified or not. The key is to ignore them; we are talking about your life here, not theirs.

Find Like-minded People

Find new friends who understand your life choices and support you along the way, even if it's just a friend. This is helpful when the world seems to be pushing for you to conform to an age-old belief or what they call their moral compass.

1. Where are there stereotypes?

____

____

2. How can we deal with certain expectations from society?

____

3. What are *like-minded people*?

____

4. How can you be around like-minded people?

____

Listening

4 Listen to some people talk about common stereotypes on the media. Match the speech to the correct options. 🔊 30

☐ gender inequality
☐ men must always look strong
☐ famous people must always look gorgeous
☐ men must take the lead
☐ age difference between famous couples

Writing

5 In your notebook, write five tips to help people break stereotypes.

Speaking

6 Talk about media and stereotypes and audio record yourself. Use the questions below as a guide.

1. What are the most common stereotypes you read or hear about in the media?
2. Why do you think stereotypes exist?
3. How can you help break these stereotypes?

Vocabulary

Crimes and Criminals

1 **Read the blog post of a teen digital influencer talking about his brother and answer the question below.**

According to the author, what has saved his brother from a life of crime?

____

____

____

My Brother Jack +

My Brother Jack

By Mark Maise

You may wonder how a young person like me can know anything about crime. The sad truth is that I have lived all my life with a [1] juvenile delinquent, my oldest brother Jack. In fact, he is a former juvenile offender.

Jack first got into trouble when he decided to join a gang that was involved in [2] graffiti. Our father confronted him and he said he was [3] innocent, but later we found out he was [4] guilty and also involved in some [5] thefts in town.

Jack was having trouble at school at the time, and my parents did not realize that this was leading him down a very negative path. At that time, Mrs. Greenway, our art teacher, invited my parents to the school. She believed in Jack, said he had a lot of talent as an artist, and together they developed a plan to motivate Jack and keep him off the streets. Because of the thefts, Jack initially did [6] community service, but now I can say that I have a great brother. And he really is an artist!

2 **Read the blog post again and match the underlined words in Activity 1 to their definitions.**

- ☐ Crimes of stealing.
- ☐ Not responsible for a crime.
- ☐ Unpaid work as a punishment for a crime.
- ☐ A young offender.
- ☐ Responsible for a crime.
- ☐ Offensive, humorous, or political writing and painting on the walls of buildings, trains, etc.

3 **Imagine you are an eyewitness to the crimes below. What do you think the right thing to do is?**

Attack	Graffiti	Theft	Vandalism

If I am an eyewitness to an attack, I think the right thing to do is to call the police immediately.

____

____

____

____

____

____

____

____

4 **Check (✓) the correct words to complete the sentences.**

1. A ________ is a person who commits a fraud.
- ☐ burglar
- ☐ fraudster

2. A ________ is a person who attacks people in a public place and robs them.
- ☐ mugger
- ☐ murderer

3. A ________ is a person who deliberately damages things, especially public property.
- ☐ terrorist
- ☐ vandal

Reading

1 **Listen to the conversation between Anna and Tim and mark the sentences T (True) or F (False).** 31

1. ☐ Tim's dad is a judge.
2. ☐ Tim's dad defends only people who have committed small crimes.
3. ☐ Tim invites Anna to meet his dad.
4. ☐ Anna is curious about Tim's dad's profession.
5. ☐ Tim wants to listen to his dad's stories all the time.

2 **SCANNING. Read part of Anna's Social Studies essay and answer the question below.**

What kind of program does Anna mention in her essay?

____

____

A Public Defender's Experience with Young Offenders

Jay Pratt works as a public defender in the United States, representing clients who may lose their freedom and cannot afford a private attorney. Public defenders are attorneys who represent defendants in criminal cases, such as minors who commit crimes like vandalism, theft, or even murder. Mr. Pratt has a great deal of experience with juvenile offenders and believes that poor academic performance, family problems, and drug use can contribute to juvenile delinquency. However, he is very hopeful that a new program in the state based on psychological counseling, yoga, and mindfulness can help many teens change their lives for the better.

3 **SCANNING. Read the text in Activity 2 again and find the crimes for the offenders below.**

1. murderer – ______________
2. vandal – ______________
3. mugger – ______________
4. thief – ______________

4 **Answer the questions below. Then audio record your answers.**

1. Do you think that everyone has the right to be defended? Why?

____

____

2. Why do some young people become juvenile delinquents?

____

____

3. How do you think a program like the one mentioned in Activity 2 can help juvenile offenders?

____

____

5 **You have been invited to create a program to help juvenile offenders. What will you include in the program? How will teens benefit from your program?**

____

____

____

____

____

____

____

____

Grammar

Indefinite Pronouns
Relative Pronouns
So for Results and Consequences
Adverbs of Manner

1 Read the dialogue and identify the indefinite pronouns. Write them down.

Anna: Let's go somewhere quieter where we can talk.
Tim: Sure! This place is really noisy.
Anna: Here is much better. So you must be really proud of your dad.
Tim: I am! Everywhere he goes he is recognized as a good person, and this is really great. He always says we must do something for other people. We need to care.
Anna: I agree, but sometimes there isn't anything you can do if a person insists on repeating the same mistakes.
Tim: Yeah... Nothing seems to work with some people...

____

____

2 Complete the sentences using *who* or *which*.

1. A fraudster is someone __________ has committed fraud.
2. This is the kind of punishment __________ he deserves.

3 Listen to Anna tell her classmates what she has learned about crime and justice. Then complete the blanks with one word. 32

My journey of trying to understand a little bit more about crime and justice started with an informal conversation with my friend Tim. Tim's father is a public defender [1] __________ has a lot of experience with juvenile offenders, which is [2] __________ amazing. I told Tim I wanted to learn more from him, [3] __________ he invited me over for dinner and we had a very interesting conversation. He told me about his experience in the area and how he believes that these young people just need help and attention. There is a reason for them to behave [4] __________ and [5] __________. I can say that Mr. Jay Pratt is [6] __________ I admire as he is making a difference in the life of many teenagers [7] __________ sometimes don't have [8] __________ to count on.

4 You have been invited to talk about crimes in the community where you live. Make sure you mention the most common crimes and how you think this problem can be resolved. Use indefinite pronouns, relative pronouns, so for results and consequences, and adverbs of manner in your text.

____

____

____

____

____

Use of English

1 PREDICTING. You are going to listen to a podcast about the reasons why it's so common for teenagers to get involved in cybercrimes. What do you think will be mentioned? Check (✓).

1. ☐ Teenagers are very familiar with the technological environment.
2. ☐ Teenagers suffer from pressure to have possessions.
3. ☐ Teenagers have a natural tendency to commit crimes.
4. ☐ It is typical for teenagers to have low self-control.

2 LISTENING FOR DETAILS. Listen and circle the correct information. 33

1. The Internet environment is far more **familiar / unfamiliar** to teens than to most adults.
2. One of the advantages of the Internet is that it has no **boundaries / disadvantages**.
3. We can see that **cybercrime / internet access** is not restricted to those who live or grow up in specific locations, and that it affects people from all walks of life.
4. Another point worth mentioning is the issue of low self-control, which may be more common among **young people / adults**.

3 Read the dialogue between two teenagers discussing the podcast. Check the correct alternative to complete the dialogue.

J: Jacob N: Noah

N: And how did you like the podcast?
J: Well, I thought it was good and ________ that was mentioned there made sense to me.
N: I know teenagers are more familiar with the Internet world than adults.
J: Absolutely! The Internet can be used for good or for bad.
N: You are right! Unfortunately, we live in a world full of temptations to have material possessions, and sometimes the Internet offers opportunities to make money.
J: Yes, but there are legal and illegal ways. Some people choose the wrong way.
N: Cybercrime can happen ________. Today we have Internet connections ________ in the world. ________ can use the Internet to commit crimes.
J: True, but I think some people are more prone to cybercrime because of their nature. Cybercriminals are very smart people!
N: That's true! They should use their expertise to help companies become more secure.
J: I agree with you. They should not commit crimes to make money. They can make a lot of money working for companies and protecting them from cybercrime.
N: Totally! Well, I have to go now.
J: All right! I'll see you at school tomorrow. Bye!

1. ☐ everything, anywhere, everywhere, anyone
2. ☐ everything, anything, everywhere, no one
3. ☐ nothing, something, everywhere, anyone

4 Go online and find information about a cybercrime that is common nowadays. Describe it in your own words. Use adverbs of manner, indefinite and relative pronouns, and so for results and consequences in your text.

____

____

____

____

____

____

____

5 Read your text from Activity 4 and audio record yourself.

Writing

1 **Read the short essay and answer the question below.**

How can a friendship influence a teenager's life?

____

____

____

____

Crime and Friendship

I am not a psychologist, but after working as a teacher for so many years, I can say that I have seen a lot, and that, perhaps, entitles me to say something about how adolescents function in life.

I became very interested in the topic of crime and friendship when a very lonely student of mine was sentenced to prison for some bicycle thefts in the neighborhood. During my studies, I found out that some psychologists say that peers and friends are a key factor in how many crimes a person commits during adolescence. Having friends leads to the advantage of developing a sense of belonging and love. When you feel safe, you are more likely to make it in life. However, there are also disadvantages when it comes to friendships. Sometimes peer pressure can be too strong, and teens may feel compelled to commit criminal acts in order to be accepted by their peers.

Despite some drawbacks, friendship is a valuable part of everyone's life. As adults, it is our job to look out for the children and young people around us and make sure they choose their friends well and follow the best possible role models.

2 **Read the text in Activity 1 again. Then check the correct statements about it.**

1. ☐ The text presents the author's opinions.
2. ☐ The text mentions the advantages and disadvantages of a situation.
3. ☐ The text is a scientific essay.
4. ☐ The last paragraph concludes the essay.
5. ☐ The text does not have an introduction.

Prepare to Write

3 **Some people believe punishment can help prevent crimes, others think punishment can only make them worse. Think of at least one advantage and one disadvantage of punishments to help prevent crimes.**

Advantages	Disadvantages

Write

4 **Write a short opinion essay about the topic of punishment. Use your ideas from Activity 3.**

____

____

____

____

____

Check and Change

5 **Read your text and make sure you included:**

- ☐ an introduction.
- ☐ advantages and disadvantages of punishment to prevent crimes.
- ☐ your opinion.
- ☐ a conclusion.

6 **Edit your text. Make sure all the elements in Activity 5 are included.**

Publish

7 **Write a clean version of your text.**

____

____

____

____

____

#ASSESS

Vocabulary

1 Complete the definitions below.

1. Someone who goes into houses, shops, etc., to steal things is a ______________
2. The release from detention before the sentence is complete if the prisoner has shown very good behavior is called ______________
3. The punishment and duration of that punishment as ordered by a court or fixed by law ______________.
4. Someone who kills another person is a ______________
5. The crime of deliberately damaging things, especially public property is called ______________
6. Someone who attacks people in a public place and robs them is a ______________

Grammar

2 Circle the correct words to complete the sentences.

1. **Anything** / **Nothing** I do seems to be working. I don't know what else to do!
2. He was found guilty, **so** / **but** he was sent to jail.
3. Do you think he is the person **which** / **who** attacked the girl last night?
4. It's dark in there. You have to move **carefully** / **careful.**
5. I can't find Sue **anywhere** / **nowhere**. Do you know where she is?

Reading

3 Read the tips on how to protect yourself against cybercrime and choose the corresponding heading for each of them.

1. Use strong passwords.
2. Keep your software updated.
3. Manage your social media settings.
4. Protect yourself against identity theft.
5. Know what to do if you become a victim.

How to Protect Yourself Against Cybercrimes.

- ☐ Never use the same password in different websites. Make them complex, and change them regularly.
- ☐ Cybercriminals often use problems in your operating systems and internet security software to gain access to your system.
- ☐ Preserve the safety of your personal and private information. Cybercriminals can easily get the information with just a few data points.
- ☐ When someone steals your identity, they access your personal information, and it involves fraud or deception. This happens when someone is tricked into giving personal data over the Internet.
- ☐ If you think you are a victim of a cybercrime, you need to let the local police and, in some cases, the FBI and the Federal Trade Commission know.

Listening

4 Listen to some people talk about some crimes they have witnessed and number the crimes in the correct order. 34

- ☐ corruption
- ☐ theft
- ☐ terrorism
- ☐ cybercrime
- ☐ graffiti

Writing

5 Write five tips for people to help them avoid being the victims of crimes in the region where you live. Use your notebook.

Speaking

6 Talk about what kind of punishment, if any, juvenile delinquents should get. Audio record yourself.

FOCUS ON CULTURE

1 **ACTIVATING PRIOR KNOWLEDGE. Look at the images related to quality education. What do they mean?**

1.

2.

3.

4.

5.

6.

Pearson has no relation of any kind with the Global Goals Organization and does not provide sponsorship to them. Also the Global Goals and none of their brands endorses Pearson's Business.

2 **Now read the text and number the extracts according to the targets in Activity 1.**

The Targets

Everyone can help to make sure that we meet the Global Goals. Use these [...] targets to create action to ensure quality education.

[...]

☐ By 2030, ensure that all girls and boys complete free, equitable, and quality primary and secondary education leading to relevant and effective learning outcomes.

☐ By 2030, substantially increase the number of youth and adults who have relevant skills, including technical and vocational skills, for employment, decent jobs, and entrepreneurship.

☐ By 2030, ensure equal access for all women and men to affordable and quality technical, vocational, and tertiary education, including university.

☐ By 2030, eliminate gender disparities in education and ensure equal access to all levels of education and vocational training for the vulnerable, including persons with disabilities, indigenous peoples, and children in vulnerable situations.

☐ By 2030, ensure that all youth and a substantial proportion of adults, both men and women, achieve literacy and numeracy.

☐ By 2030, ensure that all girls and boys have access to quality early childhood development, care, and pre-primary education so that they are ready for primary education.

Source: https://www.globalgoals.org/4-quality-education. Accessed on January 23, 2022.

3 **SCANNING. Read the text again and find the words with the following meanings.**

1. the first time a child goes to school to receive formal education – ______________________
2. the last stage of studies – ______________________
3. the ability to read and write – ______________________
4. the school years between 6 and 14 years old – ______________________
5. something related to an occupation or employment – ______________________
6. a physical or mental condition that limits a person - ______________________

4 **Work in pairs. Which of the targets can be seen in your region?**

I don't think all children have access to free education.
Yes, but I think that by 2030 this might be possible.

5 **Work in groups and write the targets for your area. Get together and discuss two things that could be changed in your area to reach SDG #4. Write a brief description for each target, using the text in Activity 2 as a model.**

1 Work in groups. Discuss how fashion can increase poverty.

2 ACTIVATING PRIOR KNOWLEDGE. Look at the image and read the caption. How does it relate to SDG #1 No poverty?

Gender Inequality

3 SCANNING. Read the text and check (✓) the true statements.

Big Brands are Keeping the Women Who Make Our Clothes Living in Poverty

The women who make our clothes do not make enough to live on – keeping them in poverty. Despite long hours away from their families, working full time plus many hours of overtime, big clothing brands do not pay garment workers enough money to cover the basics of life – food and decent shelter.

Oxfam's What She Makes campaign demands big clothing brands pay the women who make our clothes a living wage. Together, with your voice demanding action, and Oxfam's direct engagement with brands, we urge clothing companies to take the crucial next step in creating a fairer fashion industry.

[...]

Source: https://www.oxfam.org.au/what-she-makes/about-the-campaign/. Accessed on January 23, 2022.

1. ☐ The campaign focuses on women's well-being.
2. ☐ The organization that helps women is a big brand.
3. ☐ Women work long hours and don't get a living wage.
4. ☐ Everyone can help in the campaign.

4 **Write two other possible titles for the text in Activity 3.**

5 **Work in pairs. Go back to the text and discuss what changes could be implemented so that women could have better working conditions.**

They could work fewer hours per day.

6 **Go online and get more information about the *What she makes* campaign. Write a call to action inviting other students to learn about the campaign.**

#FOCUS ON CULTURE

1 **Work in groups. Discuss this question. Then present your ideas to your classmates.**

How can you help reduce hunger in the world?

2 **MAKING AND CHECKING PREDICTIONS. Look at the text below and answer: What is it about? Read and check your predictions.**

Healthy Diets...

Healthy Diets for a World With Zero Hunger

We Can All Help

Hunger is a serious problem

The number of people who don't eat well is going up. One in nine people are going hungry or do not eat the food they need. The problem is quantity but quality as well. Unhealthy diets have become a serious problem all over the world. We need to make healthy and sustainable diets cheap and accessible to all.

Working with countries

FAO, the Food and Agriculture Organization of the United Nations, is working with countries to use their expertise and help them. Here are two examples.

In the Philippines and seven other countries in Asia, FAO helps families and farmers to grow good quality foods. In these countries, fruit and vegetables are very expensive. FAO also helps them reduce prices.

In Kyrgyzstan, FAO helped them set up a logistics center. This center coordinates the distribution of fresh foods from local farmers to different schools. Small farmers can sell more, and children benefit from a good diet.

What can countries do?

Governments can educate people and teach them about healthy diets. They can work with local farmers and producers to reduce costs and produce better food. They should always consider agrobiodiversity. This helps people's health and protects biodiversity and the environment.

What can we all do?

Limit the foods that require an excessive use of natural resources for their production.

Consider the environmental impact of the food we eat.

Buy food from local farmers and producers and support biodiversity.

Read about the nutritional values of foods.

Balance our diet.

Do physical activities.

Consult specialists in nutrition.

Source: https://www.fao.org/3/ca5268en/CA5268EN.pdf. Accessed on January 23, 2022.

3 Read the text again and look for images for each of the sections of the text. Describe each of the images. Use the sample text.

A group of people collecting apples.

Section 1: ______________________________

Section 2: ______________________________

Section 3: ______________________________

Section 4: ______________________________

4 What does FAO stand for? How could they help your country?

____

____

____

5 SCANNING. Go back to your list in Activity 1 and read the text again. Are your ideas in the text? Which ones can you use in your region? Make notes.

____

____

____

6 Create a campaign. Prepare a healthy and sustainable diet campaign for the school. Include this information:

- The food you should eat.
- The food you should not eat and how to balance your diet.
- The actions you can take.
- Add images and present the campaign to your classmates.

7 Vote. Watch your classmates' presentations. Which campaign would you like to follow? Describe why.

____

____

1 Look at these pictures. Work in pairs and describe what you see. How can they be made possible?

1.

House printed with local materials

2.
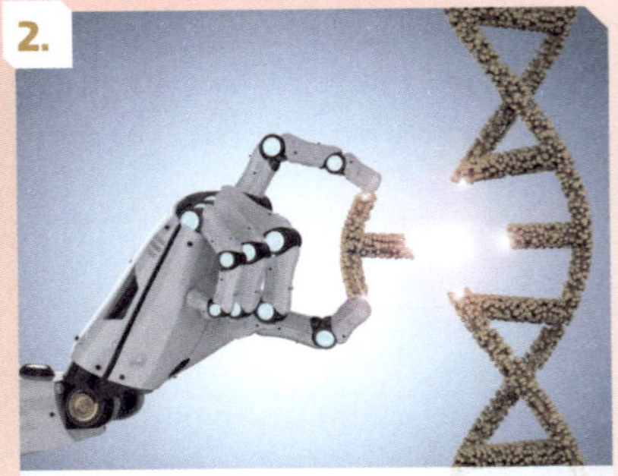
Engineering better aging

3.

Decarbonization

2 MAKING PREDICTIONS. Look at the picture. What do you think the briefing paper is about? Read and check your predictions.

Contents

Introduction

The contribution of cities to global CO2 emissions, compounded by the growing urbanization trend, positions urban ecosystems as a critical proving ground to address environmental challenges.

Foundations for an Integrated Urban Ecosystem

1. Built environment: efficient buildings, smart homes, healthy community
   Green building standards
   Low-cost green financing
   Smart energy infrastructure
2. Mobility: compact urban form and electrification of fleets
   Decarbonized public fleet
   Compact urban form and planning

Source: https://www3.weforum.org/docs/WEF_Urban_Transformation_Integrated_Energy_Solutions_2021.pdf. Accessed on January 23, 2022.

3 **READING FOR DETAILS. Read the text again and answer the questions.**

1. Is transportation related to energy solutions?

___

2. Can buildings and houses contribute to health?

___

3. Does urbanization contribute to CO2 emissions?

___

4 **Go back to the pictures in Activity 1, read the text again, and discuss.**

What can we do in our city, in our school, and at home to contribute to urban ecosystems?

5 **Make your city a more ecological place. Discuss some ideas that can be considered for where you live. Make a sketch of each of the ideas.**

6 **Give your opinion to the class. Check out your classmates' work. Ask them questions about their sketches if necessary. Decide on which is the best for you.**

#FOCUS ON CULTURE

1 ACTIVATING PRIOR KNOWLEDGE. Work in pairs. Read these headlines and make predictions about these innovations and programs.

These 20 teenagers can change our world for the better

These kids from different parts of the world are working on innovative new technologies. They think they'll change the world.

Meet Marcos Salvat, the creator of the app Say it!

This app is the basis of future technology for people with disabilities.

Teen innovation program at schools.

This program will help teens at school innovate in the area of industry and infrastructure.

2 MAKING AND CHECKING PREDICTIONS. Read the title of the text. What do you understand by "youth power"? Read and check your predictions.

By Youth...

By Youth, with Youth, for Youth

Welcome to the UNESCO Youth Programme

1 Youth have the creativity, the potential, and the capacity to make change happen – for themselves, for their communities, and for the rest of the world. UNESCO works with young people and is committed to accompany them to work together to drive social innovation and change, participate fully in the development of their societies, eradicate poverty and inequality, and foster a culture of peace.

2 UNESCO has engaged with thousands of youths to create change through its fora, built solid youth networks, reached young people to work on peacebuilding and prevention of violent extremism, and is committed to empowering underprivileged youth by providing them with spaces to participate.

3 The United Nations defines "youth" as persons aged between 15 and 24. However, this definition is flexible. According to the World Youth Report (2018), there are 1.2 billion young people aged 15 to 24 years, accounting for 16 percent of the global population. The experience of being young can vary substantially across the world, between countries and regions, and "youth" is therefore often a fluid and changing category. As such, context is always an important guide in UNESCO's definition of youth.

4 We encourage engagement of youth in UNESCO's action from design to implementation and follow-up, in their communities through the scaling up of youth-led initiatives, and in the policy agenda through the integration of youth concerns and issues.

5 To this end, UNESCO also encourages Youth Spaces aimed at empowering young people, fostering and supporting their action, promoting partnerships, and ensuring their recognition and visibility.

6 Scroll down to discover more about UNESCO's work on youth, including its Operational Strategy on Youth (2014-2021), the UNESCO Youth Forum process, and other news, events and opportunities to get involved in. Don't forget to sign up to the Online UNESCO Youth Community!

Source: https://en.unesco.org/youth. Accessed on January 23, 2022.

3 **Read again and check (✓) if each section summary is correct.**

1. ☐ UNESCO wants to help young people because they're creative and can make change happen. This will benefit their communities and the rest of the world.
2. ☐ UNESCO will start the program in the future.
3. ☐ There are different ways to define youth, or young people. Context is very important in the definitions.
4. ☐ UNESCO helps young people in different moments of their innovations: the ideas, the design, and the implementation in their communities.
5. ☐ Youth Spaces is a very important part of the Youth Program.
6. ☐ Read on and find more information about the Youth Program.

4 **Read the text again and work in groups. Brainstorm different ideas for innovation in your community. Think about what could be done to promote peace, eradicate poverty, or reduce inequality.**

5 **Decide on one idea. Write an e-mail to UNESCO's Youth Program to present it.**

CANCEL SEND

TO

SUBJECT

6 **Share your e-mails with the other groups. Work in pairs and read the e-mails. Talk about the future changes this idea could make in the community.**

1 **Match the pictures to the descriptions.**

1.

Deforestation

2.

Desertification

3.

Land degradation

4.

Biodiversity loss

- ☐ This means that millions of people can face a terrible future. Animals lose their habitats. There isn't enough fresh water. Water is polluted because of man's actions.
- ☐ This happens when the fertile land becomes unproductive. Plants can't grow because there isn't enough water, minerals, and nutrients.
- ☐ This happens when lots of trees are cut in forests and people do not replant them. They do this to create space for farms and houses, but they destroy nature.
- ☐ This happens when the land loses some of its productivity because of human activities. The process can be temporary or permanent. When it's permanent, the result is land desertification.

2 **SCANNING. Look at the title of the text. Which of the problems in Activity 1 will be mentioned? Read and check.**

Promoting the Sustainability of Terrestrial Ecosystems and Halting Desertification, Land Degradation, and Biodiversity Loss

Sustainable Development Goal 15 (SDG 15) – Protect, restore, and promote sustainable use of terrestrial ecosystems, sustainably manage forests, combat desertification, and halt and reverse land degradation and halt biodiversity loss.

- Every minute, 23 hectares of arable land are lost due to drought and desertification.
- Over the last two decades, approximately 20 percent of the Earth's vegetated surface has shown persistent declining trends in productivity, mainly due to unsustainable land and water use and management practices.
- Every year, 13 million hectares of forest are lost that are home to more than 80 percent of all land-based species and which provide livelihood to 1.6 billion people.
- The increased vulnerability to environment stresses, especially of the poor, women, and children, can lead to an intensified competition for scarce natural resources and result in migration, instability, and conflict.
- Women and girls are disproportionately and differently affected by environmental degradation, pollution, and natural and human-made disasters, and it is important to recognize the fundamental contributions of women to the conservation, protection, and management of ecosystems and natural resources.
- Increased security of tenure and gender equity can be enabling factors for the adoption and scale up of more responsible land management practices.

Source: https://wedocs.unep.org/bitstream/handle/20.500.11822/25765/SDG15_Brief.pdf?sequence=1&isAllowed=y. Accessed on January 23, 2022.

3 **SUMMARIZING. Read the text again and check (✓) the correct descriptions for each bullet point.**

1. ☐ Arable land is productive land.
2. ☐ 20 % of Earth's vegetation has grown stronger and more productive.
3. ☐ This is a serious problem for animals and human beings.
4. ☐ People who are poor and children don't suffer more than others.
5. ☐ Girls and women suffer more than others.
6. ☐ Gender equity is necessary.

4 **Read the text again and say what these numbers refer to.**

1. 23: ______________________________
2. 20: ______________________________
3. 13: ______________________________
4. 1.6: ______________________________

5 **Work in groups. Start a campaign.**

1. Prepare posters for the campaign, explaining one or two problems.
2. Suggest positive actions.
3. Include pictures.
4. Call people to action.

6 **Check on your classmates' posters. Which one is the best in your opinion? Justify your answer.**

1 Read this explanation and answer the question. What can you show visitors who want to experience your culture?

Cultural Travel

This form of travel is about experiencing life in a foreign culture, not as a temporary visitor. It is about a change of lifestyle. When you do this, you understand the new culture better.

Culture is about people, not places and things. Cultural travel is not about visiting museums and eating local food. It is about becoming a member of the new culture. Expeditions and slave trade trips are forms of cultural travel. Tourism is the opposite of cultural travel. You learn about many new places, but you are not part of the local culture.

2 Read the title of the text. Is it related to cultural travel? Read and check your predictions.

Travel the World +

Travel the World.
Make a Difference.

Earthwatch expeditions pair researchers with volunteers to address some of the world's most pressing environmental challenges. Explore our current expeditions to discover how you can make a difference.

WILDLIFE & ECOSYSTEMS
CLIMATE CHANGE

Amazon Riverboat Exploration

Help conserve wildlife within the Amazon Basin by searching for pink river dolphins, primates, macaw, caiman, and giant river otters.

South America:
Samiria River, Peru

Lead Scientist:
Richard Bodmer, Ph.D.

Duration:
8 days (avg. $306 a day)

Starting at **$2,450**

CLIMATE CHANGE

Climate Change at the Arctic's Edge

Scientists expect to see the greatest effects of climate change in the Arctic.

North America:
Churchill, Manitoba, Canada

Lead Scientist:
LeeAnn Fishback, Ph.D.

Duration:
11 days (avg. $336 a day)

Starting at **$3,695**

CLIMATE CHANGE

Climate Change in the Mackenzie Mountains

Scientists expect to see the greatest effects of climate change in the Arctic. But what, exactly, will these effects be?

North America:
Mackenzie Mountains, Northwest Territory, Canada

Lead Scientist:
Steven Mamet, Ph.D.

Duration:
11 days (avg. $336 a day)

Starting at **$3,695**

Source: https://earthwatch.org/expeditions/browse?gclid=CjwKCAiA4veMBhAMEiwAU4XRr-8HwY7uXAkXhhmw5CLRUVdQdo961UNFJNgwLaszGl4-S0mwcAXUBoC-CYQAvD_BwE. Accessed on January 23, 2022.

3 **READING FOR DETAILS. Read the text again and check (✓) the true statements.**

1. ☐ There are different expedition focuses.
2. ☐ You can find expeditions in Central America.
3. ☐ All the explorations are related to ecosystems.
4. ☐ Volunteers and researchers go on the expeditions together.
5. ☐ There are visits to museums and local restaurants.

4 **SKIMMING. Read again. Circle the information that is in the text.**

1. Name of the scientists for each expedition.
2. Price of the expeditions.
3. A short description of the expeditions.
4. Regions you can explore.
5. Weather conditions in each expedition.
6. Duration of each expedition.

5 **Work in pairs. Find information about expeditions in your country. Make a list.**

6 **Write an entry for the Earthwatch webpage about an expedition for your country. Use the information you collected and the text in Activity 2 as a model.**

7 **Work in pairs. Read all of your classmates' entries. Then make arrangements to take one of the expeditions.**

1 Read the extract. How can gender equality be promoted for young women?

Fast Facts:...

Fast Facts: Youth and Gender Equality

March 13, 2017

Women, and young women in particular, face structural discrimination due to the patriarchal nature of most societies. Young women are often amongst the most marginalized, vulnerable and – if they live in rural / remote areas, or precarious human settlements – hardest to reach young people. Young women make up nearly half of the world's population, yet are regularly prevented from accessing basic services and decent employment. Unleashing the potential of girls and young women is an effective pathway to addressing poverty, improving access to health, education and sanitation, making societies more inclusive, and reducing violence in communities.

Source: https://www.undp.org/publications/fast-facts-youth-and-gender-equality. Accessed on January 23, 2022.

2 **MAKING AND CHECKING PREDICTIONS. Look at the title of the text and the picture. What do you think it is about? Read and check your predictions.**

Leveraging the...

Leveraging the Commercial Media Sector to Promote Gender Equality: The Geena Davis Institute and the Representation Project

29 October 2021
Author: Faria A. Nasruddin
Published by: ALIGN

The Representation Project and the Geena Davis Institute work with the content-producing side of commercial media, advocating for gender-balance and quality representation on-screen in film and television.

The Geena Davis Institute was founded by the actor Geena Davis in 2004 as a response to the disparity in the on-screen representation of female characters specifically in family entertainment. The organization carries out research on the state of gender representation in family entertainment media, or entertainment targeted for children and young adolescents, and works with the entertainment industry. It uses its research to drive change that creates gender balance, fosters inclusion, and reduces negative stereotypes of girls and other groups that are under – or mis – represented.

The Representation Project was founded in 2011 by Jennifer Siebel Newson after the release of the movie Miss Representation. The Representation Project uses movies, youth filmmaker programs, research, and social media campaigns to fight intersectional sexism and other justice issues.

Source: https://www.alignplatform.org/resources/leveraging-commercial-media-sector-promote-gender-equality. Accessed on January 23, 2022.

3 **READING FOR DETAILS. Read the text again and check (✓) the true statements or cross (✗) the false ones.**

1. ☐ The Geena Davis Institute is in favor of gender equality.
2. ☐ Geena Davis founded the institute in 2004.
3. ☐ In family entertainment, there was equal representation of men and women.
4. ☐ The institute wants to eliminate gender imbalance and negative stereotypes.
5. ☐ Geena Davis also founded the Representation Project.
6. ☐ The Representation Project is in favor of gender balance and equality.

4 **Work in pairs. How does the text about the project relate to the extract in Activity 1? Can it be used to promote gender equality? Make notes.**

____

____

____

5 **Write a list of popular movies or series. Answer the questions.**

1. How many women and girls are there in each? How many men and boys? Is there a gender balance?

____

____

____

2. What could be done to have an equal number of female and male characters?

____

____

____

6 **Choose one movie or series and write the new cast. Make any changes to the description of the movie or series. Share your new movie / series with the class.**

1 **ACTIVATING PRIOR KNOWLEDGE. SDG Goal 16 is about Peace, Justice and Strong Institutions. Why are they important? Discuss in groups.**

2 **Read the title of the text. Do you think it will answer the question in Activity 1? Read and check if you are right.**

Peace, Justice, and Strong Institutions: Why They Matter

1 What's the goal here?

Promote peaceful and inclusive societies for sustainable development, provide access to justice for all and build effective, accountable, and inclusive institutions at all levels.

2 Why?

People everywhere need to be free of fear from all forms of violence and feel safe as they go about their lives whatever their ethnicity, faith, or sexual orientation.

[...]

3 How does this goal apply to me, wherever I live?

Crimes that threaten the foundation of peaceful societies, including homicides, human trafficking, and other organized crimes, as well as discriminatory laws or practices, affect all countries. Even the world's greatest democracies face major challenges in addressing corruption, crime, and human rights violations for everyone at home.

[...]

4 What would be the cost of not taking action now?

[...]

Violence affects children's health, development, and well-being, and their ability to thrive. It causes trauma and weakens social inclusion.

Lack of access to justice means that conflicts remain unresolved and people cannot obtain protection and redress. Institutions that do not function according to legitimate laws are prone to arbitrariness and abuse of power, and are less capable of delivering public services to everyone.

5 What can we do?

Exercise your right to hold your elected officials to account. Exercise your right to freedom of information and share your opinion with your elected representatives.

Promote inclusion and respect toward people of different ethnic origins, religions, gender, sexual orientations, or different opinions. Together, we can help to improve conditions for a life of dignity for all.

To find out more about Goal #16 and other Sustainable Development Goals, visit:
http://www.un.org/ sustainable development

Source: https://www.un.org/sustainabledevelopment/wp-content/uploads/2019/07/16_Why-It-Matters-2020.pdf. Accessed on January 23, 2022.

3 **SUMMARIZING. Read again and check (✓) the correct summaries for each section of the text.**

1. ☐ What's the goal here? Sustainable development, inclusive societies, justice for all, and inclusive institutions.
2. ☐ Why? Nobody should feel bad about their ethnic group, religion, or sexual orientation. They have the right to feel nobody will be violent to them.
3. ☐ How does this goal apply to me, wherever I live? This applies to me if I live in poor areas.
4. ☐ What would be the cost of not taking action now? If we don't take action now, children will suffer, people won't feel protected, and institutions can abuse power.
5. ☐ What can we do? We need to exercise our rights. We need to promote inclusion and respect to everybody.

4 **What is a synonym to "why they matter" in the title? Circle the correct option.**

1. Why they are good.
2. Why they are important.
3. Why they are interesting.

5 **Work in groups. Make a list of what you can do to promote peace and justice at school. Think about different situations which may be unfair or unjust and propose solutions.**

6 **You're going to create a poster to promote peace and justice at school. Design the poster with the information in Activity 5.**

7 **Present your poster to the classroom. Talk about the actions that need to be taken and discuss how you could promote the poster in the school.**

TEEN TALK

1 **Work in small groups and discuss. Make a list of adjectives to describe quality education.**

In many parts of the world, children and young people cannot go to school. Some can go, but their education is not good. But what constitutes good education?

2 **Do some research and find some educational courses that are aimed at your age group. Make a list of six titles. Use adjectives ending in *–ed* and *–ing* to describe them.**

Course	Description

3 **Work in pairs. Talk about the courses you chose.**

- **Student A:** Ask questions to find out more about the courses Student B chose.
- **Student B:** Answer the questions, and then say why you liked / didn't like the courses.
- Swap roles.

4 **Compare the courses you and your classmate liked the most. Use the adjectives from the box.**

bad cheap difficult easy expensive good interesting long practical short

5 **You both have to decide on one course to take. Follow the steps below and role play a conversation.**

1. Say which course you'd like to take, describe it, and compare it to your classmate choice.
2. Make a request for your classmate to join you in this course.
3. Agree on one course.

6 **Self-evaluation. Reflect on the tasks and complete this chart.**

Learning Objective	Rating
Did I follow all the steps?	☆☆☆
Did I use the structures in the unit?	☆☆☆
Did I use the vocabulary in the unit?	☆☆☆
Did I pronounce the words correctly?	☆☆☆
Did I correct any mistakes?	☆☆☆
Was I fluent?	☆☆☆

#TEEN TALK

1 **Work in pairs. Answer the questions.**

1. What words can you think of that are related to fashion and poverty? Write them down.

____

____

____

____

2. How can fashion help to reduce poverty in the world? Make notes.

____

____

____

____

2 **Make a list of clothes and accessories you could donate. Ask your classmate about his / her list and complete the chart.**

A: *Is it an accessory?*
B: *Yes.*
A: *Can you wear it on your hands?*
B: *Yes.*
A: *Gloves.*
B: *Right!*

	Clothes	Accessories
My list		
My classmate's list		

3 **Why would you donate the items listed before? Explain in a few words.**

4 **Work in groups. Go online and find pictures of clothes and accessories that have been upcycled. Describe them.**

5 **Work in pairs. Choose a picture from Activity 4.**

1. **Student A:** Give hints about the clothing item / accessory.
   It's on the head.
2. **Student B:** Ask questions to discover the item.
   Is it blue? Is it a cap?
3. Show the drawing / picture to each other. Were the descriptions correct?

6 **Self-evaluation. Reflect on the tasks and complete this chart.**

Learning Objective	Rating
Did I ask / answer correctly?	☆☆☆
Did I use the grammar from the unit?	☆☆☆
Did I use the vocabulary in the unit?	☆☆☆
Was my pronunciation appropriate?	☆☆☆
Was my description correct?	☆☆☆

1 **What do we think about when considering a healthy diet? Why? Discuss with a classmate.**

1. The kind of food.
2. The amount of food.
3. The time of the meal.

2 **In your notebook, make a list of the food you usually eat in a week. Then divide it into healthy and "every-now-and-again" (food you should not eat every day).**

3 **Talk about your diet. Read the information in the two pictures. Go over your diet list in Activity 2. Is your diet healthy?**

- **Student A:** Tell your classmate about your diet and ask if he/she thinks it is healthy.
- **Student B:** Say what you think your classmate should/shouldn't eat or drink anymore.

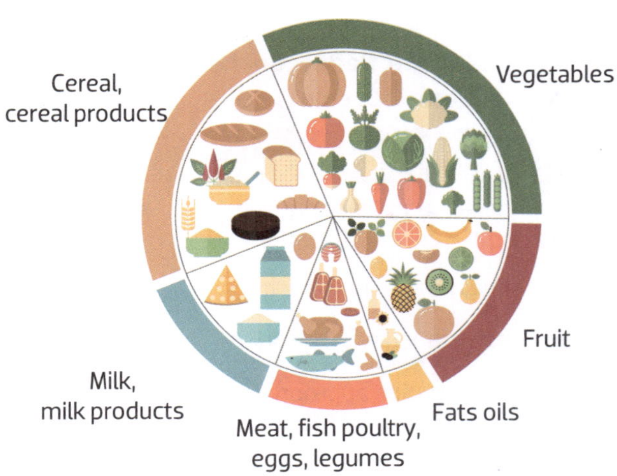

4 **Find and read the nutritional facts of the foods below. Ask and answer questions about them.**

Food	Information
candy bar	number of calories: 1 ____________
egg	% protein: 2 ____________
cookies	number of cookies in a pack: 3 ____________
milk	amount in a carton: 4 ____________

Do you know how many calories there are in a bar of chocolate?

5 **Work in groups of three. Follow the steps below. Then role play a conversation.**

1. You are at a new restaurant in town that offers organic food only.
2. One student is the server and two other students are the clients.
3. Prepare a menu together.

6 **Self-evaluation. Reflect on the tasks and complete this chart.**

Learning Objective	Rating
Did I use the grammar in the unit?	☆☆☆
Did I use the vocabulary in the unit?	☆☆☆
Did I practice the language I learned?	☆☆☆
Did I correct any mistakes?	☆☆☆
Was I fluent?	☆☆☆

1 Work in groups. Make a list of the gadgets you use every day in order of usefulness. Compare your lists.

2 Read these comments about people's favorite gadgets. Then comment on the gadget that is number one on your list.

ray89

For me, this is the best invention. I use it to clean the floor and also my desk. I think it is very useful.

5 comments

Mia_02 I don't think so. It needs electricity, and it is not environmentally-friendly.

3 Look for information about different machines, gadgets, and inventions. Which ones are sustainable? Which ones can make the environment a better place?

- **Student A:** Present your findings.
- **Student B:** Ask more questions to understand how environmentally-friendly the machine is.

4 Choose one of the devices you found in Activity 3. Tell a classmate.

1. When was it invented?
2. How did it help people?
3. How were people living without it at the time? How were they doing what the device is doing for them now?

5 Present your best gadget or device to the class. Your classmates should agree or disagree with you. Respond to them. When they present, agree or disagree with them.

6 Self-evaluation. Reflect on the task in Activity 5 and complete this chart.

Learning Objective	Rating
Did I use the language for agreeing / disagreeing?	☆☆☆
Did I use the grammar in the unit?	☆☆☆
Did I use the vocabulary in the unit?	☆☆☆
Was my pronunciation appropriate?	☆☆☆
Was I fluent and clear?	☆☆☆

1 **Look at this quote. What's your opinion about it? Discuss in groups.**

> My generation has largely failed until now to preserve both justice in the world and to preserve the planet. It is your generation that must make us accountable to make sure that we don't betray the future of humankind.
> *United Nations Secretary-General, António Guterres*

2 **You want to participate in a youth initiative against climate change. What actions do you need to take? Make notes.**

- **Student A:** Make a suggestion. Use phrasal verbs.
- **Student B:** Agree or disagree with the suggestion.
- **Student C:** Decide if the action will be included in your final list.

3 **Work in groups of three. Present your lists and give your opinion about the other lists.**

4 **Read your final list. Decide on the three most urgent actions needed. Prepare a short speech to convince the class to join your cause.**

5 **Present your speech to the class. Listen to your classmates' opinions and give yours.**

6 **Self-evaluation. Reflect on the tasks and complete this chart.**

Learning Objective	Rating
Did I use convincing arguments?	☆☆☆
Did I use the structures in the unit?	☆☆☆
Did I use the vocabulary in the unit?	☆☆☆
Was my pronunciation appropriate?	☆☆☆
Did I give my opinion?	☆☆☆
Was I clear in my speech?	☆☆☆

#TEEN TALK

1 **What are endangered animals? How are they related to the Sustainable Development Goals?**

2 **Work in pairs. Describe these endangered animals. Use the compound adjectives studied in the unit.**

1.

Giant panda

2.

Sea otter

3.

Snow leopard

4.

Gorilla

5.

Blue whale

6.

Tiger

7.

Whooping crane

8.

Tasmanian devil

A: *This is a fierce-looking animal.*
B: *A snow leopard.*
A: *No!*

3 **Find out information about these animals. Why are they endangered? Make notes.**

____
____
____
____
____
____
____
____

4 **Work in pairs. Follow the steps below.**

- **Student A:** Choose an animal from Activity 2.
- **Student B:** Ask questions to discover the animal.

A: *Is this an ocean-living animal?*
B: *Yes, it is.*
A: *Is it the sea otter?*
B: *No, it's the blue whale.*

5 **Talk about the animals you've seen. When and where did you see them?**

I've seen a giant panda. I went to a zoo in 2019.

6 **Self-evaluation. Reflect on the tasks and complete this chart.**

Learning Objective	Rating
Did I understand my classmate's information?	☆☆☆
Did I use the structures in the unit?	☆☆☆
Did I use the vocabulary in the unit?	☆☆☆
Was I clear?	☆☆☆
Was I fluent?	☆☆☆

1 **Think about different places to visit in your country for a cultural trip. Make a list.**

2 **Work in groups. Present the places you listed.**

- **Student A:** Say the place and what you can do there.
- **Student B:** Talk about a future situation that could occur if you go on this cultural trip. (for example: *If I go to Machu Picchu, I'll need to sleep in a tent*).
- **Student C:** Use the main clause of Student B and state a probable situation. (*If I sleep in a tent, I'll get a mosquito bite.*)

3 **Change groups. Share your lists and decide on a place to go.**

4 **Discuss arrangements to go to that place. Make notes.**

5 **Present your plans to the class. Follow these steps:**

1. Describe the place and say how you can get there.
2. Talk about the arrangements.
3. Talk about things you can do there.

6 **Self-evaluation. Reflect on the tasks and complete this chart.**

Learning Objective	Rating
Did I follow all the steps?	☆☆☆
Did I use the structures in the unit?	☆☆☆
Did I use the vocabulary in the unit?	☆☆☆
Was my pronunciation appropriate?	☆☆☆
Did I correct any mistakes?	☆☆☆
Was I fluent?	☆☆☆

1 **Imagine you could create a very special place of entertainment. Create a list of the different types of entertainment you would offer.**

2 **Work in pairs. Talk about the place you chose to create. Then discuss the things you must have in your place.**

- **Student A:** Say the types of entertainment you would offer in your place.
- **Student B:** Agree or disagree on what your classmate must have in his / her special place.

3 **Present one of the attractions from your entertainment place to the class. First, make notes. Use them when you speak.**

____

____

____

____

____

4 **How can you promote gender equality in your place? Think about the people and make notes. Share your ideas in small groups.**

____

____

____

____

5 **Self-evaluation. Reflect on the tasks. Then complete the chart.**

Learning Objective	Rating
Was I clear in the information I gave?	☆☆☆
Did I use the structures in the unit?	☆☆☆
Did I use the vocabulary in the unit?	☆☆☆
Was my pronunciation appropriate?	☆☆☆
Was I fluent?	☆☆☆

1 **Go over different newspapers and news websites and make a list of the most frequent crimes in your area. Take notes on numbers, dates, and other important information.**

2 **Work in pairs. Share your lists and discuss what people can do to avoid suffering from those crimes.**

Exchange phone numbers with your neighbors so you can share, discuss, and raise awareness about crime and safety-related activity in your community.

3 **Join another pair. Share what you discussed in Activity 2. Talk about the advantages and disadvantages of each suggestion to avoid such crimes.**

One positive aspect of sending everybody an instant message is that people will always be alert.

4 **Change groups. Discuss and role play a conversation. Follow these steps:**

1. Present the lists and the advantages / disadvantages you discussed.
2. Agree or disagree on them.
3. Include some more advantages / disadvantages that were not listed.

5 **Report back to the whole classroom. Show them the information you collected about the crimes in the area, the things people should do, and the advantages and disadvantages of each action.**

6 **Self-evaluation. Reflect on the tasks and complete this chart.**

Learning Objective	Rating
Did I follow the instructions to do the tasks?	☆☆☆
Did I use the structures in the unit?	☆☆☆
Did I use the vocabulary in the unit?	☆☆☆
Did I work collaboratively?	☆☆☆
Did I help my classmates?	☆☆☆
Was I fluent and clear?	☆☆☆

GAMES

1 **Work in pairs. Interview your classmate.**

1. Do you like going to the beach?
2. Do you prefer colder or hotter places?
3. Which is more exciting, the countryside or the big city?

2 **Play *Complete the Word*.**

Instructions:

1. You need a die.
2. Write numbers 1 to 6 on the board:

Number 1: An *–ed* and *–ing* adjective.
Numbers 2 and 3: Compare three elements.
Numbers 4 and 5: Talk about your likes and dislikes (activities).
Number 6: Make a request or an offer.

3 **Play in pairs.**

Instructions:

Student A: Roll the die.
Student B: Present a situation. For example, give an *–ed* and *–ing* adjective, tell Student A what to compare, etc.
Student A: Do what Student B says. Is the answer correct? Color in one letter on the board. Is it incorrect? Wait for your next turn.
Swap roles.

4 **In groups, answer the questions about the game.**

1. Was the game fun to play?
2. What was the easiest part?
3. What was difficult? Why?

1 Work in small groups. Look at the different clothing styles. Which one do you like best? Why?

1.

2.

3.

2 Play *Dress the Body!*

Instructions

1. Draw a body in your notebook.
2. In pairs, one student flips a coin.
   - **Heads:** choose a piece of clothing or an accessory for your body. Say *My character is wearing...* and draw it on the body.
   - **Tails:** tell your classmate something to draw on his / her body.

Important:
   - You can only give one element per turn, for example *My character is wearing a skirt.* You draw a skirt. *My character is wearing a green skirt.* You color the skirt green.
   - You can't repeat any words that your classmate has used.
3. If the answer is correct, draw the item of clothing on the body. If the answer is wrong, miss a turn.
   Flip the coin.
4. When the body is fully clothed with one accessory and four items of clothing from the unit, the student who completes it must describe everything.
5. If the description is correct, there's a winner.

Winner: The first student to have drawn at least four items of clothing and one accessory.

3 Discuss the following questions about the game.

1. Did you know the names of the two sides of a coin?
2. Was it easy to memorize them?
3. Did you remember all the clothing items you wanted?
4. Was it easy or difficult to play the game?
5. What was the most difficult thing about the game?

1 Work in small groups. You and your friends are organizing a picnic in the park. What food and drinks would you like to bring and why? Discuss.

2 Play *Guess the List.*

My shopping list

	Quantity

My classmate's shopping list

	Quantity

Instructions

First complete your list. Include countable and uncountable food items. Include containers in the quantity column and quantifiers.

How to play:

1. Play in pairs.
2. **Student A:** Ask B about food, for example *Do you need any...?* If the answer is *Yes*, ask about quantity and complete one line on the second shopping list. If the answer is *No*, don't write anything.
   Student B: Do the same; ask Student A about food. If the answer is *Yes*, ask about quantity.
3. To win: When the list is ready, read it out. Is the list correct? You win.

3 In groups, answer the questions about the game.

1. Was the game fun to play?
2. What was the easiest part?
3. What was difficult? Why?

1 **Work in groups. What gadgets do you usually use in your everyday life? How do they help you?**

2 **You are going to play a game called *What is it?* Read the instructions.**

Instructions

You need pieces of paper. On each one, write the name of a device, gadget, or machine.

How to play:

1. Play in pairs. Look at the example.
2. Collect all the cards, shuffle them, and put them face down on the desk, table, or floor.
   Student A: Take one card. Don't show it to Student B. Give a clue.
   Student B: Guess. Is it correct? 2 points. Is it incorrect? Student A will give you another clue.
   Student A: If necessary, give another clue.
   Student B: Guess. Is it correct? 1 point. Is it incorrect? 0 points.
3. Every time you guess correctly, write the name of the machine, gadget, or device on a sticky note on this page.
4. Switch roles.

3 **In groups, answer the questions about the game.**

1. Was the game fun to play?
2. What was the easiest part?
3. What was difficult? Why?

1 **Work in small groups. Use the phrasal verbs from the box to talk about predictions in the future.**

eat out	give up	look for	throw away	work out

I will throw away my old cell phone and buy a more modern one.

I don't care much for cell phones. I will look for a better computer.

2 **You are going to play a game called *Mime and Guess*. Read the instructions.**

Instructions

1. On pieces of paper, write down predictions, definite plans, schedules, and intentions.
2. Write at least two of each. On the other side of the card, write A or B, depending on which team you are on.

How to play:

1. Play in groups of four or six students. There are two teams: A and B.
2. Put the two sets of cards (A and B) on the desk or floor.
3. **Group A:** One member of Group A takes a B card, reads it, and mimes the sentence to his / her team. If they can guess correctly: 1 point. If they can't guess correctly: 0 points.
   Group B: One member of Group B takes an A card, reads it, and mimes the sentence to his / her team. If they can guess correctly: 1 point. If they can´t guess correctly: 0 points.

Rules:

1. The student miming can't speak.
2. The other team has to remain silent.
3. No shouting.

3 **In groups, answer the questions about the game.**

1. Was the game fun to play?
2. What was the easiest part?
3. What was difficult? Why?

1 Work in small groups. Take turns describing the following animals. Use the compound adjectives studied in the unit.

1.

2.

3.

2 You are going to play a game called *Snakes and Ladders*. Read the instructions.

Instructions

You need a die with numbers 1–6 and a small object to use as a counter (a coin, a tiny paper ball, etc.)

How to play:

1. Play in groups of four or six students.
2. First, each student gives three pieces of information using compound adjectives, for example: *Giraffes are long-necked animals*. Listen carefully. You can't write anything down.
3. Roll your die. The player with the highest number starts the game. Roll the die again and move forward the number of squares shown on the die. To remain on the square, you have to repeat some of the information provided by your classmates.

Rules:

1. If you land at the bottom of a ladder, you climb it. If you land on the head of a snake, you go down to its tail.
2. You cannot repeat the information somebody has already given.

3 In groups, answer the questions about the game.

1. Was the game fun to play?
2. What was the easiest part?
3. What was difficult? Why?

1 **Answer the following questions with a classmate. Give complete answers.**

1. What will happen if you put your hand in the fire?

____

2. If the sun rises in the east, where does it set?

____

3. What will you feel if a dog bites you?

____

4. If it rains tomorrow, what will you do?

____

2 **You are going to play a game called *Complete the Puzzle*. Read the instructions.**

Instructions

1. Play in pairs.
2. Say a sentence using the conditionals you studied in the unit. Do not complete it. Your classmate has to complete it. If it's correct, he / she can match two pieces of the jigsaw puzzle.
3. To do so, draw a line connecting the two pieces.
4. Swap roles.

Rules:

1. If you started your first statement with *If*, start your second statement with the consequence.
2. If you complete the statement with a Zero Conditional, the second time use the First Conditional.

3 **In groups, answer the questions about the game.**

1. Was the game fun to play?
2. What was the easiest part?
3. What was difficult? Why?

1 **Work in pairs. Take turns answering the following questions.**

1. What do you feel when you stroke your hair?
2. How would you describe the smell of coffee in the morning?
3. What does your favorite fruit taste like?
4. How do you feel when you see someone you really like?

2 **You are going to play a guessing game. Read the rules.**

Instructions

1. Play in groups of six. Divide the big group into two groups of three.
2. In each small group, make a list of items to describe. Include food, animals, objects, etc. Write them on individual pieces of paper. Collect all the pieces of paper and put them in a bag. Label each bag (Groups 1 and 2).

How to play:

1. A student from Group 1 picks a piece of paper from Group 2. He / She has to describe the item using verbs of senses. The other members of the group have to guess what it is.
2. Swap roles.

Rules:

1. You cannot say the name of the item on the piece of paper.
2. The team has to guess the item in one minute. If they don't, they don't score any points. If they do, they score 1 point.

3 **In groups, answer the questions about the game.**

1. Was the game fun to play?
2. What was the easiest part?
3. What was difficult? Why?

1 Look at the pictures. What do you think happened? Tell your classmates. Who has the best story?

1.

2.

2 You are going to play a game called *Memory Game*. Read the instructions.

Instructions

1. You will play in pairs.
2. First, each student has to look back over all the units. Concentrate on the videos, the vocabulary, grammar, speaking sections, and the reading texts. On the cards, write a question. The questions should be about the vocabulary, the situations on the videos, the topic of the readings, etc. Here are two examples:
   A card with these words: Name three endangered animals.
   A card with these words: If it rains next Saturday, ...
3. Create 15 cards. Put all the cards together, shuffle them, and put them face down on the table.

How to play:

1. Student 1 picks up a card from the other student's pile, reads it , and completes the instruction / sentence on the card. If the answer is correct, Student 1 scores 2 points. If it's partially correct, 1 point. If it's incorrect, 0 points.
2. Swap roles.

Rules:

1. You cannot use the same card twice.
2. When you've used all the cards, add up the points. Who's the winner?

3 In groups, answer the questions about the game.

1. Was the game fun to play?
2. What was the easiest part?
3. What was difficult? Why?

GRAMMAR GLOSSARY

Comparatives and Superlatives

Base Form	Comparative	Superlative
Short adjective	short adjective +er than	*the* short adjective +est
Long adjective	more + long adjective than	the most + long adjective
Irregular adjective: good	better than	the best
Irregular adjective: bad	worse than	the worst

1. We use comparative forms when we compare two elements (two people, two objects, two places, etc.)
2. We use superlative forms when we compare more than two elements.
3. In all comparative forms we use *than* after the comparative adjective.
4. In all superlative forms, *the* goes before the superlative adjective.

*The first course is **shorter than** the second course. The third course is **the shortest**. It's **the best**, too.*

*The second course is **more interesting than** the third course, but I think **the most interesting** course is the first one. I think it's **better than** the third course, too.*

*Course number four is **worse than** other courses. It's **the worst** course for me. It doesn't have any practical activities.*

Likes and Dislikes + *-ing*

Likes / Dislikes	Object / Person / Place	Activity
Like / dislike	+ noun	+ verb + -ing
Hate / love	+ noun	+ verb + -ing

1. *like / dislike / hate / love* + noun: the noun is plural when it's **countable** and singular when it's **uncountable**.

*I like **books**. I hate **milk**.*

2. *like / dislike / hate / love* + verb + *-ing*: just add *-ing* to the verb.

*I like **reading**. I love **studying**.*

Spelling

When the verb ends in *-e*, we delete the *-e* and add *-ing*.

*I **ride** my bike in the morning. I like **riding my bike**.*

Would like for Requests and Offers

Requests		Offers	
For something	For an activity	For something	For an activity
I'd like + noun	I'd like to + verb	Would you like + noun?	Would you like to + verb?

1. We use *would like* when we make a request (= want something).

***A:** I'd like a glass of water, please.*
***B:** Sure! Here you are.*
***A:** I'd like to start at 5 o'clock.*
***B:** I'm sorry, I can't.*

2. We also use *would like* to make an offer.

***A:** Would you like to play?*
***B:** Sure. I love video games.*
***A:** Would you like a sandwich?*
***B:** No, thanks.*

Simple Present vs. Present Continuous

Simple Present	Present Continuous
routines	activities in progress
likes and dislikes	exceptions to routines

1. We use the Simple Present to refer to habits and routines. We also use it for likes and dislikes.

I like chocolate.
I have chocolate and cookies for breakfast.

2. We use the Present Continuous for activities in progress. We can also use it together with the Simple Present to show exceptions to routines or habits.

A: *What are you doing, Sam?*
B: *I'm doing my homework.*
I usually do my homework in the evening, but today I can't. I'm doing it now.

Subject and Object Questions

Question Word	Subject	Object
What	What is that? What could happen?	What are you doing?
Who	Who's your best friend? Who can ride a bike? Who likes chocolate?	Who can you help? Who do you like?

1. When we ask about the subject, we don't use the auxiliary verb.
2. We can ask about the subject using different tenses and verbs.
3. When we ask about the subject, we don't know the answer, so the verb is in the singular.

What ***is*** *happening?*
Who ***likes*** *chocolate?*

4. When we ask about the object, we use an auxiliary, then the subject and the verb.
5. We can ask about the object using different tenses and verbs.

What **do you like?**
Who **are you describing?**

Countable and Uncountable Nouns

Countable Nouns	Uncountable Nouns
Things in the singular or plural	Only in the singular

1. Countable nouns refer to objects we can count using numbers. They take *a / an* in the singular, for example: *an apple, a cookie, a pizza, an orange*. And take numbers in the plural: *two oranges, three pizzas*.
2. Uncountable nouns refer to things we cannot count, such as substances, abstract ideas and qualities. Some examples are: *orange juice, air, beauty, safety*. As they don't have a plural form, there's no need to use *a / an* with uncountable nouns. To count them, we use containers or quantifiers. For example: *a bottle of milk, a pot of yogurt, a loaf of bread, a liter of water*.
3. Sometimes uncountable nouns are used as countable; here the meaning is not the substance but the object. For example: *one ice cream*, meaning *one ice cream cone*; *a coffee*, meaning *a cup of coffee*.

Quantifiers

Countable Nouns		
Affirmative	**Interrogative**	**Negative**
Some	Any	Any
	How many	
		Many
A lot of		

Uncountable Nouns		
Affirmative	**Interrogative**	**Negative**
Some	Any	Any
	How much	
		Much
A lot of		

1. *How many* and *How much* are used to ask about quantity. For the answers, we use quantifiers, containers, or measure words.

__How many__ apples are there? Two, some, a kilo, not many.
__How much__ milk is there? Two liters, a bottle, a lot, not much.

2. *A lot of* shows big quantity.

There is __a lot of__ people in the park today.

3. *Much* and *many* are usually used in the negative and in questions.

There isn't __much__ food in the refrigerator.
There aren't __many__ cookies in the jar.
Is there __much__ food in the refrigerator?
Are there __many__ cookies in the jar?

Indirect Questions

Direct Question	Indirect Question
What time does the supermarket open?	Can you tell me what time the supermarket opens?
What time is it?	Can you tell me what time it is?
How much sugar do you need?	Can you tell me how much sugar you need?

1. Indirect questions are more polite and a little more formal. We usually use them when we talk to a person we don't know, for example, when walking in the street, in a store, etc.

Do you know where the nearest park is?

2. We don't use auxiliary verbs in indirect questions.

Can you tell me where you bought the ice cream?

Past Continuous

Subject	Aux. verb	Main verb
I / He / She / It	was	verb + -ing
You / We / They	were	

1. We use the Past Continuous to show activities in progress in the past.

At 4:30 yesterday, I **was studying**. My mom and dad **were working**, and my sister **was playing** in the garden. My brother **wasn't studying**. He **was playing** video games.

2. In the Past Continuous, the activities start before the time reference and we don't know whether the activities are complete or not.

I started studying before 4:30. My mom and dad started working before 4:30, and my sister started playing in the garden before that, too. My brother started playing video games before 4:30.

Simple Past and Past Continuous

When	Simple Past	Past Continuous
While	Past Continuous	Simple Past

1. We use the Past Continuous and the Simple Past to refer to two simultaneous actions in the past.

   The action expressed by the Past Continuous was in progress when the action in the Simple Past happened.

While I **was studying** last Friday, my grandma **arrived** home.

I was studying

My grandma arrived

2. *When* introduces the action in the Simple Past.

When she arrived, I was studying.

3. *While* introduces the action in the Past Continuous.

She arrived **while** I was studying.

4. We can refer to the action in the Past Continuous first, or to the action in the Simple Past.

While I was studying, she arrived. = She arrived while I was studying.

When she arrived, I was studying. = I was studying when she arrived.

Future Plans and Intentions

Will	Going to	Present Continuous	Simple Present
predictions	intentions	plans	schedules

1. We can use all these forms to refer to the future.
2. *Will* is used to express a prediction. When we make a prediction, we indicate a time reference.

*In 30 years' time, people **will fly** to work. They **won't use** gas for cars.*

3. *Going to* expresses an intention for the future.

*When I finish school, **I'm going to start** university.*
***I'm going to work**, too, but **I'm not going to work** outdoors.*
*Susan **is going to help** her mom at home.*

4. The Present Continuous is used to talk about definite plans. A person or a group of people make the plan. We can change the plans, but we need to say when.

*We**'re visiting** the Technology Museum on Wednesday.*
*We **aren't traveling** by bus, we're taking the train.*

5. The Simple Present is used for future time reference when we talk about schedules. We can't change them.

*We have to hurry up, our train **leaves** at 8:00.*

Too and *Enough*

Too		
Too + adjective	*Too much* + uncountable noun	
	Too many + plural noun	

Enough	
Enough + noun	Adjective + *enough*

1. We use *too* and *enough* to indicate quantity.
2. *Too* indicates that something is not acceptable, and *enough* indicates it's acceptable.

*It's **too cold**, we can't play outside. The temperature is not high.*
*We have **enough food** for the picnic, we don't need to go to the supermarket.*

3. *Too* has a negative meaning.

This sweater is very big. (it means it's oversized, but you can wear it)
*This sweater is **too big**! (it means you can't wear it)*

4. We use *too much* + noun with uncountable nouns.

*This hamburger has **too much salt**.*

5. We use *too many* + plural countable nouns.

*There are **too many cars** in this city. We can't move around.*

Present Perfect + *ever / never*

Questions	Sentence with a verb in the affirmative
Present Perfect + *ever* ?	Present perfect + *never*

1. We use the Present Perfect with *ever* to ask about experiences. We don't use *ever* in affirmative or negative sentences.

A: *Have you* ***ever*** *seen an okapi?*
B: *No, never.*
A: *Has your sister* ***ever*** *seen a tarantula?*
B: *Yes, she has.*

2. When we answer *Yes...*, we may add information using the Simple Past.

Yes, she has. She saw one when we were in the mountains in the south of the country.

3. We use *never* with the Present Perfect to refer to experiences we have not had, with a verb in the affirmative.

*We****'ve never traveled*** *by plane.*

Present Perfect + *for / since*

For	Since
Period of time	Point in time

1. We use the Present Perfect to indicate a period of time up to the present.

I've studied *English for six years.*
My parents ***have worked*** *in this office since 2016.*

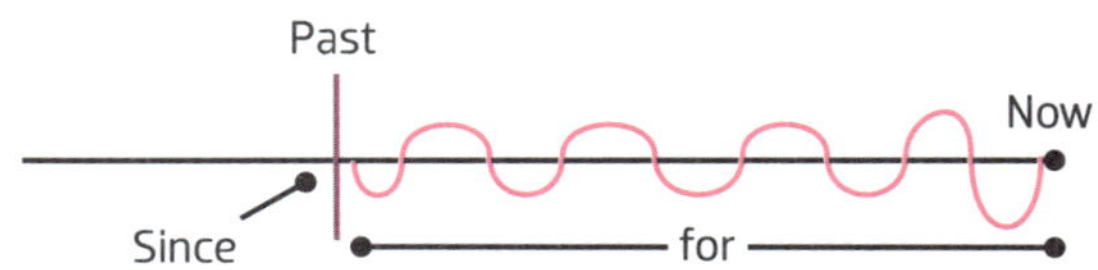

2. The actions may be complete or not.

3. We need a reference to a period of time after *for*, for example: *for two weeks, for seven years, for two months.*
4. We need a point in time after *since*, for example: *since yesterday, since 7:00 o'clock, since my birthday.*

I've lived *in this house since 2018. I'm still living in this house.*

*We****'ve visited*** *our grandparents three times since the beginning of the year.* (We aren't visiting them now, each action of visiting them is complete, but the period of time is not complete. Maybe we'll visit them again.)

Zero Conditional

If clause	Main clause
Simple Present	Simple Present

1. In conditional sentences, an action depends on a condition, and the main clause shows a result. For instance, *if you travel to another country*, you *need a passport*. The condition is *traveling to another country*, and the result is that *you need a passport*. So we say: *If you travel to another country, you need a passport.*
2. In zero conditional sentences, the time reference is general. This means it's true now, it was true in the past, and most probably will be true in the future. You needed a passport in the past, you need it now, and most probably you'll need one in the future.
3. We can begin the sentence with the *if* clause or the main clause. The meaning is the same.

If you travel to Antarctica, you must wear warm clothes.
You must wear warm clothes if you travel to Antarctica.

Prepositions with Means of Transportation

By	Land, air, water
	Bus, boat, bike, car, taxi, coach, plane

1. We use the preposition *by* to refer to means of transportation.

*We go to school **by** bus, we never go **by** train.*

2. There are two exceptions: *on foot* and *on horseback*.
3. We can refer to the specific means of transportation, for example: *by subway*, *by car*, or the general means, *by water*, *by land*, *by air*.
4. When you travel on a ship, you say *by boat*.

First Conditional

If clause	Main clause
Simple Present	Will

1. In first conditional sentences, the time reference is future and the situation is probable.

*You'**ll need** to buy a backpack if you go camping. (You'll probably go camping.)*

2. We can begin the sentence with the *if* clause or the main clause. The meaning is the same.

*If you take a big suitcase, it **will be** very heavy.*
*It **will be** very heavy if you take a big suitcase.*

3. You can use modal verbs too, without will.

*You **must buy** a backpack if you go camping.*

Must not

Obligation	Prohibition
Must	Must not

1. *Must not* expresses prohibition to do something.

*We **must not talk** in a library.*
*We **mustn't take** photos with flash in a museum.*

2. We use *can't* to express no permission and *must not* to express prohibition.

*We **can't play** outside, it's raining.* (when it's not raining, we have permission to play outside)
*We **must not** play outside.* (a prohibition at all times)

3. We use *should* and *shouldn't* to express moral obligation and to give advice. *Shouldn't* expresses a moral obligation *not* to do something, but it isn't a prohibition.

*I **shouldn't eat** candy, it's bad for my teeth.*

Verbs of the Senses and Adjectives

Verb	Adjective
Look	beautiful
Smell	awful
Sound	interesting
Taste	sweet
Feel	soft

1. We use verbs of senses + adjectives to describe people, objects, and places.

*My city **looks** nice. It **smells** fantastic because there are lots of trees and flowers.*
*That cake doesn't **look** nice, but it **tastes** delicious.*
*Your idea **sounds** boring, let's do something different.*
*This teddy bear **feels** very soft.*

2. The adjective depends on the sense. Some adjectives can be used with more than one sense, such as *nice* or *salty*. Something sounds nice, looks nice, tastes and smells nice.

*This food **smells** good but **tastes** salty.*

3. These verbs are not used with the Present Continuous, only with simple tenses.

*That perfume **smells** awful, but the bottle **looks** beautiful.*
*My grandma's food was super. It always **tasted** nice.*

Indefinite Pronouns

	People	Objects	Places
Every			
Some	body / one	thing	where
Any			
No			

1. These pronouns are impersonal because they do not refer to a person, thing, or place in particular.
2. We use *some...* and *every...* in affirmative sentences.

Somebody *has committed a crime.* ***Everybody*** *has to be careful these days.*

3. *No...* takes the verb in the affirmative, but the meaning is negative.

There's ***nothing*** *here. We can go* ***nowhere***, *we have to stay at home.*

4. We use *any...* in the interrogative and negative.

Is there ***anybody*** *in the garden? I can't see* ***anything***!

5. All of them take a verb in the singular.

Nobody was *absent yesterday.*
Is there anywhere *we can go?*

Relative Pronouns

Person	Object / Thing
who, that	which, that

1. Relative clauses give information about a noun.

The man ***who was here yesterday*** *is a thief.*
The thing ***that he stole*** *is a watch.*

2. The pronouns *who, that,* or *which* refer to the noun mentioned before.

The crime ***that*** *he committed is awful.*
*(****That*** *refers to the crime)*
I saw a man ***who*** *was suspicious.*
*(****Who*** *refers to a man)*

3. We can use *that* for people or things.

So for Results and Consequences

Result	Because	Reason
He is the best student	because	he studies a lot.
Reason	**So**	**Result**
He studies a lot,	so	he is the best student.

1. **So** – is used to show the results of an action.

I have to study all weekend ***so*** *I can pass my test.*

2. ***Because*** – is used to show the cause of an action.

We are listening to music ***because*** *we are excited.*

Adverbs of Manner

Adjective	Adverb
quick	quickly
nice	nicely
bad	badly
good	well

1. Adverbs of manner give us information about the way in which an activity is performed or carried out.

She sings ***beautifully***. *I can dance very* ***well***.

2. Adverbs of manner are formed by adding *–ly* to the adjective.

She ***quickly*** *helped me with the books.*

3. There's an exception to the rule: *well* is the adverb for *good*.

#AUDIO TRACKS

Unit	Tracks	Page	Activities
-	01	Introduction	
0	02	6	1
	03	7	3
	04	10	4
1	05	12	1
	06	13	4
	07	16	4
2	08	18	1
	09	19	4
	10	22	4
3	11	24	1
	12	25	3
	13	25	4
	14	28	4
4	15	30	1
	16	31	3
	17	32	2
	18	32	3
	19	34	4
5	20	36	1
	21	37	3
	22	40	4
6	23	42	1
	24	44	1
	25	46	4
7	26	48	1
	27	49	4
	28	50	2
	29	50	3
	30	52	4
8	31	54	1
	32	55	3
	33	56	2
	34	58	4

UNIT ZERO

Activity 1 02

I feel like I need to develop my artistic skills. I've decided this is what I want to do in life. Maybe a basic course on drawing would help me now.

Activity 3 03

N: Noah

N: Guys, I have the list of summer courses with me. They are courses you can do in one week or two. There are so many courses, I am going to register for three or four. I want to do a poetry reading course. I love reading poetry! Hey, Janice, why don't you take the course with me? I know you like writing poetry, too. I also want to take a data analysis course. I hate studying math, but I need to practice, so this course is great for me. Hey, Ron, do you want to join me? I know you don't like math very much, but I think you need some extra classes, too. Well, there are two other courses I like, so maybe I can register for them, too. I like dancing, so I think I can do the tango lessons. Oh, and I like singing, too. There is a course called *Become a Singer*. Linda, it would be great to have you with me in this course. Then we can finally get ready to start our band! What do you say, guys? Let me know, OK?

Activity 4 04

N: Nancy **E: Elliot**

N: Elliot, I want to take a language course. Would you like to take a course with me?

E: Sure! Is it online?

N: Yes, it is completely online. I'm thinking about taking French or German. What do you think?

E: Hmm... I like French, but in my opinion, German is more important for my future career. I want to be an engineer and work for a large car manufacturer in Germany.

N: I prefer French, but alright. Let's do German then. They offer the course two evenings per week or on Saturday mornings.

E: I have a lot of free time, but I prefer evenings.

N: Oh... But it is on Monday and Wednesday evenings. I can't on Wednesdays. Is it OK for you to have this class on Saturdays?

E: Sure, that also works for me. But can we start next month? I have a lot of tests this month.

N: Hmm... The next class starts at the end of this month... There is another class in three months, but I think it's better to start now than later.

E: No problem. I can organize myself to start at the end of the month.

N: Deal! Thanks, Elliot.

UNIT ONE

Activity 1 05

D: Don **L: Lara**

D: Lara, I'm thinking of donating some of these clothes. What do you think?

L: I think it is a great idea! Let me see, what clothes are you talking about?

D: These shirts and jeans. What do you think?

L: Don, they are full of holes and ripped. They are no good for donation.

D: Oh... So what do I do with these clothes?

L: I don't know... We need a solution for clothes that are not good for donation. There are so many people with no clothes. They need help.

Activity 4 06

G: George **B: Brenda**

G: Welcome back to *The Show is Now*, and today I'm talking to Brenda, the creator of the website *New Use for the Old*. Brenda, welcome to our show.

B: Hello! I'm glad to be here and to show you my website.

G: So Brenda, what is on your website?

B: Oh, you can find everything there, old T-shirts, jeans, jackets...

G: But why do people look for your website? They can just donate their clothes to charity.

B: No, they can't. These clothes that just arrived are no good for donation. They are not just old. They usually have holes in them and are in very bad condition.

G: Oh, I see. Who posts on your website?

B: All kinds of people, not only poor people. Sometimes we like some clothes or accessories very much, and we want to find a new use for them, so my website offers a solution.

G: OK, and how do you offer the solution?

B: Well, I don't, other users offer the solution. They post ideas, and you can read all the ideas before you make a decision.

G: That's really great! Congratulations!

Activity 4 07

A: Amós **L: Lauren**

A: Did you see the clothes sale on our favorite fashion store website?

L: Are you kidding me? Of course, I did. But there are a lot of vintage clothes. Not my style.

A: I'm more trendy, too. But the boots are amazing.

L: Which boots do you like the most? Show me.

A: These ones, the brown ones. Take a look at the price. Just $20. That's really cheap.

L: Nice, but they seem old fashioned, with these stains and holes right here.

A: That's exactly what makes them stylish and fashionable. Without the holes they would be boring and traditional. And the stains are perfect! I think they are original.

L: Hmm, I don't know. I prefer to buy durable shoes...

UNIT TWO

Activity 1 08

E: Emily M: Mia

E: Hey, Mia, check out this online menu on the Learn a Bit and Eat it app.

M: Wow! They have foods from all over the world! Look, Brazilian feijoada. I love it! Let's order some.

E: Wait, let's see the other options they have. Hmm... Fish and chips?

M: Yuck! I am not a big fan of fish. Last time I had fish and chips I felt really sick.

E: OK... Let's not order any fish and chips then.

M: Look, they offer ceviche. You can get three portions for a special price.

E: Yeah... But I'm not very much into raw fish. I think your first option is the best one. Let's order some feijoada.

M: Agreed. And see if they have grape juice, too. I'd love to have some!

E: All right.

Activity 4 09

Hi, Celia. Can you stop by the supermarket on your way home? How much money do you have on you? I want to make a key lemon pie, but we don't have all the ingredients. So I need you to buy eight limes to make some lime juice and... Oh, yes, I need some sweetened condensed milk, too. And eggs... No, you don't need to buy any eggs or butter. How many eggs do we need to make this pie? Let me check... Well, we have four eggs here. I guess that's OK. I also need some sugar and a pack of crackers. All right, I think that is all... No, wait. I also need some milk. I guess I have all the rest. Thanks, darling. See you in a while.

Activity 4 10

I'd like to talk about *The Wow's snacks* in Phoenix. I really like sandwiches and they have some interesting choices, like the special spicy sandwich and the four-cheese sandwich. These are my favorite and I recommend them. The place is also very good. They have a bar where you can have some special drinks before you eat. The service is good, too. I just think they need more servers there. There are only three and the space is very large, so there are a lot of people, but not many servers. Oh, and I think it's a little expensive, especially the drinks. But I still recommend it to friends and family.

UNIT THREE

Activity 1 11

E: Emily M: Mia

E: Mia, look at this picture my dad took last weekend.

M: Wow! That's awesome! But, wait. Does he have a drone?

E: My dad is a tech geek! He loves all kinds of tech devices and gadgets.

M: Drones take really awesome pictures, but I was reading a text for a school assignment and they can do so much more than that.

E: Really? What else can they do?

M: They're used for all kinds of aerial inspections.

E: Well, that makes sense.

M: Yeah, and my mom works for a company that's testing the use of drones to deliver packages.

E: That's so cool! I think drones are a very useful invention. When they start delivering things, they'll help a lot of people.

M: What do you mean?

E: For example, they could deliver medicine or vaccines to dangerous places, like war zones.

M: Brilliant, Emily!

Activities 3 and 4 12 and 13

G: George C: Chloe

G: Good morning everyone! Welcome back to *The Show is Now*, and today I'm talking to Chloe. She's a history teacher, and she's going to talk about a great inventor. So, Chloe, who's this great inventor you want to talk about today?

C: Good morning, George. Well, I want to talk about a very special inventor. Her name is Maria Telkes. She was a Hungarian inventor who made a great contribution to humanity.

G: That's great! What did she invent?

C: Among other things, she invented the first solar-powered heater.

G: That's very interesting. Nowadays, many cities around the world use solar systems in their homes.

C: Exactly!

G: And how did you become aware of Maria Telkes's work?

C: I was reading about solar energy because I wanted a more sustainable house. When I was researching, I found an article about her and became interested in her work. Maria has also invented other devices to store solar energy.

G: She's really made a great contribution to a more sustainable world.

Activity 4 14

M: Matthew R: Rebecca

M: One day, in 2016, I was looking at some things in an electronics store when I saw this wonderful scientific calculator. It looked so technological that I thought: I want one of those! So I bought it. When I showed it to my friends, I was really excited until one of them said, *That's cool, but you can just type 'scientific calculator' into a search engine and get something with the same functions as this*. That's when I realized I hadn't spent the money well...

R: Four years ago, I joined a book club. My friends from the club had the idea to buy an e-reader, which is like a tablet, but you can read digital books with it. I went online and bought one. At first I was amazed because most of my friends from the club had one. But then one day I told my cousin about it and she asked, *Why did you buy an e-reader? You can use your phone or your tablet to download an e-reader app. It's basically the same thing.* I tried it, and the apps are very similar to an e-reader, but not the same. I used my e-reader for a while when I was part of the book club, but after that my e-reader had no use.

UNIT FOUR

Activity 1 15

Hi, Xavier. Sorry for sending you a message so late, but I was at my grandpa's and just forgot my cell phone. Listen, I can't go to the movies with you on Saturday. I'm going to the mall with my grandpa. He needs help picking out a new smartphone. Are you free on Sunday?

Activity 3 16

Hmm ... An e-mail from Max. Let's see...

Hello, Joyce. How are you? I hope all is well. I'm going to be in Cartagena next Tuesday and wanted to check something with you. Can you pick me up at the airport? My flight arrives at 4:20 p.m. and I'm meeting John for dinner at 7:00pm. I think he'll be at work before then, so I need this favor from you. I also have something I want to tell you, but I'm only going to tell you in person, so maybe we can grab a coffee when you pick me up? Please let me know. Love, Max.

Max is coming to Cartagena... I think he has some great news to tell me... I'll send him an e-mail explaining that I won't be able to pick him up until 6:00.

Activity 2 and 3 17 and 18

Z: Zack V: Vivian

Z: Wow, Vivian, this list is really long. Do you have enough money to buy all these gadgets?

V: Oh, of course not! It's more of a list of things I'd like to buy, not things I'm going to buy. For example, I'm not going to buy a new smartphone.

Z: Then why is it on your list?

V: Because... because... I don't know. But the phone I want to buy is too expensive; it's the SPX Plus model, and I think I can get a good phone for less money.

Z: In my opinion, this phone isn't worth its price. But look, this smartwatch is great and you can get a discount if you pay cash.

V: Yeah... But I don't have enough money. I have to pay for these things with a credit card.

Z: What about the tablet for Maya? Are you going to buy it?

V: I'm not sure... The operating system is too old. Also, I don't think this brand offers good quality products.

Z: All right, so the tablet for Maya and the smartwatch for Grandma... Wait a minute, a smartwatch for Grandma?

V: Yes, I want to give it to her as a gift.

Z: I don't think she'd use a gadget like that.

V: Well, you obviously don't know Grandma. She can teach you how to set up a smartwatch or your smartphone. She knows a lot about technology. I think she's the smartest person in my family.

Activity 4 19

1. I think the next device I'm going to buy is an e-book reader. I'm very interested in literature, especially mystery novels, and I have too many print books that I don't read anymore, so maybe digital books can help me save trees.
2. I don't really want to buy anything, but my best friend always says I need a smartwatch. I go jogging three times a week and sometimes I'm late for my appointments because I never pay attention to the time when I exercise. So, yes, maybe I should get a smartwatch.
3. A new gadget? I don't need anything. I think people buy too many digital gadgets. It's like they never have enough technology with them. Maybe I need a new phone, but I don't want to buy it now. I prefer to wait until this phone stops working.
4. I don't want to buy anything now, but I really want my sister to get me a new virtual assistant. She says that I'll get one for my birthday. Well, let's see... My birthday is in two months. Fingers crossed!
5. I want to buy new wireless headphones to listen to music at school, but my mom says I can't. The headphones I want are too expensive, and we don't have money for them now. But I really want to save money and buy these headphones one day.

UNIT FIVE

Activity 1 20

Good afternoon, everyone. We are here today with Dr. Lasso from the Central College of Ecuador. Dr. Lasso is a specialist in unusual animals in the Galapagos Islands, and he is here today to talk about the giant tortoise, a very interesting animal that can live well over a hundred years...

Activity 3 21

Hello, everyone. It's a pleasure to talk about this city that I love. I have lived here for five years and have had the opportunity to do many interesting things. Over the last five years I have made many good friends, and we have experienced many things together. We have tried mountain biking together, and we have also organized some skating competitions. I have never been to the city museum, but I plan to visit it soon. It has been a great experience to live in this wonderful city!

Activity 4 22

M: Mia J: Josh

M: Josh, will you watch the documentary that the science teacher suggested?

J: Of course! I cannot wait to learn more about Antarctica.

M: I bet it'll be really interesting. Last week I saw the movie about the grasslands, but I think a polar habitat is more interesting.

J: I think so, too. Ms. Jay also mentioned a documentary about deserts around the world. Have you guys seen it?

M: Yes, I have. Really interesting stuff. I am sure you'll enjoy it.

UNIT SIX

Activity 1 23

C: Caleb G: Grace

C: Hi, Grace. I'm glad I ran into you. There's something I want to ask you.

G: Hey, Caleb. Sure, shoot.

C: I'm going to Singapore next month with my family and I remember you were there a year ago with your family, right?

G: Yes, we were! The place is amazing, but it was a really long trip! How are you guys going to travel?

C: By plane, of course! And we will be driving around on the tour bus, I think.

G: Hmm... You do not have to just take a tour bus around, Caleb. There's the MRT, a subway network there, and it's good and fast.

C: See? That's why I wanted to talk to you. You must have some great tips to give me!

G: Oh, I read a guide about traveling in Singapore. I think I saved the link on my dad's computer.

C: Thanks! Hey, let's talk a little more after class. I can buy you an ice cream, and then you can give me some more tips.

G: Sure! And if I find the guide, I'll send you the link.

Activity 1 24

Ma: Marianne Mi: Michael

Ma: Michael?

Mi: Yes, this is me. Hello, you!

Ma: Hi! Are you going to the Natural History Museum?

Mi: Yes, I have a school presentation there in 30 minutes, but I forgot my laptop, so I had to cancel my first trip and then call for another one.

Ma: Don't worry about it. Traffic is light today. We'll be there in 20 minutes if I take Fifth Street.

Mi: Oh, that's great. Thank you so much.

Ma: So a presentation? What is it about?

Mi: It's about the origin of species and human evolution. We are going to present it to other schools. The museum is running a project to get schools to learn more about the history of the country.

Ma: That's cool! Are you guys nervous before this presentation?

Mi: A little bit. But I know I have all the information I need, and if I forget something, I will just look at the slide presentation to remember things. I also drank two glasses of chamomile tea, so I am pretty calm now. That's my ritual when I have presentations or things like that.

Ma: Chamomile tea? When I am nervous, I just do some breathing exercises, like before I drive a car, I always breathe in and out three times.

Mi: Wait. Are you afraid of driving? You are such a good driver! And you don't look nervous.

Ma: Thank you! But my anxiety is well under control today. I drive every day in the city, and now I'm only afraid of long distances.

Mi: And what do you do if you have to go to another city with a passenger? Are you afraid, then?

Ma: Yes, but then I do it like always: breathe in, breathe out... not just three times, ten times or more. That really works. My fear's still there, but I can drive well and the passenger doesn't notice anything.

Activity 4 25

J: Jill L: Lucca

J: Lucca, can you take me to our language class tomorrow? My mom's car broke down and I don't like taking the bus.

L: Sure... But I'm going by bike. I need to get some exercise and I love biking! I have an extra bike if you want...

J: By bike? No, thanks. I'm not that into biking.

L: OK, so you don't like buses or bikes. I like both, so I can ride my bike to class or take the bus. The only thing I don't like is cabs, but that's just because of the price.

J: Haha! I know. Maybe we could walk there together... I really like to walk. What do you say?

L: Jill, it's a 50-minute walk. Are you sure about that? I don't like walking very much, but for 50 minutes? That's even worse!

J: Oh, come on! It's good exercise.

L: All right. I don't have anything planned before class. Let's walk there, then.

J: Great! I'll see you in front of the park.

UNIT SEVEN

Activity 1 26

A: Amanda P: Phil

P: Oh, just some entertainment articles. Look at this one: "Famous couples with a big age difference".

A: Why do people care so much about this? If they love each other, let them be! Scroll down a little more. Look! What about this article: "Famous Hollywood actresses who are taller than their male partners"? So what? These websites look desperate to get readers, so much so that they write about stereotypes in a very disrespectful way.

P: At least nowadays there is a movement in favor of gender equality and deconstructing stereotypes. Emma Watson, for example, is part of this movement. She is an ambassador for the UN's campaign *HeForShe*.

A: I know. Thanks to people like her I believe things will change one day. I don't understand why these websites publish things like that. They sound so cruel!

P: Well, I guess it's because people like me read it... Anyways, have you read about Tom Holland and Zendaya when people asked them about their height difference?

A: No, I haven't. Let's check it out ...

Activities 2 and 3 28 and 29

B: Ben H: Heidi

B: *Solar System – the Big Bang Experience*. It sounds interesting ... Oh, but you must wear a VR headset. I don't like them. They look uncomfortable.

H: Oh, come on, Ben. It's for five minutes. I'm sure it's fine. Here, put it on. And remember, you mustn't take it off until you have finished the experience.

B: All right. It's not bad. It feels OK, not heavy or uncomfortable.

H: See? Now, let's ask that assistant to start the experience. I'll be right here, next to you.

B: Wow! Check this out, Heidi! I'm in the Solar System! And I can control it! I feel so powerful right now!

H: So, what can you see? Is it cool?

B: It's so cool! I can see all the planets and the stars. Some of them look small... Hey, I can make them bigger! And I can move them, too.

H: Do you feel hot when your hand is next to the Sun?

B: No, of course not. Virtual Reality is not perfect, you can see things, but you can't smell anything, or feel heat or taste things, for example. Wow! It's like I'm flying in empty space now.

H: Really? I don't like this... Do you feel scared?

B: No, but only because I know this is virtual reality. OK, I moved Jupiter closer to the Sun and ... Oh, it's over. I want to try this again.

H: Again? Oh, Ben, this is no fun. I like VR, but this experience looks boring. Let's find another VR experience, but a more fun one.

B: Girls don't usually like virtual reality...

H: That's a very sexist stereotype, Ben. You mustn't say these things. Besides, girls can like anything they want, and boys can, too.

B: You're right. Sorry. Let's go.

Activity 4 30

1. I don't like to read entertainment news about couples with a big age gap. So what? Are they happy? Are they in love? So let a 30-year-old marry a 50-year old!
2. Whenever people see celebrities dressing like normal people, no makeup or anything, it's a reason for paparazzi to take loads of photos. Why do people think celebrities need to be celebrities 24/7?
3. I like to read about women defending their rights, but sometimes I see the media making fun of this. If women are fighting for equal rights, it's because the fight is necessary.
4. My daughter says that men need to invite women to dance, and not the other way around. Why does she think like this? Because the movies she watches say that. This stereotype is very present in the media, especially in cartoons.
5. My son came to me this morning saying that men must always look strong. He says that his favorite cartoon character said that, so it has to be true. We need to be careful about the stereotypes we expose our children to.

UNIT EIGHT

Activity 1 31

A: Anna T: Tim

A: Tim, is it true that your father is a lawyer?

T: Yes! He works in the criminal law field. He defends people who have committed a range of crimes, from small ones to big ones like murder or even terrorism.

A: Wow! That's so interesting! I would love to meet him. I am sure he has lots of interesting stories to tell and I could use them in my social studies essay.

T: You can have lunch with us next week. He'll be happy to tell you his stories. We are kind of tired of them...

A: Thank you, I would love to do that. I would like to ask him how he feels about defending someone he thinks is guilty.

T: Everyone asks him that question. I can answer that question. He always says that his job is to defend and the judge's job is to judge. The judge is the one who decides whether the person is guilty or innocent and what the verdict will be.

A: Hmm... That makes sense to me.

Activity 2 33

P: Presenter **D: Dr. Sanjay Purang**

P: Good afternoon, everyone! We have a very special guest with us in the studio today: Dr. Sanjay Purang.

D: Good afternoon! Thank you very much for having me here in the studio today.

P: Dr. Sanjay is a cybercrime specialist, and today she's going to tell us why she believes that young people are more likely to be involved in this type of crime than adults. Dr. Sanjay, what can you tell our listeners about this topic?

D: First of all, it's important to point out that teenagers are much more familiar with the Internet environment than most adults. This can be a big advantage for them because they were born and raised in the age of new technologies, so they have been juggling computers, tablets and smartphones, accessories, etc. from a young age. Of course, that alone does not make them criminals, but what I am saying is that they have much more knowledge about the cyber world than anyone else. A positive aspect of the Internet world is that it has no boundaries. But there is also a disadvantage. We see that not only people who live or grow up in a poor area witness or participate in cybercrime, as it is not geographically limited. Another aspect that should be highlighted is the issue of low self-control, which is typical for young people. They have no patience and act impulsively to get everything they want, and this can sometimes mean that they engage in criminal acts. Finally, I would like to mention that adolescents tend to compare themselves on a materialistic basis, which creates pressure for possessions, and some adolescents try to acquire new possessions by committing crimes that might end up sending them to jail later on.

P: Thank you very much, Dr. Sanjay...

Activity 4 34

1. It was not very late at night, but the streets were quiet and I could hear the sound of paint splattering. They were spraying the church walls, and when they saw me, they left the place.
2. Can you imagine that they charged an extra fee for using the sports club at night? They kept the money for themselves, and the club found out only after many months.
3. How stupid of me! I used a very simple password, and someone gained access to my files and stole some photos I had there.
4. I heard that they placed a bomb in a car in the middle of a very busy street.
5. I parked my car and went to the gym. When I left two hours later, my car was not there.

NOTES

NOTES

PICTURE CREDITS

Front cover (A) F8 Studio/Shutterstock/Shutterstock / (B) Supphachai Salaeman / Shutterstock/Shutterstock / (C) StockStyle/ Shutterstock/Shutterstock / (D) the_rocket_booster / Shutterstock/Shutterstock / (E) Good Job/Shutterstock/Shutterstock / (F) Meliun/Shutterstock/Shutterstock / (G) OrangeVector/ Shutterstock/Shutterstock; Page 5 Daisy Daisy/shutterstock/Shutterstock; Page 6 bowie15/123rf/Asset Library; Page 7 VH-studio/shutterstock/ Shutterstock; Page 11 (A) Karkas/Shutterstock/Asset Library / (B) tamy Jeong/123rf/123RF / (C) sommersby/123rf/123RF / (D) Serhii Kucher/123rf/ Asset Library / (E) mawielobob/123rf/Asset Library / (F) Vlad Teodor/Shutterstock/Asset Library / (G) Neamov/Shutterstock/Asset Library / (H) Lexa_1112/ Shutterstock/Asset Library / (I) sripfoto/Shutterstock/Asset Library / (J) Chiyacat/Shutterstock/Asset Library / (K) sommersby/123rf/123RF; Page 12 (A) Red Alami/Shutterstock/Asset Library / (B) Anna Koldunova/123rf/123RF / (C) Anna Koldunova/123rf/123RF; Page 13 Seasontime/Shutterstock/Asset Library; Page 14 Navistock/Shutterstock/Asset Library; Page 15 IMG_191 LLC/Shutterstock/Asset Library; Page 18 (A) Ricardo Villasenor/shutterstock/Shutterstock / (B) Africa Studio. Shutterstock/Asset Library; Page 20 limonzest. 123rf.com/Asset Library; Page 21 Ferveez Mohideen. Shutterstock/Asset Library; Page 23 (A) dreamnikon/123rf.com/Asset Library / (B) narongpon chaibot/Shutterstock/Asset Library / (C) Andrey_Popov/ Shutterstock/Asset Library / (D) Matej Kastelic/Shutterstock/Asset Library / (E) Stanisic Vladimir/ Shutterstock/Asset Library / (F) Cultura Motion/Shutterstock/Asset Library; Page 24 Budimir Jevtic/ Shutterstock/Asset Library; Page 26 Shutterstock/Asset Library; Page 29 goodluz/shutterstock/Shutterstock; Page 30 Sasha Ka/ Shutterstock/Asset Library; Page 35 (A) Michael Rosskothen/123rf/Asset Library / (B) Lee Yiu Tung/Shutterstock/Asset Library / (C) Jurgen Vogt/Shutterstock/Asset Library; Page 36 Fotos593/Shutterstock/Asset Library; Page 38 Olesia Bilkei/Shutterstock/Asset Library; Page 39 STILLFX/Shutterstock/Asset Library; Page 40 (A) Nipa Noymol/Shutterstock/Asset Library / (B) Nico Smit/123rf/Asset Library / (C) Ondrej Prosicky/Shutterstock/Asset Library / (D) Sebastian Duda/Shutterstock/ Asset Library; Page 41 (A) Shutterstock/Asset Library / (B) Introwiz1. Shutterstock/Asset Library; Page 42 anek.soowannaphoom. Shutterstock/Asset Library; Page 50 dbrinda/Shutterstock/Asset Library; Page 51 glazok90 / Shutterstock/Asset Library; Page 53 KeyStock/Shutterstock/Asset Library; Page 54 Wavebreakmedia/Shutterstock/Asset Library; Page 60 (A) Goal_1_CMYK_TARGET 1.1.eps / (B) Goal_2_CMYK_TARGET 1.2.eps / (C) Goal_3_CMYK_TARGET 1.3.eps / (D) Goal_4_CMYK_TARGET 1.4.eps / (E) Goal_5_CMYK_TARGET 1.5.eps / (F) Goal_6_CMYK_TARGET 1.6.eps; Page 62 (A) LOVE YOU/Shutterstock/ Asset Library / (B) Kzenon/Shutterstock/Asset Library; Page 64 Maitree Boonkitphuwadon/ 123rf/Asset Library; Page 65 4zevar/shutterstock/Shutterstock; Page 66 (A) belekekin/Shutterstock/Asset Library / (B) Phonlamai Photo/Shutterstock/Asset Library / (C) Scharfsinn/Shutterstock/Asset Library / (D) Riedl Lukas/Shutterstock/Asset Library; Page 68 Peter Probst / Alamy Stock Photo/Alamy; Page 70 (A) franz12/Shutterstock/Asset Library / (B) Triff/Shutterstock/ Asset Library / (C) iliuta goean/Shutterstock/Asset Library / (D) NeverSettle/shutterstock/Shutterstock; Page 74 (A) Andrey_Popov/Shutterstock/Asset Library / (B) Stefano Politi Markovina / Alamy Stock Photo/Alamy; Page 76 Tribalium/Shutterstock/Asset Library; Page 79 insta_photos/shutterstock/Shutterstock; Page 80 Uplight pictures/shutterstock/Shutterstock; Page 81 (A) Marina Solva/Shutterstock/Asset Library / (B) Nina Puankova/Shutterstock/Asset Library; Page 82 (A) Monkey Business Images/shutterstock/Shutterstock / (B) hakinmhan/ 123rf/Asset Library; Page 84 (A) kstuart/Shutterstock/Asset Library / (B) Menno Schaefer/Shutterstock/Asset Library / (C) Bildagentur Zoonar GmbH/Shutterstock/Asset Library / (D) Andreas Rose/Shutterstock/Asset Library / (E) Michael Rosskothen/ 123rf/Asset Library / (F) Arif Wicaksono/Shutterstock/Asset Library / (G) Nancy Bauer/Shutterstock/Asset Library / (H) Jason Benz Bennee/Shutterstock/Asset Library; Page 85 MS Mikel/shutterstock/Shutterstock; Page 86 Sean Pavone/shutterstock/Shutterstock; Page 87 Vitalii Vodolazskyi/shutterstock/Shutterstock; Page 89 MilletStudio/Shutterstock/Shutterstock; Page 90 (A) hifashion/Shutterstock/Asset Library / (B) crystalfoto/ Shutterstock/Asset Library / (C) Hnatyk/Shutterstock/Asset Library / (D) crystalfoto/Shutterstock/Asset Library; Page 91 eakkachai halang/Shutterstock/ Asset Library; Page 93 Ground Picture/Shutterstock; Page 94 (A) Kurit afshen/Shutterstock/Asset Library / (B) Nicola_K_photos / Shutterstock/Asset Library / (C) aaltair/Shutterstock/Asset Library; Page 96 andresr/123rf/Asset Library; Page 97 (A) Ernest Prim/ 123rf/Asset Library / (B) Shi Yali/Shutterstock/Asset Library; Page 99 Pressmaster/shutterstock/Shutterstock; Page 100 (A) Prostock-studio/shtterstock/Shutterstock / (B) 4zevar/shtterstock/Shutterstock; Page 102 Prostock-studio/shtterstock/Shutterstock; Page 103 (A) Happy Poppy/shtterstock/Shutterstock / (B) wizdata/ Shutterstock/Asset Library; Page 104 (A) Jiri Hrebicek/shtterstock/Shutterstock / (B) Alena Ozerova/shtterstock/Shutterstock / (C) metamorworks/shtterstock/Shutterstock; Page 105 Duet PandG/shtterstock/Shutterstock; Page 106 (A) OTIN NKS/shtterstock/Shutterstock / (B) mStudioVector/Shutterstock/Asset Library